Oxford Socio-Legal Studies

Small Claims in the County Courts in England and Wales

OXFORD SOCIO-LEGAL STUDIES

Oxford Socio-Legal Studies is a series of books exploring the role of law in society for both an academic and a wider readership. The series publishes theoretical and empirically-informed work, from the United Kingdom and elsewhere, by social scientists and lawyers which advances understanding of the social reality of law and legal processes.

SMALL CLAIMS IN THE COUNTY COURTS IN ENGLAND AND WALES

The Bargain Basement of Civil Justice?

JOHN BALDWIN

CLARENDON PRESS . OXFORD
1997

Oxford University Press, Great Clarendon Street, Oxford OX2 6DP
Oxford New York
Athens Auckland Bangkok Bogota Bombay
Buenos Aires Calcutta Cape Town Dar es Salaam
Delhi Florence Hong Kong Istanbul Karachi
Kuala Lumpur Madras Madrid Melbourne
Mexico City Nairobi Paris Singapore
Taipei Tokyo Toronto Warsaw
and associated companies in
Berlin Ibadan

Oxford is a trade mark of Oxford University Press

Published in the United States by
Oxford University Press Inc., New York

British Library Cataloguing in Publication Data
Data available

Library of Congress Cataloging in Publication Data
Baldwin, John, 1945–
Small claims in the county courts in England and Wales: the bargain basement of civil justice?/John Baldwin.
p. cm. — (Oxford socio-legal studies)
Includes bibliographical references.
1. Small claims courts—Great Britain. 2. Small claims courts—Social aspects—Great Britain. 3. County courts—Great Britain. 4. Justice, Administration of—Social aspects—Great Britain.
I. Title. II. Series.
KD7228.B35 1997 347.42'04—dc21 97–25117

ISBN 0–19–826477–1

1 3 5 7 9 10 8 6 4 2

Typeset by J&L Composition Ltd, Filey, North Yorkshire
Printed in Great Britain by
Bookcraft Ltd., Midsomer Norton, Somerset

General Editor's Introduction

One of the great challenges for a legal system is to devise ways in which the legal problems of ordinary people may be resolved in a relatively simple, quick and cheap fashion. Disputes occur frequently. Most do not raise complex legal problems. What is at stake may often seem to the outsider to be banal or to involve a trivial amount. Nonetheless, some disputes do become matters of great concern to the people involved.

The small claims regime in England and Wales is relatively new, but has grown substantially in recent years, to the extent that it now accounts for the great majority of defended actions in the county court. The small claims procedure has generally been viewed very positively in official enquiries, and it is widely believed that it is by its expansion that greater access to civil justice can be achieved. How the present regime actually works in practice, however, is not well understood. John Baldwin's new book, which is based on an analysis of the experience of the litigants, lawyers and judges involved in the small claims regime, deals with this question. Professor Baldwin not only documents the operation of the small claims court but assesses how well it works. The careful evaluative research in this book is to be welcomed as an important contribution to the debate about the future scale and shape of civil justice in England and Wales, and in particular about whether the small claims procedure is something to be further developed.

KEITH HAWKINS

Acknowledgements

In carrying out the study of small claims procedures reported in this book, I have been indebted to a number of people and organizations. I should mention first my sincere gratitude to the three bodies which generously funded the study—the Lord Chancellor's Department, the Office of Fair Trading, and the Economic and Social Research Council.

I would also like to thank Ms Melissa Morse of the Lord Chancellor's Department, her former colleague, Mr Christopher Tye, and Mr Bill Davey of the Office of Fair Trading for the practical assistance, advice, and encouragement that they offered to me as the research proceeded. The staff in the county courts involved in the study were also extremely helpful, and, though frequently hard pressed, they were very willing to do whatever they could to facilitate the conduct of the research. The study would not have been possible without the co-operation offered to me by the litigants who brought small claims to the county courts. They uncomplainingly gave up their time, often in difficult and stressful circumstances, to answer questions about their experiences.

I was extremely fortunate in being able to recruit over a dozen research assistants, many of whom were the recent graduates of the Birmingham University Law School, who worked for short periods of time on the study. They helped both in the collection of information from the county courts and in the interviewing of litigants. I am particularly grateful to the following for the care and conscientiousness they showed in carrying out this work: Mr James Baldwin, Ms Clare Bradley, Ms Amanda Broadbent, Ms Jane Creaton, Mr Edward Crosse, Mrs Virginia Davis, Mr Tim Greenald, Ms Yvette Tinsley, Ms Rebecca Trupp, Ms Stephanie Vellins, Ms Rachel Ward, Ms Anna Watkins, Ms Sarah Whittaker, and Mr Daniel Wright. Mr William Baldwin also assisted with the coding of the statistical information collected from the courts. I also owe an enormous debt to my friend and colleague, Mrs Sue Deebank, who was herself actively involved in the collection of data and in the interviewing of litigants. Mrs Deebank also assumed responsibility for liaising with the courts in organizing the researchers' visits to the courts and offered a great deal of assistance in supervising the work of the research assistants.

The success of the research also hinged upon the co-operation I received from the district judges whose hearings I observed. It is no exaggeration to say that, in all the research I have conducted in the past twenty years, I have not found a group of respondents who were quite so affable or so accommodating. The judges I approached spoke to me with commendable frankness and good humour about their experiences of hearing small claims, and I found none of the defensiveness to academic research that I must confess I anticipated. Indeed, I was greatly encouraged by the constructive response that I encountered both from the individual district judges with whom I came into contact and from the Association of District Judges. I say with considerable feeling that the attitude towards research displayed by the district judges stands in refreshing contrast to that I have often encountered from several of the other groups and organizations which have been the focus of my research in the past.

My loyal and long-suffering secretary, Mrs Judy Cohen, typed numerous transcripts of interviews and helped me in many different ways with the preparation of the manuscript. Mrs Denise Lees was also of enormous assistance when problems arose in the final stages with the manuscript. My colleagues, Professor Brian Harvey and Dr Adrian Hunt, generously agreed to read the manuscript in draft and both offered many valuable insights and suggestions about ways it could be improved. My wife, Kay, did the same, and, while probably regarding my preoccupation with small claims as curious, she nonetheless put up with it with remarkable forbearance.

It goes without saying that the views expressed in this book are mine alone and are not to be attributed to any of the organizations or the individuals to whom I am indebted.

PROFESSOR JOHN BALDWIN
University of Birmingham
March 1997

Contents

1 Introduction and Background: The Development of Small Claims in England and Wales

The background

There have been some remarkable developments of late in the way that civil actions are dealt with in county courts in England and Wales. It is hardly an exaggeration to say that a silent revolution has taken place in the civil courts over the past twenty years in which the small claims regime has been greatly expanded. In the process, the face of civil justice administration has been radically changed. The proportion of civil actions handled by the county courts as small claims has increased inexorably in the past twenty-five years, and we have reached the position where the vast majority of defended actions are now being dealt with under the small claims procedure. The massive and unprecedented rise in the small claims limit from £1,000 to £3,000 in January 1996, following the Lord Chancellor's acceptance of the recommendation to this effect by Lord Woolf in his inquiry into the civil justice system, seems certain to accelerate this trend.[1] All the indications are, then, that the domination of the small claims regime in the administration of civil justice in the county courts will continue in the future and, indeed, will become more pronounced.

Yet our knowledge of how the small claims regime operates in practice is disconcertingly slight. No one can make an informed assessment of whether its dominance is to be welcomed or not. We do not know how lawyers or judges regard small claims procedures, still less what the litigants who experience them at first hand make of them. The author has been carrying out research into small claims in the past four years and has spent many hours talking to the people involved about them. This book, which reports the results of this research, represents one of very few attempts that have been made in England and Wales to evaluate the operation of the small claims procedure. The writer will seek to describe what happens at small claims hearings, to examine what the parties think of them, to identify

[1] Lord Woolf (1995) at ch. 16.

the problems that they create, and to assess the implications of the expanded small claims regime for the future of civil justice in England and Wales.

At the time of writing, the great majority of defended claims in the county courts for less than £3,000 are automatically referred to the small claims procedure and are then heard in private by a district judge.[2] Small claims hearings cover an almost infinite range of disputes and complaints. Most claims involve relatively small sums of money—considerably less than the £3,000 limit—and few raise issues that carry constitutional import. It is at these hearings that those disputes that are part and parcel of everyday life are sorted out. They are the kind of arguments that could affect almost anybody, and they include (to take some common, if disparate, examples) the resolution of disputes about liability in road accidents; people declining to pay what are seen as the excessive bills of solicitors, accountants, or estate agents, or else voicing dissatisfaction about the quality of workmanship of builders, electricians, plumbers, and the like; complaints about equipment that has not worked, clothes that have been wrecked in the process of dry cleaning, or holidays that have not gone according to plan.

Having observed a great number of small claims hearings, the author can testify to the passion frequently generated by what may appear on the surface to be simple and relatively humdrum disputes. Cases that involve expensive animals that have died shortly after purchase or wedding arrangements that have been botched seem to generate particular acrimony. There may not be huge sums of money at stake in these disputes, but to the parties they are frequently matters of almost obsessional concern. 'We do not need to call on psychiatrists or clinical psychologists', Chief Justice Warren Burger once wisely stated, 'to tell us that a sense of injustice rankles and festers in the human breast and the dollar value of the conflict is not always the measure of tension and irritation produced'.[3] Although the kind of cases heard at small claims hearings are often dismissed by practising lawyers as unimportant, even trivial, one should be wary of minimizing the significance of disputes of this kind, and sums of up to £3,000 are far from trivial to most people. It is, indeed, doubtful whether use of

[2] Since the research reported in this book was conducted before January 1996, however, the small claims limit was set at that time at £1,000.

[3] Chief Justice Burger, cited in Nader (1979) at p 1001.

the word 'small' can any longer be considered appropriate to describe these claims.

Before discussing the outcome of the research, it is worth pausing to consider the background against which it was conducted. In outlining this background, it will be clear that there has never been a better time to be researching small claims in England and Wales than in the past four years. Devising small claims procedures has been part of a relentless, world-wide search for simplified legal processes to deal with civil cases, and extending the scope of small claims has not been by any means confined to England and Wales. The adoption of simplified and informal procedures reflects a growing disenchantment with traditional court processes and a recognition that we need cheaper solutions to legal problems than those customarily provided by the formal courts. Politicians, administrators, and the general public are united in wanting to devise ways of dealing with civil cases that are cheaper, quicker, and less off-putting than those that the courts have provided in the past. And, in many jurisdictions, treating more and more civil actions as small claims has proved a main way of attaining these objectives.

It is not difficult to describe the ways in which small claims hearings differ from traditional court hearings. The former tend to be much more informal, more relaxed, and less adversarial; the role of legal representation is greatly diminished; litigants are expected to present their own cases, and the judges are encouraged to be much more 'interventionist' in approach. The mechanisms adopted in dealing with small claims in England and Wales have been applied in varying degrees in almost all jurisdictions which have introduced such procedures. Small claims in England and Wales are heard in the judge's own chambers, and wigs and gowns are dispensed with.[4] (It is, however, strange that, even in England and Wales, small claims hearings continue to be held in private.[5]) The underlying assumption is that the

[4] Small claims procedures in Scotland are much more formal than they are in other parts of the United Kingdom and, indeed, in most parts of the world. In the main Scottish study of small claims (Scottish Office, Central Research Unit, 1991: 67), it was noted that 'there has been comparatively little relaxation of formalities here to date'. The study demonstrated that, to a much greater extent than in England and Wales, small claims proceedings in Scotland continue to conform to adversarial court traditions. Judicial wigs, gowns, and other trappings of the formal adversarial approach are, for example, preserved at hearings, as they are in a few other countries.

[5] The writer agrees with Sir Jack Jacob (1987: 263) who argued in favour of small claims hearings being held in public 'in compliance with the fundamental principle of publicity governing judicial proceedings' and to increase 'public knowledge of the system and public confidence in its operation'.

costs involved in civil litigation will be reduced if legal proceedings are made simpler and less legalistic so that lay people can play a much more prominent part in them. The inevitable corollary is that the participation of professional lawyers at small claims hearings is much less significant, and in some countries it has been entirely eliminated.

Searching questions are increasingly being asked about the kinds of procedures that are needed to deal with civil actions, very many of which do not involve particularly large sums of money or complex legal issues. The possibility of extending the principles adopted in small claims hearings to other kinds of civil actions is also being canvassed. The role of legal representatives is slowly being redefined, and their indispensability at court hearings is no longer taken for granted. Do-It-Yourself solutions in civil justice have become the order of the day in the 1990s, and, in consequence, very large chunks of the business of the civil courts have been carried out without the involvement of legal representatives.[6]

The need for lawyers and the fear of the high costs they generate are very relevant issues when one considers small claims, since the costs incurred in pursuing such actions through the formal courts can quickly come to exceed the sums of money in dispute. 'It takes no great understanding of the mysteries of high finance to make obvious the futility of spending a thousand dollars to get a thousand dollars' is how Justice W. O. Douglas expressed this simple truth in 1934.[7] The understandable fear of litigants that they may run up legal bills that exceed the sums of money at issue has greatly encouraged the spread of small claims procedures. It is widely accepted that Rolls Royce solutions are inappropriate in dealing with everyday disputes involving small sums of money. The call nowadays is for 'proportionality' in legal costs, by which is meant that legal costs must bear a sensible relation to the sum of money at issue in the case.[8] However, as will be

[6] None of this should be taken to imply that civil disputes should invariably be resolved in the courts. Most people involved in civil disputes resort to other methods of settling them, if they are settled at all. The last few years have seen a burgeoning interest in what has become known as 'Alternative Dispute Resolution' (or ADR) and in procedures such as arbitration, conciliation, and mediation. The civil courts are tending to recede in importance in the disposal of numerous types of civil action: see the perceptive discussions of these developments in Menkel-Meadow (1991); Glasser and Roberts (1993); Twining (1993), and Freeman (1995).

[7] Cited by Thomas (1982) at 52–3. In one survey, conducted under the auspices of the Civil Justice Review (1988), it was estimated that legal expenses in personal injury cases accounted for 84 per cent of the damages recovered: see further Rickman and Gray (1995).

[8] This emphasis on 'proportionate costs' is very strong in the reports prepared by Lord Woolf (1995, 1996).

seen in the course of this book, whether unrepresented litigants are capable of putting forward a competent legal case in court is the critical question, and how far lawyers can safely be dispensed with remains a matter of considerable dispute.

The history of small claims

It is interesting that, despite its dominant position in the county courts, the small claim procedure has a comparatively short and undistinguished history in England and Wales. While it is possible, as Ervine (1993) has noted, to trace the origins of small claims courts in the United States to the early years of this century, the small claims movement in England is, by contrast, little more than a quarter of a century old. Publication in 1970 of the report, *Justice Out of Reach*, by the now defunct Consumer Council is usually acknowledged as providing the initial impetus.[9] The Council had noted that 'the individual simply does not take his dispute to a court for decision' (1970: 5), and argued that the county courts were as a result virtually irrelevant as far as the small claims of consumers were concerned. To encourage individuals to pursue such actions, the Council recommended the introduction of special small claims courts—a solution that had already been adopted in several other countries.[10] But as many commentators have observed since then, there has always been a curious resistance to the idea of setting up such courts in England.[11]

Although people commonly refer to English Small Claims Courts, there is in reality no such institution. All that has happened is that county court procedures have been modified over the years to accommodate small claims: there has been no wholesale restructuring of the civil courts of the kind that has occurred in many other jurisdictions. A special procedure, known universally, if somewhat misleadingly, as 'arbitration', for use in dealing with small claims was introduced in

[9] Small claims procedures in many other countries have a much longer pedigree: see Whelan (1990) at 208–12. For detailed discussions of the historical background to small claims in this country, see further Applebey (1979); Whelan (1990) at 99–106; and Harvey and Parry (1996) at 211–17.

[10] Small claims courts existed, for example, in Australia, the United States, and Canada. A good indication of the range of approaches adopted in dealing with small claims in different jurisdictions is given in the collection of essays compiled by Whelan (1990).

[11] The lack of official enthusiasm for specific small claims courts has been the subject of frequent criticism: see, for example, Economides (1980) and Whelan (1990).

England and Wales under the Administration of Justice Act 1973, and Order 19 of the County Court Rules 1981, as revised, sets out the provisions that are now in force. This solution to the small claims conundrum (which has applied in a somewhat similar form in Northern Ireland and in Scotland)[12] has been at once cautious and modest, with small claims procedures simply grafted on to the existing county court structure.[13]

Furthermore, the small claims procedure has itself been used rather sparingly in England and Wales in comparison with many other countries. The enthusiasm one finds nowadays for small claims in official circles is a comparatively recent phenomenon, and it is easy to overlook the point that, for most of the time that the small claims procedure has operated in England and Wales, official attitudes to it were decidedly low-key. This is clearly seen in the relatively low limits set for small claims. When the small claims procedure was introduced in 1973, for instance, the limit was fixed at only £75. Although this was increased five times subsequently,[14] the scope of the small claims procedure changed little in the fifteen years before 1996, once adjustments in the Retail Price index were taken into account.[15] And though the limit throughout the 1970s and 1980s was in real terms about two and a half times higher than its 1973 value, it was still low compared to that in other countries.[16]

The major change in small claims in England and Wales occurred in January 1996 when the limit was suddenly trebled to £3,000. This followed acceptance of the recommendation made by Lord Woolf

[12] Procedures for dealing specifically with small claims were not introduced in Northern Ireland until 1979 or in Scotland until 1988. For discussions of small claims procedures as they apply in Scotland and Northern Ireland, see Bland (1987); Mulvaney and Greer (1987); Paterson and Stedward (1989); Greer (1990); Scottish Office, Central Research Unit (1991); Ervine (1991, 1993); Office of Fair Trading (1991) at 25–8; and General Consumer Council for Northern Ireland (1992).

[13] See, however, Applebey (1979), 743–54; Whelan (1990), 119–24; and White (1985), 151–3, who discuss the voluntary schemes operating in Manchester and London which dealt with small claims outside the official court structure in the 1970s. These experiments were eventually abandoned because of shortage of funds.

[14] The level was raised to £100 in October 1974, to £200 in July 1978, to £500 in October 1981, to £1,000 in July 1991, and to £3,000 in January 1996.

[15] The writer is grateful to Ms Melissa Morse, Head of the County Court Policy Branch of the Lord Chancellor's Department, for making available to him the information on the changing real value of the small claims jurisdiction.

[16] In many parts of the United States, for example, the limit had been set at $5,000 or higher, and comparable figures applied in many parts of Australia and Canada as well: see further Cranston (1995), at 52.

(1995) who had conducted a major review of the operation of the civil justice system in England and Wales. Lord Woolf regarded a great expansion in the small claims regime as the best way of securing greater access to civil justice, and the Lord Chancellor seized the opportunity to expand the scope of small claims.[17] However, given the cautious use of the small claims procedure before then, this unprecedented increase might be seen more as a move to bring the limit in England and Wales into line with that in many other countries rather than as a dramatic change of direction in the way that civil actions should henceforth be handled. If, however, the government were to raise the small claims limit to £5,000 (as Lord Woolf himself has proposed[18]), then it would be significantly higher than the small claims limits found in most other countries.

Judicial interventionism

From the time that the small claims procedure was introduced in England and Wales (and in similar forms in a number of other jurisdictions, including Scotland and Northern Ireland), litigants have been encouraged to present their own cases in court and the judges have been urged to intervene in a pro-active way in proceedings so as to elicit from the parties the relevant evidence on which to base their decisions. In simplifying court procedures and encouraging district judges to play an interventionist role at hearings, a main objective has been to offset any disadvantage that might be suffered by litigants who are unrepresented and even to make legal representation redundant.[19] The judges have been given very considerable latitude in the way they conduct small claims hearings and have been able to adopt whatever methods they think will best achieve a just and expeditious outcome. Order 19 of the County Court Rules 1981 (as amended) indicates how much freedom they have been allowed:

[17] He announced the rise in the small claims limit in a press release on the very day that Lord Woolf's interim report was published.

[18] Lord Woolf (1995) recommended that the effects of the increase to £3,000 be monitored, and, if no serious problems arise, that the limit be raised to £5,000. At the time of writing, the writer is himself conducting a study in which the effects of the increased limit are being evaluated.

[19] There has been some dispute about the extent to which this objective can realistically be fulfilled. Genn and Genn (1989), in a study of tribunal adjudication, for example, argued that the greater participation of a chairman, even when a lawyer, did not by any means obviate the need for legal representation.

The hearing shall be informal and the strict rules of evidence shall not apply. . . . At the hearing the arbitrator may adopt any method of procedure which he may consider to be fair and which gives to each party an equal opportunity to have his case presented; having considered the circumstances of the parties and whether . . . they are represented.[20]

The district judges (who have an almost exclusive jurisdiction to hear small claims[21]) are expected to lend a helping hand to litigants who seek to present their own cases. With weighty encouragement from the Review Body on Civil Justice (1988), and latterly from the Woolf Inquiry (1995), district judges have come to play a role at hearings that bears certain similarities to the inquisitorial judge found in civil law jurisdictions, often assuming the sole responsibility for examining the parties and their witnesses, entering the arena of the dispute whenever they wish, and abandoning the aloof judicial role that judges in England and Wales have by tradition played.

The idea that English judges might be induced to adopt an 'inquisitorial' role would probably have been unthinkable even in the relatively recent past. But after a lengthy period of hesitation and unease when considerable variations in the propensity of registrars (the immediate forerunners to district judges) to intervene at small claims hearings were noted,[22] many district judges, as the results in Chapter 3 show, are playing the interventionist role with considerable skill and enthusiasm. Legal representation is permitted at small claims hearings in England and Wales, but, since legal aid is not normally available,[23] parties who wish to have lawyers present have to pay for them themselves. Legal representation is further discouraged because successful parties in these proceedings are not entitled to recover the costs involved from the other party because of the 'no costs' regime that applies in small claims.[24] What this means in practice is that, beyond

[20] Order 19 of the County Court Rules 1981 at 7(3) and (4).

[21] The only exception—and one that as yet rarely arises—is in cases in which both parties request that a claim in excess of the small claims limit be dealt with by 'arbitration' and the district judge takes the view that the matter would be better heard by an outside arbitrator with specialized expertise. This may become somewhat more frequent in the future, following the recommendation by Lord Woolf (1995) that the district judges' discretion to transfer cases into (and out of) the small claims procedure be widened.

[22] See, for example, the Civil Justice Review (1988) at para. 488.

[23] Preliminary legal advice may be available to litigants who are eligible under the advice and assistance scheme (the so-called green form scheme). But this does not extend to representation at hearings: see Baldwin (1988).

[24] In civil proceedings, the traditional rule is that the legal costs of both parties usually have to be paid by the losing party. Under the 'no costs' regime in small claims, this rule does not apply. For a fascinating discussion of the deterrent effect on civil litigation of the rules on costs, see Zuckerman (1996).

the sum involved in the claim itself, the most a successful small claims plaintiff can hope to recover from the other party are modest loss of earnings, travelling expenses, the costs as stated in the summons, and the court fee.[25]

Because of the 'no costs' rule, then, most litigants involved in small claims are put off hiring representatives. Where there is legal representation, it is generally a junior member of the profession who provides it. In the author's study of small claims, lawyers appeared for one side or the other in less than a quarter of all small claims hearings, and there were very few hearings in which both of the parties were legally represented. Lay representation, though permitted at such hearings since 1992,[26] is rarer still. As will be seen in Chapters 3 and 4 of this book, the absence of legal representation, the presentation of cases by inexperienced lay litigants, and the extremely flexible role that district judges play, all make for the adoption of judicial procedures at small claims hearings that are decidedly rough-and-ready. As district judges are themselves fond of observing, the justice dispensed at small claims hearings almost invariably falls well below a Rolls Royce standard. Unlike the situation in certain jurisdictions in other parts of the world that the writer has observed, district judges in England and Wales strive to announce the decision immediately at the end of the hearing when the parties are present in court. Yet litigants' rights of appeal are extremely limited. There is no appeal on errors of fact at all in small claims in England and Wales, and all that is left to a disgruntled litigant is to allege that the judge made a material error of law or was guilty of misconduct.[27] The whole idea behind the adoption of small claims procedures is that they will provide a cheap, simple, and

[25] Plaintiffs have to pay an issuing fee to the court in order to issue a summons to start proceedings. This fee is calculated on a sliding scale according to the size of the sum that is claimed. At the beginning of 1997, county court fees were revised, and the minimum fee in small claims was set at £10 and the maximum at £80. Defendants who wish to make a claim against a plaintiff—a counterclaim—have to pay fees on the same scale. (There is also a separate scale of court fees for plaintiffs who wish to issue enforcement proceedings.) Litigants who are in receipt of income support automatically qualify for exemption from the court fee, and, at the discretion of the Court Manager, the fee may be remitted where paying it would cause undue hardship because of the exceptional circumstances of the case.

[26] The Lay Representatives (Rights of Audience) Order 1992 removed the restrictions on the appearance of lay representatives: see Applebey (1994), at 88–91.

[27] A plaintiff or defendant may, however, apply to have the judgment 'set aside' if, for instance, he or she had no knowledge that the hearing was taking place. With such applications, parties have to attend the court and satisfy the district judge that this was indeed the case: see Applebey (1994), at 69–71.

speedy resolution of disputes in which the decision is final. It is believed that these objectives would be thwarted if the parties were allowed endlessly to pursue remedies for their grievances.

Under traditional civil procedure in England, party autonomy rules and the judge's role at hearings tends to be a passive one. The situation is very different in small claims where it is the hearing itself that is all-important. As will be argued throughout this book, this presents a major problem to the small claims regime because lay litigants, since they lack legal expertise and guidance, frequently fail to appreciate the meaning of 'proving' a legal case. Indeed, they commonly adopt a casual approach to case preparation, particularly as far as the collection of evidence is concerned, and merely turn up to the hearing ready to explain everything orally to the judge. As will be discussed in Chapter 3, this often means that, if the hearing is to go ahead at all, it will be for the judge to seek to remedy a litigant's failure adequately to complete the summons (or defence) or to produce the necessary supporting evidence. There is no requirement that litigants take legal advice before hearings, and in practice very many of them do not trouble to do so. Nor do court staff fill this legal void, because, while they are enjoined under the Courts Charter to give advice to litigants on procedural matters, they are not allowed to offer legal advice.[28] The assistance that members of the county court staff are able to give to the parties is, thus, narrowly circumscribed.[29] In some county courts, staff might help litigants to complete the court forms, but in others the only assistance they have time to offer is to hand out copies of the relevant leaflets that the Lord Chancellor's Department has issued.[30]

So what do district judges do when they are confronted by litigants who are unfamiliar with legal procedures and are ill-prepared for the hearing itself? The answer reveals a basic truth about small claims

[28] The Courts Charter states: 'Where possible, court staff will advise on technical procedure and help you fill in forms. They cannot, however, give legal advice.' As far as the procedural assistance offered by court staff is concerned, positive views were expressed by court users in the National Survey of Court Users, published by the Lord Chancellor's Department in March 1995: see the discussion of these findings in the Woolf Inquiry (1995), at 122.

[29] In some other jurisdictions, court staff are able to offer legal advice to litigants: see, for instance, Weller *et al.* (1984).

[30] The Department has prepared seven straightforward leaflets, written specifically for litigants in person, each of which deals with a discrete stage in the process of pursuing a small claim. These leaflets (approved by the Plain English Campaign) have been supplemented by other leaflets which deal with paying the judgment, enforcement, and the like.

procedures and is a point that immediately strikes any observer: this is that pragmatic good sense is much more often used by district judges to resolve matters than refined legal procedures.[31] McBarnet's (1981) observation that 'the courts are there not to indulge in the impossible absolutes of philosophy or science but to reach decisions—quickly' (*ibid.*: 13) applies with particular force to small claims hearings. Indeed, as will be seen in Chapter 3, common sense on some occasions triumphs over application of the law itself.

Despite the flimsy evidence available in England and Wales about the operation of the small claims procedure, the system tends nowadays to be viewed very favourably in official circles. The Review Body on Civil Justice (1988), for instance, concluded that the small claims procedure was 'substantially sound in that it is able to produce results, without major delay and cost, which satisfy a large number of those who use it' (*ibid.*: paragraph 507), and it regarded the procedure as having 'fulfilled its aim of providing a suitable forum for use by the general public' (*ibid.*: paragraph 505).[32] Seven years later, Lord Woolf (1995) described the small claims procedure as providing 'a forum which is fair and appropriate to litigants in person' (*ibid.*: 104). These sanguine assessments are supported by a dramatic increase in the number of small claims processed in the county courts. The number in England and Wales more than doubled between 1990 and 1993, and figures published by the Lord Chancellor's Department show that over 88,000 small claims were disposed of in 1995, a figure that represents nearly 80 per cent of all trials held in the county courts.[33]

Academic interest in small claims

For an academic observer, examining the way that small claims are dealt with in the courts is endlessly fascinating, especially because the legal ground rules have been dramatically changed and many established working assumptions have been swept aside. It is particularly interesting to discover how lay people fare in this kind of relaxed legal

[31] As Lord Bingham CJ (1994: 7) observed when he was Master of the Rolls, small claims are 'resolved relatively informally and, perhaps, with more regard to common-sense than the letter of the law'.

[32] The recommendations of the Civil Justice Review (1988) had a considerable effect in accelerating changes in district judges' approaches in dealing with small claims: see Applebey (1993) on the main ways that these recommendations affected county court procedures.

[33] See Table 4.7 in *Judicial Statistics Annual Report 1995.*

setting. One should not underestimate the social importance of the questions that these changes in procedure raise. Even eight years before the unprecedented trebling in the small claims limit in 1996, the Review Body on Civil Justice (1988) had noted that the modifications to small claims procedures represented 'the most widespread and radical innovation in civil justice in the last 15 years' (*ibid.*: paragraph 457). Since then, the central place of small claims in county courts has become ever more pronounced, a situation that has been brought about not only by the very large rises in the small claims limit, but also because judicial interventionism is increasingly being urged upon judges in contexts beyond small claims[34] and is seen as having a growing applicability to the disposal of civil business in general.[35]

As was noted above, it is curious, given the prominent place that the small claims procedure occupies in the administration of civil justice, that we do not know much about how it operates. Little research has ever been conducted in England into small claims. By contrast, the growing importance of small claims courts in the United States has been matched by the quantity of empirical research conducted into their workings. Indeed, in their review of the research, Yngvesson and Hennessey (1975) referred to small claims courts in the United States as 'the least forgotten of the lower courts today . . . no other lower court has received such widespread attention from lawyers, social scientists and the concerned public in the past decade' (*ibid.*: 220). Yet in England and Wales, small claims procedures have scarcely attracted the interest of researchers at all.[36] Apart from Applebey's early pioneering work (1978, 1979), a postal questionnaire study of small claims litigants conducted by the National Audit Office (1996),

[34] Parallel developments have occurred, for example, in relation to the network of tribunals that has been created to resolve many kinds of dispute surrounding administrative decision making: on this, see Genn and Genn (1989) and Baldwin *et al.* (1992).

[35] In the years since publication of the Report of the Review Body on Civil Justice, the idea of a judiciary exercising a greater responsibility for the disposition of civil business (particularly by the adoption of case management techniques as practised in certain other jurisdictions) has become much more widely accepted in England. Even before Lord Woolf's (1995, 1996) enthusiastic advocacy for the 'procedural judge' with responsibilities for the management of cases, support for such moves had been voiced by some of the most senior members of the English judiciary and legal profession: see in particular Browne-Wilkinson (1988); Purchas (1993); Heilbron (1993); and Bingham (1994).

[36] There is a similar paucity of research on small claims in Scotland and Northern Ireland. In Scotland, there have been only a couple of studies: see Ervine (1993) and the Scottish Office Central Research Unit (1991). In Northern Ireland, Professor Desmond Greer has worked virtually single-handedly on small claims: see Mulvaney and Greer (1987); Greer (1990); and the General Consumer Council for Northern Ireland (1992).

and a rather clumsily executed survey by management consultants on behalf of the Review Body on Civil Justice,[37] there is nothing that begins to compare with the wealth of North American research and writing on the subject.

This lack of interest reflects a more general neglect of civil justice by academic researchers in England. Socio-legal researchers for a generation have been preoccupied with the issues that surround criminal justice, and it has only belatedly been recognized that the questions raised in the administration of civil justice are of comparable importance.[38] There has also been a corresponding absence of theorization about civil justice issues in general and about small claims in particular. As with much of the writing in the field of judicial administration, the bulk of the literature on small claims has been written from a legal or policy perspective: broader theoretical concerns have been almost entirely neglected. If one looks for relevant theoretical insights about the operation of the small claims regime in the literature on civil justice, they are to be found in the writing on the subject of alternative dispute resolution or ADR as it has become universally known. Even in this literature, however, it is very evident that the focus has been upon pragmatic concerns, not abstract theorizing. It is nonetheless worth briefly examining some of this writing to see what light it might shed on small claims.

Although the author was familiar with a number of theoretical positions as he commenced his research, and, indeed, used them to inform the design of his study, it has to be said that they proved to be of limited utility in making sense of the operation of small claims procedures as he observed them. At the time the research was being planned, there were three main theoretical stances that he viewed as being particularly relevant. These concerned the objective of expanding informal procedures in the civil courts as a means of enhancing access to justice; the way that the spread of 'informalism' has served to foster the interests of the economically powerful and reinforced inequalities; and the process by which informal procedures promote settlement through 'private ordering'. It is worth saying a little about each of these positions.

[37] Touche Ross (1986). See the detailed critique of this study by Whelan (1987, 1990, at 111–18).

[38] As far as the average citizen is concerned, such issues are likely to carry much more immediate significance than the questions that arise in relation to criminal cases: see Bell (1969), at p. xiii.

The first view—that procedures like small claims facilitate citizens' access to justice—is a recurrent theme in much of the writing on small claims. It is assumed, explicitly or otherwise, in most of this literature that the simplification of legal procedures will of itself extend citizens' access to justice. The corollary—that no redress for citizens' grievances will be available if these mechanisms do not exist—is also widely accepted. 'The concept of a small claims court appears to be based on two fundamental tenets' is how Greer (1990) neatly expresses the point, 'that simplicity achieves access, and that access achieves justice' (*ibid.*: 158). The distinguished Italian comparative lawyer, Mauro Cappelletti, has become the name most closely associated with the 'access to justice' movement,[39] and a main focus of his work has been concerned, directly and indirectly, with the operation of small claims procedures.[40] The somewhat hackneyed description of small claims courts as 'peoples' courts', accessible to all-comers, indicates the purpose they are seen as fulfilling. 'Access to justice' is a prominent theme which runs through the current debate surrounding the future of small claims in England, following publication of the wide-ranging review of the civil justice system which Lord Woolf completed in 1996, the very title of which was 'Access to Justice'. In his interim report, Lord Woolf (1995) stated unequivocally that he saw 'the small claims scheme as the primary way of increasing access to justice for ordinary people' (*ibid.*: 100).

The assumption that informal legal procedures like small claims facilitate access to justice is, then, extremely important. Yet the capacity of the small claims procedure to enhance access to justice is one about which this writer remains sceptical. The concept, 'access to justice', is itself profoundly problematic because it can easily become a slogan, bandied around as self-evidently desirable, yet in reality without much substance.[41] The extensive literature on the subject,

[39] Cappelletti's analysis of the barriers that limit citizens' access to the courts has now become a classic in the socio-legal field. The Florence Access-to-Justice Project that he directed was a genuinely comparative attempt to tackle the question of the barriers to securing justice.

[40] Cappelletti and Garth (1978) noted, for instance, how the barriers to achieving justice were most pronounced for small claims and for isolated individuals, especially the poor, and they saw possible antidotes to the inequalities in the resources of litigants as lying in particular in state provision of legal services, the restructuring of legal processes, and the adoption of new procedural mechanisms.

[41] Access to justice is, as Silbey and Sarat (1989: 45) put it, 'a rhetorical symbol of undeniable attractiveness and mobilizing power'.

amassed over the past thirty years, demonstrates convincingly that, whatever efforts are made to create informal judicial procedures, very substantial 'barriers to justice' remain and these severely impede access to justice.[42] Furthermore, it is commonly assumed that, with the promotion of informal legal procedures like small claims, members of a much wider public will be induced to turn to the civil courts to resolve their disputes. But there is not much evidence in the study of small claims reported in this book (or in other sources known to the author) to indicate that this happens much in practice. Indeed, it seems that the extent to which the small claims procedure has succeeded in facilitating access to justice has been at best limited. The evidence in this and other studies shows instead that, while such mechanisms provide a means whereby access to justice might be extended, in practice they continue to be used by very limited sectors of the population, particularly by professional people or those representing business interests. In so far as ordinary people are involved in small claims, they are likely to appear as defendants—in other words, as those who are 'taken' to court—rather than as litigants seeking to assert a right or remedy a wrong. And any hopes that the small claims context might provide an avenue through which the poor might find redress for their grievances seem to have no empirical support whatever.

This brings us to the second perspective which looks on the operation of informal legal procedures from a standpoint that is almost diametrically opposed to the first. Seizing upon the fact that the civil courts are heavily used by professional, commercial, and business interests, several writers have adapted conflict theory to argue that those with economic and political muscle inevitably emerge as the principal beneficiaries of civil justice.[43] (This emphasis is reflected in the title of the celebrated paper by Marc Galanter, 'Why the 'Haves' Come Out Ahead', published over twenty years ago.) There is a good deal of empirical evidence suggesting that small claims procedures have been mobilized to serve powerful commercial interests by providing a convenient mechanism through which commercial organizations can pursue small debts.[44] The tendency for such organizations to

[42] On these barriers, see in particular Morris, White, and Lewis (1972); Abel-Smith, Zander, and Brooke (1973); Byles and Morris (1977); Genn (1984, 1995); and National Consumer Council (1995).

[43] See, for instance, the perceptive discussions in Nader (1979) and Holland (1982).

[44] Cappelletti and Garth (1978: 71) themselves recognized that small claims courts can operate so as to 'facilitate the wholesale trampling on the rights of debtor-individuals'.

'colonize' small claims procedures to the detriment of individual litigants, which is well documented in the literature,[45] has prompted the observation that there are serious dangers for individual litigants in the proliferation of informal procedures. A number of writers have argued that 'informalism' itself is more likely to weaken the lay litigant's position than to strengthen it,[46] and, far from viewing the development and expansion of informal mechanisms as enhancing citizens' rights, they have argued that they have served to extend the coercive arm of the state.[47] The way that law operates so as to buttress the position of the powerful rather than to protect the rights of the weak has, indeed, become a main focus in what has become known as the 'critical legal studies movement'.[48]

But, as the present research proceeded, the author came increasingly to question this position. The notion that the small claims procedure provides little more than a convenient debt collection mechanism for business concerns is often presented as the received wisdom on small claims. Yet it emerged in this study as something of a caricature. Although it is true that the vast majority of small claims involve disputes about monies that are said to be owed, there is (as will be demonstrated in Chapter 2) much more than simple debt collection to most cases. This applies even to those cases classified by the courts or the parties as 'debts', 'unpaid invoices', or 'outstanding amounts'. Furthermore, in the author's view, it may well be misleading for most purposes to dichotomize users of the court into individual litigants and business interests. In the small claims setting, there is often in practice little real distinction between litigants who appear on their own account and those who appear on behalf of commercial concerns, or at least the differences between the two groups are in most cases less striking than the similarities. As is revealed in this study, the commercial interests involved in small claims are overwhelmingly small businesses and individual traders. Few small claims involve large organizations of any kind. Most litigants, whether individuals or the representatives of businesses, are unrepresented at hearings and likely

[45] The phenomenon has been observed in many jurisdictions: see, for example, Sarat (1976); White (1985); Greer (1990); Ramsay (1990); Rohl (1990); Weller *et al.* (1990); Scottish Office Central Research Unit (1991); and McGuire and Macdonald (1994).

[46] See in particular Auerbach (1976); Abel (1982); Trubeck (1984), and Matthews (1988).

[47] 'Coercion serves to "persuade" parties to submit to informal justice, to "agree" to the outcome, and to comply with it' is how Abel (1982: 271) puts it.

[48] See, for instance, Merry (1990), at 7–11.

to share similar anxieties about the hearing, the judge's decision and its consequences, and problems that may arise in relation to enforcement. In other words, the argument that one group is able to wield coercive power over the other is a far cry from the situation that is normally encountered at small claims hearings.

A final perspective, not unrelated to the last, emerges as a clear strand in this body of literature. This concerns the way that informal legal mechanisms can facilitate the settlement of claims through what has been called the 'private ordering' of justice. According to this view, the parties, with or without the help of lawyers, are encouraged to seek their own solutions to legal problems, particularly through informal negotiation. The procedures of the civil courts are indeed frequently portrayed as being specifically designed to produce settlement,[49] even though the fiction that matters will proceed to a full court hearing is maintained.[50] 'Parties who want peace and want it on good terms', Genn (1995) cleverly observes, 'have no alternative, within the context of adversarial court procedures, but to prepare for war' (*ibid.*: 406). It is, indeed, argued that in assessing the efficacy of the civil justice system, it is not so much the number of disputes that the courts actually determine that is important as the number that are settled before the court processes are invoked.[51] 'Bargaining in the shadow of the law' is the evocative phrase used by Mnookin and Kornhauser (1979) to describe the way in which legal processes may be used to facilitate negotiated strategies. They argue that the primary function of law is to

[49] Writing about the courts in New England, Merry (1990: 35) notes that:

> 'courts exert slow but sustained pressure on the parties to work out the situation themselves. At every step of the court process, they are urged again and again to settle, to drop the case, or to come to an agreement before a trial. They are pressured to settle in the clerk's hearing, at the pre-trial conference, and at the day of the trial before the hearing in the small claims court'.

[50] The pressures which impel the parties in civil actions towards settlement are particularly potent in England and Wales because of the operation of the indemnity rule of costs and the 'payment into court' rule: see generally Cranston (1986, 1995); Jacob (1987); Merry (1990); Zander (1989); Bundy (1992); and Genn (1995). Roberts (1995: 447) notes that 'in litigation two conceptually distinct goals have become entwined with each other—resolution through settlement and resolution through authoritative third-party determination—sharing a common procedural route'. He (1995: 456) sees the emphasis in the Woolf Report (1995) that the philosophy of litigation should be to encourage early settlement of disputes as leaving 'the divergent objectives of settlement and judgment sadly entangled'. On the relation between judicial adjudication and settlement, see also Galanter and Cahill (1994), at 1341–2.

[51] Galanter and Cahill (1994: 1379) make the point as follows: 'Courts do more than resolve disputes, they broadcast messages to various audiences about the conduct of disputes and about the norms of conduct underlying those disputes'.

provide a framework within which the parties themselves determine outcomes.[52] The courts' function as a backdrop to pre-court negotiations is seen as being as relevant in civil cases as in the bargaining practices which have for many years been a major preoccupation of criminal justice researchers,[53] and, indeed, one prominent writer has viewed settlement in civil cases as 'the civil analogue of plea bargaining' (Fiss, 1984).[54]

But it soon became apparent in this study that informal negotiation (whether in the shadow of the law or otherwise) was not a common characteristic of the disposal of small claims. Out-of-court settlements in small claims in England and Wales are much less common than in other kinds of civil action. The reason for this is not difficult to determine: it is that settlement discussions in civil cases are primarily conducted on the initiative of lawyers, and when, as in small claims, lawyers are largely excluded, settlement becomes an infrequent occurrence. Lay litigants themselves rarely engage in pre-trial discussions unless prompted to do so. In so far as informal negotiations take place at all in small claims, they tend to be fostered by individual judges who may well have greater regard to immediate pragmatic concerns than the 'shadow of the law'.

The general conclusion to be drawn from this brief theoretical excursus is that, while each of these perspectives may have some relevance in the small claims context, none is of great value in understanding the many underlying tensions—some writers have called them contradictions[55]—in the small claims jurisdiction. The author's

[52] Although Mnookin and Kornhauser applied the concept of 'private ordering' to divorce cases, they saw it has having wide applicability to other kinds of dispute as well.

[53] There is a vast literature on the subject of informal settlements of plea (or plea-bargaining) in criminal cases: see, for instance, Baldwin and McConville (1977) and McConville *et al.* (1994).

[54] It is also established that court endorsement of informal settlements can amount to thoroughly coercive pressure on lay litigants. The plea bargaining literature shows how defendants in criminal trials are frequently pressured into accepting plea arrangements worked out behind closed doors. (See generally Baldwin and McConville, 1977; and McConville *et al.*, 1994.) We know much less about settlement mechanisms in civil cases, but the limited research evidence available (for example Genn, 1987) indicates that settlement processes may well favour certain kinds of litigant over others. As Fiss (1984: 1075) put it: 'Consent is often coerced. . . . Like plea bargaining, settlement is a capitulation to the conditions of mass society and should be neither encouraged nor praised'.

[55] See, for instance, Yngvesson and Hennessey (1975); Economides (1980); and Whelan (1990), at 124–9. Yngvesson and Hennessey (1975: 257) argue that:

> 'problems in the way small claims courts are operating today are linked not so much to who is using them, although this is a legitimate cause for concern, but to contradictions in the small claims model itself, contradictions linked to the "cross-cutting interests" of those most involved in planning and setting up the courts'.

own position is that it is the application of the law in informal legal settings that sets limits on the expansion of procedures like small claims, and it is this factor that principally handicaps unrepresented litigants. It consistently emerged throughout this research that lay litigants, since they lack legal expertise, experience difficulty in establishing the legal validity of their claims and defences and in arguing a coherent case in court. On this view, legal procedures like small claims, based as they are upon the principle of Do-It-Yourself justice where litigants are encouraged to do without lawyers, are problematic, even ultimately contradictory. It is not enough, therefore, to simplify court proceedings, to make hearings more relaxed and informal, or to encourage judges to play a facilitatory and interventionist role at hearings. The truth is that the law itself is complex, it does not by any means always conform to lay notions of justice, and it certainly cannot be conveyed to lay people in a few simple explanatory leaflets written in straightforward English.

The pervasiveness of law sets a definite limit on the extent to which it is feasible to expand the small claims jurisdiction, and, if litigants do not receive prior legal advice, it is unrealistic to expect judges to sort out the legal difficulties at the hearing itself. 'The procedure and protocol in these cases have changed, and the formality of the court has been removed, but nobody has altered the law' is how one district judge aptly expressed the point in an interview with the author. As will be argued in Chapters 3 and 4 of this book, litigants, who may well have been perfectly satisfied with the way that the hearing has been conducted, are nevertheless sometimes mystified by the decision that the judge eventually reaches because it does not square with their common sense conception of 'justice'. The picture presented by Sherr (1986) of the lawyer as 'the "High Priest" of the law handing down mystical pronouncements to grateful recipients' (*ibid.*: 356) might be extended to the district judge's role at small claims hearings.

One consequence is that, while it would not be accurate to regard the expansion in the scope of small claims as operating to the detriment of lay litigants, it would be naïve to see it as an unexceptionable development, or even as one that inevitably enhances citizens' access to justice. Attention needs also to be paid to the legal problems confronting litigants who decide to go it alone in the small claims setting. In this book, therefore, a number of key questions surrounding the operation and expansion of small claims will be explored. These questions have hitherto been largely neglected in the literature, and they include the extent to which lay litigants can be expected competently to prepare and present a legal case; whether legal advice is needed before and during hearings; the flexibility that district judges assume in applying the principles of English law, and the vexed question of the enforcement of judgments.

Conclusion

The striking feature in the resolution of small claims in England and Wales is the pragmatism of the judges who adjudicate them.[56] It is pointless to compare the small claims arena with a notional legal arena in which a Rolls Royce standard of justice is meted out. The whole point about civil procedure in general, and small claims in particular, is to devise a system which, in the words of Lord Woolf (1996), is 'proportionate but workable . . . not one which is theoretically impeccable but unaffordable' (*ibid.*: 106).[57]

The expansion of simplified legal procedures to deal with small claims in settings that are to a large extent free of legal representation is of great political significance, not least because the procedure has proved increasingly attractive to policy makers in coping with the alarming rise in the costs of civil litigation. The legal and political expediency of expanding the small claims limit in order to ease the crisis within the civil justice system and to counter the damaging effects of the diminishing availability of legal aid is very evident. How far small claims procedures are capable of continued expansion is a central concern of the study discussed in this book.

[56] The resolution of small claims in England and Wales is, however, impressive in that a highly paid judicial figure conducts the hearings. As will be seen in Chapter 3, although district judges are on the whole anxious to expedite matters, small claims hearings are rarely dealt with in a cursory manner.

[57] As Menkel-Meadow (1995: 228), one of the leading American authorities in the ADR movement, has argued: 'the greatest challenge for the transformation of the civil justice system is not *whether* it should be engaged in . . . alternative ways of doling out justice, but *how*' (emphasis in original).

2 Background to the Study: the County Court Files

The available research evidence on the operation of small claims in England and Wales is small-scale and fragmented. Commentators are as a result almost completely ignorant about what happens at small claims hearings in England and Wales. The *Judicial Statistics*, published annually by the Lord Chancellor's Department, provide a good deal of intriguing information about the work of the county courts in general and shed a little light on cases dealt with under the small claims procedure. But they cannot show—nor are they designed to—anything at all about how well small claims procedures operate in practice or about whether they are able to offer a standard of justice that is acceptable to the people who use them.

Publication of the *Judicial Statistics* has shown that the number of 'plaints' (the somewhat arcane term used for civil claims) entered at the county courts has been steadily increasing for at least half a century. Although there have been some strange fluctuations from year to year—in particular a marked reduction in numbers of plaints since 1992[1]—the trend over the last fifteen years has shown substantial overall increases in the numbers of cases dealt with in the county courts. But the *Judicial Statistics* reveal little of substance about the actual workload of the courts.[2] The great majority of judgments are entered without any court hearing—'by default' in the official vernacular—because the court has received no response from the defendant within fourteen days of service of the summons.[3] This means that, in 95 per

[1] Table 4.1 of the *Judicial Statistics: Annual Report 1995* (Cm 3290, 1996) shows, for instance, that the number of plaints entered in 1995 was 8 per cent lower than in 1994 and that the 1994 figure was 11 per cent lower than that for 1993.

[2] See the interesting discussion on this point in Camley (1995).

[3] Little is known about what happens in those cases in which judgment is entered by default, and it was beyond the resources of the present project to examine such cases. It is, however, clear that, in many cases, legal procedures are initiated without much optimism on the plaintiff's part that the other party will respond to the summons, and sights may well be set on later enforcement stages. There are probably also a substantial proportion of default judgments where the defendant pays up or makes an offer of payment to the plaintiff when the summons arrives. In many such circumstances, the parties do not trouble to inform the court. In one study conducted in New York City,

cent or more of all cases, the plaintiff is automatically granted judgment, without making any appearance in court.[4] The workload of the county courts is in consequence to a large extent administrative and bureaucratic in character rather than adjudicatory.[5] It is still a common misconception about the county courts, as Ison observed in 1972:

> that they are engaged primarily in the task of adjudication. So far as consumer transactions are concerned, it is nearer the truth to describe the county courts as being like collection agencies, enforcing the claims of sellers and finance companies regardless of their legitimacy. Only occasionally and by way of exception is there an inquiry into the merits of the case [*ibid.*: 18].

In one sense, small claims are a strange collection of cases. They are officially (and perhaps curiously) defined as those plaints which, up to a prescribed financial limit, happen to be defended in the county courts. It is well established that only a tiny proportion of all civil disputes ever reach the courts,[6] and, of those that do, small claims make up only a minority. However, small claims have formed an increasing proportion of county court business over the past twenty years, and they have come to dominate the disposal of defended civil actions. The figures given in the *Judicial Statistics* on this are striking, and show that an increase in the proportion of cases disposed of under the small claims procedure has occurred in virtually every year since it was introduced. The rise has been inexorable and remarkably consistent. When, for example, the small claims procedure was introduced in England and Wales in 1973, well over ten times as many judgments in the county courts were entered after trial (i.e. following a hearing in open court) as by arbitration (i.e. by the small claims procedure). Five years later, this

Sarat (1976) sent questionnaires to litigants who failed to attend hearings in the small claims court, and he found that over half of those who replied said they had been able to reach an out-of-court settlement. See also the study conducted by Caplovitz (1974), in Chicago, Detroit, and New York, which also sheds light on the reasons debtors fail to turn up to court hearings.

[4] It is important to bear in mind that, even if there is no court hearing, time still has to be spent by court staff in processing the paperwork in such cases: see Cranston (1986), at 133–4. There is generally no need for judges to be involved in these cases, however, since the County Court Rules do not specify who enters the default judgment.

[5] This point is forcefully made by Cain (1983).

[6] In its quarterly journal, *Fair Trading*, the Office of Fair Trading publishes the results of its Consumer Complaints Surveys. This gives the detailed breakdowns of consumer complaints reported by trading standards departments and advice agencies. The results of these surveys demonstrate that only a very small proportion of consumer complaints reach the county courts: see further Office of Fair Trading (1986, 1991) and the discussion at 165.

figure was reduced to three times as many. By 1982, rather more judgments were being entered under the small claims procedure than by trial, a trend that has accelerated ever since. Nowadays about 80 per cent of all defended actions in the county courts are dealt with under the procedure.

In numerical terms, the increase has been no less extraordinary, and it is scarcely an exaggeration to say that there has been something of an explosion in the numbers of small claims hearings in the 1980s and 1990s. In the fifteen years between 1978 and 1993, a ten-fold rise occurred in the number of small claims, and by 1993, almost 106,000 cases were heard under the small claims procedure. It was, therefore, surprising to find that in 1994, just under 88,000 cases were disposed of under the procedure, a reduction of no less than 17 per cent from the 1993 figure. The *Judicial Statistics* show that the 1995 figure was only slightly higher than that for 1994.[7] 1994 was, indeed, the first year in the history of small claims in England and Wales when there had been no increase in the number of hearings, and a reduction of 17 per cent suggests that the massive increase in numbers of small claims that many people assume will attend the raising of the limit to £3,000[8] may not occur. The capacity of the county courts to hold small claims hearings is finite, and one wonders whether, after years of rapid and sustained expansion in numbers of small claims hearings, the county courts have now reached saturation point in the numbers that district judges are able, or indeed prepared, to conduct.

This reduction notwithstanding, it can be confidently asserted, on the basis of the figures given in the *Judicial Statistics*, that the small claims procedure provides the predominant method of dealing with defended actions in county courts in England and Wales. The progressive raising of the small claims limit (with consequent automatic referral of claims within that limit to the small claims procedure) has reinforced that trend and has had the effect of reducing the numbers of traditional trials—or 'open court' trials as they are known—in the county courts. Although it is possible to do no more than speculate at the time of writing about the effects of increasing the small claims limit to £3,000, the official policy objective is clear: it is to divert ever more

[7] The number of small claims disposed of in the county courts was, according to the *Judicial Statistics*, 87,885 in 1994 and 88,170 in 1995.

[8] See, for instance, the *New Law Journal*, 23 June 1996, where the editor anticipated that the rise in the small claims limit to £3,000 will 'provide a simple procedure for hundreds of thousands more cases each year with no legal costs' (*ibid.*: 913).

cases to the small claims regime and to have far fewer determined by means of formal court adjudication.

Examining county court files

Considerable efforts were made in this study to find out what district judges and litigants thought about small claims procedures, and the author attended many courts throughout the country to see for himself what happened at the hearings. The author was the beneficiary of what has become known in the trade as 'syndicated' funding in that more than one organization supported the project. The Lord Chancellor's Department, the Office of Fair Trading, and the Economic and Social Research Council generously contributed to the funding of the research at different stages, and this allowed for a more extensive examination of the operation of small claims procedures (including the enforcement of judgments) than might otherwise have been possible. Having the Lord Chancellor's Department as one of the sponsoring organizations proved an enormous benefit, not least because it considerably eased the problems of gaining access to interested parties and enlisting their support. Problems of 'access' have in the past greatly limited the scope of socio-legal research, and being allowed to examine court files, to involve court staff at the county courts, to observe hearings and to interview district judges was extremely important.

In the course of the study, some 1,800 court files were examined, and, although this paper exercise seemed at first a rather dreary part of the project, it was nonetheless surprising to discover how much useful information could be unearthed simply by reading through court documents. It is true that the exercise yielded mainly statistical data, but many of the files contained much interesting information and anecdote, and they allowed comparisons to be made which would not have been possible using smaller numbers of cases. Court files represent an invaluable source in assessing the way that legal processes like small claims procedures operate, and the material extracted from the files that is discussed in this chapter complements the predominantly qualitative information unearthed in other parts of the inquiry. Material from interviews and court observation (which will be discussed in the following chapters) will be used to put some flesh on the bare statistical bones derived from scrutiny of the court files.

In this statistical exercise, the aim was to investigate the characteristics of a representative national sample of small claims. Given the resources available, it was not possible to include all county court summonses in this sample, since, as was noted above, 95 per cent or more of them are undefended actions which never reach the stage of being treated as a small claim.[9] Information relating to the processing of actions in which defences were filed was collected from a total of 1,800 files held at a dozen county courts in England and Wales. A random sample of 150 small claims, all of which were heard in 1993, was drawn from each court. To provide a broad mix of courts, two county courts in each of the six Circuits in England and Wales were included in the sample.[10] Information was systematically extracted from these 1,800 court files on factors such as the nature of the claim and the defence; the type of plaintiff and defendant involved; whether the parties turned up to a hearing; whether they were legally represented; the amount of money in dispute; the outcome of the hearing; the length of time taken to conclude the matter, and the court record of enforcement procedures. This information provided a broad factual framework within which detailed aspects of the procedures could be explored in later qualitative aspects of the enquiry.

Who makes use of the small claims procedure and for what purposes?

It is important at the outset to determine who is involved in small claims and what kind of issues arise in these disputes. As discussed in Chapter 1, there has been a great deal of discussion in the academic literature about whether the small claims procedure has been hijacked by commercial and business interests from the individual consumers for whom it was originally devised. It has become fashionable in this literature to depict the small claims arena as one in which business organizations can pursue small debts cheaply, and American writers often refer to small claims courts as being 'colonized' by business interests.[11] Table 1

[9] See, however, Whelan (1990), at 214–15 who stresses the importance of examining undefended as well as defended claims.

[10] In this part of the study, the sample of courts was drawn so as to include a relatively large and small court from each of the six Circuits in England and Wales. The county courts in question were: Northampton, Worcester, Cardiff, Chester, Manchester, Preston, Leeds, York, Portsmouth, Exeter, Edmonton, and Cambridge.

[11] There is now an extensive literature dealing with this phenomenon: see particularly Yngvesson and Hennessey (1975); White (1985), at 144–53; and Weller *et al.* (1990). The predominance of business users of small claims procedures has also been noted in other jurisdictions: see Jettinghoff (1986) and Whelan (1990) *passim.*

TABLE 2.1 *Who sues whom in small claims*

Plaintiffs Defendants		%
Large firm/org. *v.* other large firm/org.	5	0.3
Large firm/org. *v.* small firm/trader	70	3.9
Large firm/org. *v.* individual	188	10.4
Small firm/trader *v.* large firm/org.	10	0.6
Small firm/trader *v.* other small firm/trader	429	23.8
Small firm/trader *v.* individual	440	24.4
Individual *v.* large firm/org.	48	2.7
Individual *v.* small firm/trader	238	13.2
Individual *v.* other individuals	362	20.1
Other types of party	10	0.6
	1800	100.0

shows the kinds of plaintiffs and defendants involved in the small claims hearings included in the 1,800 files examined. These results highlight the very important point about the small claims arena that it is extensively used by small firms, traders, and individuals.

Table 1 shows that small firms featured as plaintiffs or defendants (or both) in about two thirds of all hearings in this sample. Indeed, in almost a quarter, small firms appeared against other small firms. Public organizations (like local authority departments, hospitals, and universities) and large commercial or business concerns (like banks and building societies) appeared much less commonly, whether as plaintiffs or defendants. But individuals featured in over 70 per cent of all hearings, albeit almost as often as defendants as plaintiffs. The small claims procedure is not, therefore, monopolized, as some writers have argued, by big business or, indeed, by other large and powerful organizations:[12] it is used mainly by small business concerns and by private individuals.

It is worth considering carefully the role of individuals in this picture because the small claims procedure in England was, after all, primarily

[12] Vidmar (1984: 528), refers, for instance, to the common depiction in the literature of 'large corporate entities . . . using the court to pursue individuals who . . . are intimidated and outgunned by their powerful adversaries'. His own study in Canada failed to support this picture, as do the results set out in Table 1.

created to serve their interests. Have private individuals become the victims of the procedure rather than the beneficiaries? While it is true that they were more likely to be involved in actions as defendants than as plaintiffs, private individuals still activated the procedure in a considerable proportion of all claims. The fact that well over a third of plaintiffs were individuals rather than business organizations clearly indicates that considerable use is still being made of small claims procedures in England by those for whom it was originally intended. Again, the figures presented in Table 1 scarcely support the common portrayal of the small claims procedure as subjugated to the requirements of large business users.

Nor do the findings support the other common characterization of small claims procedures given in the academic literature as offering a cheap and easy debt-recovery mechanism for businesses. While this picture applies in large part to county court actions taken as a whole,[13] only a small minority of such actions eventually turn into small claims. While almost all small claims involve the recovery of some debt or other (in that plaintiffs are claiming that there is money that is owed to them), the defences that are put forward may well transform the issue in contention from one of straight debt collection into something very different. Few defendants involved in small claims appear in court simply because they have declined to pay an outstanding bill. A good reason—or, more accurately, an arguable case—is generally offered by defendants for why they have not paid. In that sense, small claims are probably actions of a very different character from the myriad of all county court actions.[14]

In examining further the extent to which the interests of individual litigants are subordinated to those of business concerns, it is worth trying to determine who are the main beneficiaries in small claims. Who comes out ahead—individuals or the representatives of commercial and business concerns? This is a more difficult question to answer than might at first appear, particularly because the outcome of many court cases is not clearcut. It may as a result be misleading to talk of the proportions of plaintiffs winning or losing their cases since a significant proportion of them are successful only in part. About three-quarters of claims in this sample ended in a winner-takes-all decision (when either the plaintiff was awarded all that was sought or the claim was dismissed

[13] See further Cain (1983), and Whelan (1990), at 207–34.
[14] See the discussion in Whelan (1990), at 118–19, on this point.

TABLE 2.2 *The outcome of hearings for different groups of plaintiffs*

Type of plaintiff	Succeeds (wholly or in large part)		Less than 50% successful		Fails (wholly or in large part)		Total	
		%		%		%		%
Large public org.	54	63.5	6	7.1	25	29.4	85	100.0
Large firm	62	66.7	7	7.5	24	25.8	93	100.0
Small firm	330	62.0	45	8.5	157	29.5	532	100.0
Individual trader	64	58.2	14	12.7	32	29.1	110	100.0
Individual	304	62.4	51	10.5	132	27.1	487	100.0
	814	62.3	123	9.4	370	28.3	1307	100.0

outright), and, in just over a quarter of judgments, the sum awarded to plaintiffs was significantly less than the amount claimed.[15] Calculations involving proportions of winners and losers are in consequence bound to be somewhat complex. The exercise is further limited by the fact that no account could be taken of the relative strength of the respective legal cases or the performance of the parties on the day in court.[16] Despite these inevitable limitations, it was nonetheless interesting to investigate whether any broad patterns could be discerned in the outcome of hearings involving different types of plaintiff. As Table 2 indicates, no clear patterns at all emerged. Business users of the court did not appear to be any more successful than were private individuals.[17] This is surprising, particularly in the light of the academic

[15] This point was strenuously argued by Vidmar (1984: 518–19) who noted that:

'Studies that judge outcomes by whether or not the plaintiff receives any award are likely to report that plaintiffs almost always prevail. Studies that look at awards as a proportion of the amount sought are likely to report that plaintiffs typically win some of what they seek and that contested court cases often compromise between the two parties' positions'.

[16] It is doubtful whether such an exercise could ever be satisfactorily conducted. Large numbers of hearings would need to be attended by someone sufficiently experienced and knowledgeable to make such assessments. Such an exercise was well beyond the resources available in this study.

[17] The table excludes 493 hearings which were adjourned or in which the outcome was decided without a court hearing.

literature on small claims which suggests that the procedure is easily exploited by business interests familiar with its operation.

It is clear from this discussion that one needs to be wary of jumping to simplistic conclusions about the processing of small claims. The figures in Table 2 do not support the depiction of the small claims procedure as a mechanism which operates overwhelmingly to the benefit of powerful business concerns and at the expense of the lay litigant: rather they show that rates of success and failure are about the same for all groups.

The 1,800 files also revealed that the great majority of claims contained, on the surface at least, a real issue of substance raised in the defence for the court to determine. It is important to re-emphasize the point that small claims are not primarily concerned with debt recovery. In very many of these files, the defence that was submitted transformed the matter from a claim for payment of a debt into something different, and the description of the issue as 'debt recovery' may well mask a much more complex dispute. 'A claim by a business for non-payment may in essence be a consumer claim for defective goods or service', Whelan (1990: 219) rightly observes, and 'the refusal to pay represents the dissatisfaction felt by the consumer'. The category of 'quasi-debt' recovery case was used in this study to describe such claims, and it included claims for money which were defended on the grounds that a bill was excessive or inaccurate, or had already been paid, or related to shoddy goods, poorly performed services, unauthorized work, or else should not have been sent in the first place. In other words, parties labelled as 'defendants' may well be defending the case on the basis that they have received a raw deal themselves, and indeed frequently they see themselves as more sinned against than sinning and wanting to 'defend their good name' in the face of false accusations. Such quasi-debt cases were very prominent in this sample, comprising almost a third of all claims.[18]

Table 3, which presents the details relating to the types of claim that arose in this sample of 1,800 cases, shows that small claims cover a variety of issues, few of which can be described unequivocally as ones of straight debt recovery. Indeed, to characterize small claims procedures as representing mere debt collection mechanisms is to understate

[18] Caplovitz (1974), in a major study of debt in the United States, noted that 35 per cent of debtors gave reasons for their default that implicated the creditor.

TABLE 2.3 *Issue in dispute at small claims*

		%
Consumer goods and services	381	21.2
Quasi-debt recovery	560	31.1
Road accident	278	15.4
Straight debt recovery	164	9.1
Credit sale	32	1.8
Dishonoured cheque	28	1.5
Employment	45	2.5
Housing	114	6.3
Other type of claim	198	11.1
	1800	100.0

the importance of what is, in reality, a much more complex and socially significant operation.

Special small claims procedures were originally devised in England and Wales as a response to the 'consumer movement', and the procedural rules were relaxed primarily to encourage consumers to bring their disputes before the courts.[19] Yet as has just been seen, the boundaries between consumer claims and claims from businesses for non-payment are often very difficult to draw, and Table 3 indicates that only about a fifth of the 1,800 claims were classed in this study as specifically consumer disputes.[20] Consumer claims fell into four main categories: disputes about goods (28.1 per cent), consumer services (34.6 per cent), trade services (18.4 per cent), and professional services (18.9 per cent). However, in only a minority of these claims (40.4 per cent) was the plaintiff an individual—the rest were businesses or other commercial organizations, almost always a small firm or individual trader. A similar profile emerged in relation to defendants involved in consumer claims, where only a third were individual litigants, and a majority were drawn from small business concerns. This means that the original conception of the small claims procedure being of particular benefit to private individuals bringing consumer disputes to the courts has scarcely been realized: the procedure is used more by other groups and for other purposes.

[19] On this, see the report of the Consumer Council (1970) and the discussion in Whelan (1990), at 99–102.

[20] Further details of the outcome of 'consumer' claims is given in Baldwin (1996).

TABLE 2.4 *Amount of money claimed by the plaintiff*

		%
Less than £50	106	5.9
£50 less than £100	164	9.2
£100 less than £200	292	16.4
£200 less than £300	265	14.9
£300 less than £400	211	11.8
£400 less than £500	143	8.0
£500 less than £750	287	16.1
£750 less than £1,000	206	11.6
£1,000 or more	108	6.1
Amount not specified	18	–
	1800	100.0

As one would expect, the amount of money claimed in small claims varies greatly. This study was completed before the small claims limit was raised to £3,000 in January 1996, and the limit was set at £1,000 throughout the period that the study was conducted. But as the figures in Table 4 show, even with the limit at £1,000, two-thirds of all small claims included in this national sample were for less than £500. Indeed, almost a third were for amounts under £200. This suggests that raising the small claims limit might not have a dramatic effect on the number of claims dealt with under the expanded small claims procedure since, even shortly before the rise, the great majority of claims were already well below the limit. It is perhaps also revealing that, although there were a number of claims which involved sums in excess of £1,000 (which could still be dealt with under the former regime if the plaintiff so requested and the other party and the court agreed), there were no indications that large numbers of plaintiffs were seeking to do so. Table 4 presents the overall figures.

In just over a fifth of all cases, the defendant issued a counterclaim (i.e. a separate claim against the plaintiff). Counterclaims were on average for lesser amounts than the sums claimed by plaintiffs. Over 40 per cent of counterclaims were for less than £200, and only a quarter were for more than £500. However, no more than forty-one (10.8 per cent) of all counterclaims succeeded, wholly or in part. It was not difficult to see from the court files why rates of success were so low. The main reason was that the relevant law was frequently misunderstood by defendants.[21] Many counterclaims were no more than vague assertions that some compensation should be paid to the defendant for the stress that had been caused by the plaintiff pursuing the action in the first place. In other words, they fell short of being legal claims at all. This is a crucial point in understanding the operation of the small claims regime, and is an illustration of the argument advanced in the previous chapter that the application of the law itself sets a critical limitation on the operation of simplified procedures like small claims in which lawyers are as a rule involved only as adjudicators. The following quotes relating to defendants' counterclaims, which are taken directly from the court files, provide examples of the kinds of difficulty that lay litigants, when unaided, experience in making out a legal case:

The defendant will claim costs in defending what is a claim without foundation at law [Midland and Oxford Circuit, Case 117].

If this matter proceeds I wish to claim my costs of defending this action off the plaintiff [Midland and Oxford Circuit, Case 288].

£100—costs incurred [Wales and Chester Circuit, Case 152].

£50—nuisance value since I have told [the newspaper] and their agents that I have never placed any advertisement [Wales and Chester Circuit, Case 230].

£50—the plaintiff owes my father this sum for a previous loan [Wales and Chester Circuit, Case 64].

£100—because no matter how much effort I've gone to to sort the matter out, their accounts department have not at all responded [Northern Circuit, Case 2].

£250—time and costs involved in dealing with matters that should have been dealt with by the plaintiff [Northern Circuit, Case 53].

The only counter claim I will have, will be for any costs involved defending this case [North Eastern Circuit, Case 155].

I claim the amount of £307.20 as compensation for loss of reputation as I can prove beyond a shadow of a doubt that my vehicle was not in this collision. I request that this case be discussed forthwith [North Eastern Circuit, Case 187].

£67—by reason of the plaintiff's breach of the covenant for quiet enjoyment. The defendant has suffered loss and damage, wasted telephone installation,

[21] See Applebey (1994), at 71. For a judicial view of the vagueness of defendants' counterclaims, see Dickinson (1994).

fees, bank charge for cancelling cheques, 'distress and inconvenience' [Western Circuit, Case 224].

Yes, I would like to make a counterclaim against the plaintiff for wasting my time, and causing distress and strain, anxiety and nuisance. The amount I would leave to the Court's discretion. The following letters bear testimony to my case [South Eastern Circuit, Case 60].

£350—this Counterclaim is for the cost of my holiday which Mr D 'RUINED'. I think it's fair, because I am not claiming aggravation money, Ferry and Petrol Compensation [South Eastern Circuit, Case 92].

I verily believe that I have a valid defence and counterclaim to the Council's claim [South Eastern Circuit, Case 126].

£66—I counterclaim because I cannot be responsible for the plaintiff's incompetence and therefore would argue the costs involved [South Eastern Circuit, Case 199].

The above quotations from the court files provide examples of the kinds of misunderstandings that lay litigants may encounter in completing the court forms.[22] It is not that these forms are particularly difficult to complete, but rather that lay litigants frequently complete them in a casual, superficial, or inappropriate manner. There is also a common inclination (evident in some of the quotations above) to use English that borders on the Dickensian. Although this is no doubt intended to impress, it nonetheless often betrays misunderstandings of the law. The district judges are for the most part remarkably sympathetic to the difficulties that lay litigants face, and many of them say that they will 'lean over backwards' to ensure that litigants receive a fair deal. Indeed, as will be seen in Chapter 3, some judges concede that they are prepared on occasions to 'stretch' the law, even to ignore it, where they fear that its strict application would produce injustice. But district judges are obliged to set the key points raised by litigants into some kind of legal context, and the examination of these 1,800 files revealed (in the judgement of the solicitor employed on the study to examine them[23]) that it sometimes requires considerable mental and legal agility to determine what exactly is the case that a litigant is attempting to develop. This said, in the great majority of

[22] These difficulties are elaborated in the study by Cain (1983).

[23] Mrs Sue Deebank, a qualified solicitor, assumed the responsibility for evaluating the legal validity of claims and defences.

cases included in this sample, the litigants had developed at least the kernel of a legal case, and to that extent they gave the judges something to work on. In the author's view, however, a legal mind needs to be applied at an early stage in proceedings if litigants are to do justice to themselves at hearings.

The hearings

Not all the claims in this sample were determined by a district judge at a small claims hearing. In one in six defended claims, matters had been resolved informally between the parties beforehand and the court did little more than countenance the agreement already reached without the need for a formal court hearing.[24] In some of these cases, settlement was reached as soon as the parties met face to face, something that often happens only on the day of the hearing itself. In that sense, the mere existence of a court and the fixing of time for a hearing can serve to prompt a settlement between the parties. It is somewhat strange that the parties in small claims are not officially encouraged at any stage to seek to resolve their differences through settlement, and the leaflets that are issued by the Lord Chancellor's Department make only a passing reference to that possibility. The interviews that were conducted with litigants in this study showed that many lay people thought that initiating contact with the other side would be regarded by the authorities as improper. This is paradoxical since settlement in civil proceedings tends to be viewed by the legal professionals as a very desirable result and preferable to litigation and a court-imposed resolution.[25] But different considerations apply in small claims, and lay litigants, if left to their own devices, rarely engage in settlement discussions.[26]

The main reason that small claims hearings do not proceed as anticipated is that one of the parties does not turn up on the day. As with many other kinds of court and tribunal, these hearings are dogged

[24] These cases are very similar to those cases, classified as judgments by default, in which the defendant reaches an out-of-court agreement with the plaintiff. Whether a case is officially recorded as a judgment by default or a defended civil action (i.e. as a small claim) depends upon whether the court initially receives a response from the defendant to the summons.

[25] Early settlement of civil actions was strongly endorsed, for example, in Lord Woolf's Inquiry (1995, 1996).

[26] A few district judges actively seek to prompt it themselves at small claims hearings: see 62–6.

TABLE 2.5 *Who turns up to small claims hearings*

		%
Both parties attend	509	40.2
One party attends and the other sends a representative	80	6.3
Both parties send a representative	14	1.1
Plaintiff alone present	317	25.0
Defendant alone present	106	8.4
Representative for one of the parties attends	58	4.6
Neither party attends	182	14.4
Not relevant—resolved by the parties beforehand	302	–
Not clear from the file who attends	232	–
	1800	100.0

by the non-appearance of the parties. This phenomenon is extremely important in relation to small claims hearings,[27] and, in the present sample, over a half of the cases failed to go forward to full hearings with both the parties (or their representatives) in attendance. Table 5 shows the detailed picture.

There were marked (and statistically significant) differences from group to group in their propensities to attend hearings. Not surprisingly, plaintiffs were more likely to attend or to send their representatives than were defendants (76.4 as against 56.9 per cent), and individuals were more likely to attend hearings, whether as plaintiffs or defendants, than were litigants from small or large businesses. 83.3 per cent of individual plaintiffs attended the hearing as against 72.3 per cent of businesses, and for defendants the proportions were 58.6 per cent and 54.8 per cent respectively.[28]

Attendance is of the greatest significance in relation to the outcome of small claims hearings, since it consistently emerged throughout this study that, where only one party attended, success was all but assured for that party. The mere fact of attendance was, it seemed, sufficient in most cases to determine the outcome, whatever might be the legal and evidential strengths and weaknesses in a litigant's case. Or to put it another way, non-attendance was very closely associated with failure,

[27] The non-attendance of one or both parties is also a frequent occurrence at other kinds of court and tribunal: see, for instance, Baldwin *et al.* (1992), at 103–9.

[28] These differences were statistically significant at the 1 per cent level, indicating that there was a probability of only a one in 100 that the differences could be due to chance.

regardless of the strength of the litigant's case on paper. In those hearings in which plaintiffs alone or their representatives attended, only thirty-seven (10.8 per cent) were decided wholly or substantially in favour of the defendant. Absent plaintiffs fared even worse: only five (4.5 per cent) succeeded when the defendant or a representative turned up to the hearing. The implication of this finding is clear: when litigants seek preliminary guidance about how they may succeed with a claim, the best single piece of advice they can be given is, it seems, simply to turn up to the hearing.

It has often been stated in the academic writing about small claims that plaintiffs are likely to come out on top. Yngvesson and Hennessey (1975: 243), for example, in their celebrated review of the research literature, cite the findings of numerous empirical studies to support the general proposition that 'the plaintiff almost always wins'. However, as Yngvesson and Hennessey themselves recognized, this bald statement is somewhat misleading, since there are other independent variables that might produce this result. Account needs also to be taken, for instance, of the fact that plaintiffs are also more likely to attend hearings, that their claims may be more firmly grounded in law, and that a substantial proportion of decisions are neither wholly in favour nor against the plaintiff. Non-attendance was found to be so frequent an occurrence in the present study and so closely tied to success that it would obviously have been meaningless to have considered rates of success for either party without taking it into account. In the 548 hearings in which both parties (or their representatives) attended and where there was a full hearing, only 64.4 per cent of plaintiffs were successful wholly or in large part. Even this proportion may exaggerate the success of plaintiffs, since it does not take account of those cases in which there was an informal settlement between the parties.[29] This means that defendants were successful in a surprisingly high proportion of cases. This finding runs counter to the received wisdom in the small claims literature and offers a measure of support for the viewpoint advanced by Vidmar (1984) whose study in Canada showed that, once account was taken of non-attendance and of the fact that small claims disputes did not always result in all-or-nothing outcomes, defendants were not less successful than plaintiffs.

[29] Although no information could be collected in this study on the details of these agreements, it is nevertheless likely that there were a number of plaintiffs who decided to settle for much less than they had originally claimed.

A number of litigants sought to mitigate the effects of non-attendance by sending letters (even occasionally affidavits) to the court in which they gave reasons for their failure to turn up to the hearing or attempted to explain their case in further detail. Seventy-nine of the court files contained letters submitted by one or other of the parties. Fifty of the letters were from absent plaintiffs,[30] twenty-five from absent defendants, and four from both absent parties. However, few of these letters had the effect of countering the negative effects of non-attendance. They only ever seemed to tip the scales when, by good fortune, the other party failed to turn up at the hearing. There were only three instances in which the party submitting a letter was successful (wholly or in part) when the other party attended. Yet where neither party attended, the party that sent a letter to the court was successful in almost 70 per cent of instances. It seemed, then, that a letter to the court might have had some effect in influencing the outcome of a case in exceptional circumstances, but it clearly could not offset the more general disadvantages of non-attendance.

An issue that is frequently raised by litigants in relation to non-attendance is whether it is fair to hold hearings in the court in the district where the defendant resides or carries on business, as is the practice in England and Wales.[31] Where the two parties involved in a small claims dispute live in different parts of the country, nearly all hearings are automatically transferred from the county court at which the summons is issued to the court nearest the defendant's home or place of business. This can present serious difficulties to those plaintiffs who have to travel considerable distances to have their claims heard. In this sample, as many as a third of all claims were transferred to the defendant's court. In one in twelve of all claims, this would have involved plaintiffs travelling to a court that was over 100 miles away, and one in seven to a court over thirty miles away. One wonders whether plaintiffs whose cases have been transferred to a distant court are less likely to attend the hearing as a result. The figures on this are interesting and show that a transfer of venue seemed to have no effect upon plaintiff attendance as long as the distances were no more than about thirty miles. In these circumstances, the rate of attendance by plaintiffs was about 80 per cent regardless of the distances they were required to travel. For journeys in excess of thirty miles, however,

[30] Eleven of the letters submitted by plaintiffs and two by defendants had been written by solicitors.

[31] See Applebey (1994), at 49–50.

attendance fell to less than 60 per cent. Not surprisingly, defendant attendance rates were much less affected by such transfers, although, as an overall trend, defendants were significantly less likely to attend hearings than were plaintiffs. And even when the transferred hearing involved a journey of over 100 miles for the plaintiff, a higher proportion of plaintiffs nevertheless attended hearings than did defendants.

As this study proceeded, it was apparent in all the author's discussions with judges, litigants, lawyers, court administrators, and others that legal representation at small claims hearings remains a critical question. As will be seen in subsequent chapters, it is also a subject on which views widely differ. There is an obvious and unresolved tension here. On the one hand, the involvement of lawyers can be seen as desirable, maybe even essential, because the small claims arena is a legal setting in which lay people are bound to be at a disadvantage; on the other hand, it needs to be recognized that the costs of employing lawyers can rapidly defeat the object of the small claims procedure. The ostensible purpose of relaxing the rules of evidence and procedure in the civil courts and encouraging interventionism on the part of district judges has been to facilitate the presentation of cases by unrepresented parties and to reduce the need for legal representation. In seeking to encourage lay people to use the civil courts, a few jurisdictions have taken the radical step of banning lawyers altogether from small claims hearings.[32] While this has never been seriously contemplated in England, litigants' reliance upon lawyers at small claims hearings in England is probably lower than in most other countries where representation is allowed.[33] Table 6 shows the frequency with which legal representatives appeared at the small claims hearings in this sample.

It is clear from the table that, in the great majority of the small claims hearings included in these samples, neither of the parties was legally represented. There were very few cases in which both of the parties were legally represented. Lay representation at hearings is even more of a rarity: only forty-six of the hearings (3.1 per cent) in this large sample involved a lay representative appearing for one side or the other, and there was not a single hearing in which both of the parties had lay representation.[34] Table 6 also shows that three times as many

[32] See below at 76.

[33] The available research is discussed by Weller *et al.* (1984) and Whelan (1990), at 221. The study conducted by the Scottish Office Central Research Unit (1991) also shows that rates of legal representation are much higher in Scotland.

[34] The study conducted by the National Audit Office (1996) also showed very low rates of lay representation.

TABLE 2.6 *Legal representation at small claims hearings*

		%
Neither party is legally represented	1224	81.6
Plaintiff alone is legally represented	183	12.2
Defendant alone is legally represented	61	4.1
Both parties are legally represented	31	2.1
Not relevant because not resolved by small claims procedures	301	–
	1800	100.0

plaintiffs were represented at hearings as were defendants. Not surprisingly, there was an identifiable trend for representation to be associated with the amount of money at stake in the claim—the larger the amount, the more likely it was for the parties, in particular plaintiffs, to be represented.[35] Whereas only 10 per cent of plaintiffs (and 3 per cent of defendants) were legally represented in claims of less than £100, this proportion increased to a quarter (12 per cent for defendants) in claims in excess of £500.

It is more frequently assumed than demonstrated in the academic literature that litigants who appear on behalf of business interests or other organizations are more likely to be represented at small claims hearings than are individuals, and it is argued that this reinforces power differentials between these groups.[36] This association was, however, only weakly confirmed in the present study. Public organizations (like local authority departments, hospitals, and banks) and the largest firms were certainly more likely to have legal representation at hearings than were other kinds of litigant. Indeed, some of these large organizations had an in-house solicitor who turned up to all hearings in which the organization was a party. Even so, in three-quarters of all small claims hearings in which such organizations were involved, the case was presented by a representative of the organization rather than by a solicitor.[37] The smaller firms and traders were, if anything, even

[35] The same phenomenon was noted by Weller *et al.* (1984) and by Touche Ross (1986).

[36] See, for example, the discussion in Whelan (1990), at 221–3.

[37] Although it was not recorded in the court files, it was apparent from court observation that some of those staff members who appeared on behalf of organizations had acquired a considerable amount of experience in presenting cases in this kind of setting.

TABLE 2.7 *Rates of legal representation by type of litigant*

	Represented		Not represented		Total	
		%		%		%
Where plaintiff is:						
Large public organization/ large firm	39	23.5	127	76.5	166	100.0
Small firm/individual trader	97	15.4	531	84.6	628	100.0
Individual	77	16.3	394	83.7	471	100.0
	213	16.8	1052	83.2	1265	100.0
Where defendant is:						
Large public organization/ large firm	10	25.6	29	74.4	39	100.0
Small firm/individual trader	30	5.7	496	94.3	526	100.0
Individual	51	7.4	638	92.6	689	100.0
	91	7.3	1163	92.7	1254	100.0

more likely to represent themselves than were individuals. Table 7 shows the proportions of litigants in the different groups who were represented at the hearings.[38]

But does legal representation make a difference to the outcome in court? This is a very tricky question to answer, not least because no account can be taken in a statistical examination of the relative strength of the legal case in question. However, the effect of representation is an extremely interesting issue to examine in the small claims context. There is some research evidence to suggest that legal representation is associated with a successful outcome before certain kinds of tribunal,[39] and, in the largest study of small claims courts carried out in the United States by Steven Weller and his colleagues (1984, 1990), it emerged that representation was more important to defendants than it

[38] The totals in each part of the table are slightly different because of the small number of hearings in which other types of party appeared. The differences shown in Table 7 in the likelihood of different types of plaintiff and defendant being represented reach a level of statistical significance. In both cases, however, this is because of the higher proportions of large firms and public organizations which had legal representation at hearings.

[39] See the studies of tribunals by Bell (1975) and Genn and Genn (1989), and the discussion in Cranston (1995), at 52–4.

was to plaintiffs. But it was apparent from observing small claims hearings in the present study and from talking to the district judges concerned that representation was not something that many judges welcomed. It is worth examining whether the prevailing judicial view that lawyers are only of limited value to small claims litigants is supported by the evidence.

Researchers have always found it extremely difficult to separate the effects of representation from the other variables that influence the outcome of cases. There is no satisfactory way of taking account of the likelihood that parties with the strongest cases may also be the ones most likely to engage the services of lawyers. There is in addition an unknown number of weak cases that never reach the courts because they are dropped on the advice that a lawyer has offered. There was no possibility of controlling for these kinds of complication in this study. Testing the hypothesis that represented parties are more likely to be successful than those who are unrepresented could, therefore, only be done crudely. The results showed clearly, however, that there was a strong (and statistically significant) tendency for litigants with legal representation to be more successful than those without.[40] Representation seemed to improve litigants' chances of success by about 10 per cent. It also emerged that, as Weller *et al.* (1984) had found in the United States, defendants benefited more than plaintiffs from representation, and, where represented defendants faced unrepresented plaintiffs, judgment was awarded against them in less than a third of hearings. It is difficult to know what weight to attach to these results, but they do support the author's general conclusion that, while the small claims arena has been devised with litigants in person firmly in mind, having legal assistance is of considerable benefit to those litigants who seek it.

There has been a great deal of debate—and no little research—in recent years concerned with the subject of court delay.[41] Very little is known, however, about the length of time that it takes for cases to be dealt with in the county courts. No fixed standards are laid down by the county courts, and it is still widely accepted that it is the parties who are in control. Even with the advent of the managerial or 'procedural' judge,[42] the parties (and their lawyers) exert a considerable influence

[40] This association was not found in the Touche Ross study (1986) in which it was noted that legal representation made little, if any, difference to outcome.

[41] See particularly the research conducted in the United States by Church, Carlson, Lee, and Tan (1978) and in England by Plotnikoff and Woolfson (1993).

[42] See Woolf (1995, 1996).

TABLE 2.8 *Length of time taken from issue to conclusion*

		%	Cumulative percentage
Within 12 weeks	293	16.6	16.6
12 weeks under 16 weeks	310	17.5	34.1
16 weeks under 20 weeks	246	13.9	48.0
20 weeks under 6 months	297	16.8	64.8
6 months under 9 months	326	18.5	83.3
9 months under 12 months	156	8.8	92.1
12 months or over	140	7.9	100.0
Not known	32	–	
	1800	100.0	

over the time it takes for civil cases to be finalized by the courts. There is, however, at least a tacit expectation that matters will be dealt with expeditiously under the simplified small claims procedure. The court files provide some useful information on court delays, and Table 8 shows how long it took to deal with the claims included in the sample.

Table 8 shows that only slightly more than a third of all claims were concluded within four months of the date of issue of the summons, and almost one in twelve took over a year to be concluded. There were also dramatic variations from court to court.[43] For instance, while less than a tenth of claims had been concluded in Edmonton and Manchester within sixteen weeks, almost two thirds had been dealt with in Cardiff in that time. And although a half of cases in Worcester, Manchester, and Edmonton had not been concluded within six months, the proportion was less than a quarter in Cardiff and Exeter. No overall patterns were evident according to the size of the court in terms of delays in hearing claims, and there was no indication whatever that large courts took any longer to deal with them than the smaller ones.

As noted in Chapter 1, finality of result is regarded as being of utmost importance in the hearing of small claims. Litigants' rights of appeal are in consequence very limited, being confined to errors of law or judicial misconduct. In this sample, only two appeals—both unsuc-

[43] Similar variations between courts were noted in the survey conducted by Touche Ross (1986). It would, however, be misleading to attempt to draw direct comparisons between the two studies since important changes of procedure (in particular the virtual elimination of preliminary hearings in small claims) have occurred since the Touche Ross study was completed.

cessful—were launched out of these 1,800 cases. (It is, however, common at hearings for the losing parties immediately to tell the district judge, as soon as the decision is announced, of their intention to appeal.) But litigants do have a right to seek to have judgments set aside, and a district judge may agree to that course and order that a fresh hearing be held if one of the parties is able to demonstrate that they were unaware that the hearing was to take place on a particular date. In small claims, this procedure is far more significant than appeal, and, in this sample of 1,800 small claims, judgments were set aside in no fewer than 118 (6.6 per cent). There were even seven cases in which judgment was set aside on more than one occasion.[44]

Cases do not end with the court hearing: successful plaintiffs also need to enforce the judgment if they are to recover any money. The issue of enforcement will be examined in some detail in Chapter 5, and the county court files provide some limited information about what happens at that stage. The files show that, in 80 per cent of cases in which the claim was resolved, no formal action was initiated by plaintiffs to enforce the court order. In the cases in which some action was taken, by far the most common step was by means of a 'warrant of execution'—in popular parlance, 'sending the bailiffs in'. The other possible steps that parties might take to enforce judgment (which include measures such as the attachment of earnings orders, garnishee orders, and charging orders[45]) were hardly used at all. However, it should not be inferred from these figures that only 20 per cent of plaintiffs experienced problems in enforcing the court's judgment. On the contrary, it will be argued in Chapter 5 that it is often at the enforcement stage that the really serious problems in pursuing a small claim become apparent. There is no doubt that many more plaintiffs face difficulties at this stage than the official figures suggest. The files at several of the county courts visited in this research contained only superficial information about enforcement procedures, and it is very noticeable that these parts of the court files are often poorly kept. There may indeed be considerable under-recording of enforcement action at some county courts where details of enforcement procedures

[44] Applebey (1994: 97) observed that seeking to have a judgment set aside is a technique cynically employed 'all too often . . . by those who know how to manipulate the rules' in order to drag out proceedings. Lord Woolf (1996), at 160, proposed that applications to have judgments set aside should be subject to a preliminary paper consideration stage.

[45] The available methods of enforcement are described at 142–4.

are sometimes recorded in a casual manner,[46] perhaps reflecting the generally half-hearted attitude towards enforcement that is evident in many courts.

Conclusion

The objective of this chapter has been to examine who uses the small claims procedure and with what result. In some respects, the results of this statistical exercise contradict assumptions commonly made about small claims, not only by court personnel but by academic writers too. While this analysis shows something of the diversity of small claims, there are nonetheless certain underlying patterns that are found at all county courts. These relate particularly to the predominance of small businesses, the relative infrequency of representation, and the importance of attendance as a key determinant of outcome.

What is missing, however, from this statistical description is any idea of the drama of small claims hearings and the human and psychological dimensions of appearing in court to present or defend a claim. As will be seen in subsequent chapters, the power inequalities that are frequently assumed to exist between lay litigants on the one hand and business users of the court on the other are, in most cases, more apparent than real, since a majority of all those involved in small claims hearings have little, if any, prior experience of the procedure. Much the same might be said of many of the lawyers who appear at hearings. Most litigants inevitably rely upon their common sense to see them through, and, while this might be thought to be appropriate in relation to procedures that are designed to be informal and flexible, it can nevertheless provide a precarious basis on which to ground judgements about the law itself.

[46] In one court in the sample, for example, there was no record of any enforcement action at all in any of the 150 claims that were examined.

3 The District Judge's Role at Small Claims Hearings

At the time of writing, there are over 350 permanent district judges sitting in county courts in England and Wales and over twice as many deputy district judges.[1] These are the judges who conduct small claims hearings, and, in common with small claims adjudicators in other parts of the world, they have been encouraged to intervene to an increasing extent at small claims hearings. Publication both of the Report of the Review Body on Civil Justice in 1988 and of the interim report of the Woolf Inquiry in 1995 has given considerable impetus to this development.[2] The Civil Justice Review Body had noted in a consultation paper that there was considerable hesitancy on the part of many registrars (the forerunners to district judges) in playing a truly interventionist role, and it was evident that some of them were stuck in an adversarial rut.[3] The Review Body strongly favoured expansion of the small claims procedure and enthusiastically supported the idea of an interventionist judiciary 'dispensing with the formal rules of evidence and procedure, and assuming control of the questioning of the parties and their witnesses' (1988: paragraph 527).

In playing an interventionist role, district judges are expected to ensure that the relevant evidence is elicited from the parties and that litigants appearing in person are assisted in presenting their own cases. The concept of judicial interventionism is vital to the successful operation of small claims procedures, and represents the unifying thread in the arrangements made in virtually all countries that have grappled with the question of small claims. Although there may be wide variations between jurisdictions in the methods of reaching decisions and in the procedures adopted, the idea of the adjudicator freely entering the

[1] The former are in the main based at a particular court, whereas deputies are expected to sit at county courts around the Circuit.

[2] The recommendations relating to small claims are set out in chapter 8 in the Civil Justice Review (1988) and in chapter 16 of the Woolf Inquiry (1995).

[3] See Lord Chancellor's Department (1986). In its examination of small claims, the Review Body relied heavily upon the study conducted by the management consultants, Touche Ross (1986).

arena of the dispute and lending a helping hand to unrepresented litigants is, thus, fundamental in almost all thinking about small claims.

Judicial interventionism is not, however, always easy to achieve, particularly for judges who (as in England) have been reared according to adversarial principles. Judges have in the past been discouraged from playing a pro-active role at hearings, and the traditional role of judges is nicely captured in the following passage written by Glanville Williams (1963: 26): 'The classic advice to a newly appointed judge is that he should take a sup of holy water in his mouth at the beginning of a case and not swallow it until the evidence on both sides has been heard'. Times have changed a great deal since that passage was written, yet, despite the increasing importance of alternative forms of dispute resolution based upon mediation, conciliation, and arbitration, playing the interventionist role remains foreign to the thinking and the traditions that English judges have absorbed in their training and experience. Nor is it a role that they would naturally welcome, since it is one that bears remarkable similarities to that played by inquisitorial judges found in many civil law jurisdictions. Yet it can be asserted with some confidence that, unless adjudicators play an interventionist role—and, what is more, play it competently and enthusiastically—small claims procedures simply will not work.

Dilemmas with small claims

Although the small claims procedure is now firmly established in this country, there are a number of legal and conceptual questions that remain unanswered after twenty-five years of its operation. The meaning of 'interventionism' itself is, for example, unclear. There are difficulties with the underlying theory of judicial intervention as well as unresolved dilemmas, even contradictions, in the small claims model itself.[4] One main uncertainty relates to whether the judges at small claims hearings are obliged clinically to apply the law in reaching decisions or whether the flexibility and informality of procedures allow them the latitude to substitute their own broader notions of social justice. As will be seen later in this chapter, some district judges argue that a determination to adhere coldly to the letter of the law and to preserve the aloof and dignified detachment that is still so much part of

[4] For a perceptive discussion of some of these dilemmas, see Yngvesson and Hennessey (1975).

English judicial traditions runs directly counter to the spirit of small claims. They contend that, if small claims procedures are to operate satisfactorily, it will be because their robust and pragmatic good sense supersedes the strict application of law to their decisions.

Another dilemma surrounds the role of legal representatives. There is no generally accepted view on how lawyers, who themselves remain for the most part adversarial in orientation and thinking, are to fit into the inquisitorial ethos of the small claims regime. Nor has any definitive answer been given to the question whether litigants in person should consult lawyers before they make or defend a claim or whether they should be legally represented at hearings. The court leaflets that are available to litigants are ambivalent on the point, stating that a solicitor is 'probably' not necessary.[5] As seen in the previous chapter, the participation of a lawyer does improve a litigant's statistical prospects of success at small claims hearings, and, in the opinion of this writer, the provision of competent legal advice at the outset, even if it is only to dissuade a litigant from proceeding further with the case, is vital.

Similar dilemmas arise at the hearings themselves. Whilst district judges are in principle expected to assist litigants to present their cases in court, it is difficult to see the value of this exercise where the case being advanced is without legal validity and is doomed from the outset to fail. No rule exists to guide judges on whether they should merely go through the motions of a full hearing (which may merely serve falsely to raise litigants' hopes) or whether they should intervene as early as possible to put them out of their misery. Any district judge who takes the latter course—'going for the jugular' in the judicial vernacular—may well find that this leaves lay litigants complaining that the hearing has failed to address the key issues in their case and that the judge was unwilling to allow the grievance fully to be aired in court. However, the alternative of engaging in a charade in which litigants are given free rein (and indeed assisted in developing specious arguments) is perhaps even more unsatisfactory.[6]

[5] Similar ambivalence pre-dates the current leaflets: see White (1958), at 145–6, and Whelan (1990: 125) at 124–5. In a perceptive discussion, Whelan dissects the contradictory messages given in the earlier publication of the Lord Chancellor's Department (Birks, 1984) about the importance of legal representation. He notes that this booklet 'rather than boost the confidence of the potential litigant-in-person, makes clear instead that self-reliance for claimants is a risky business'.

[6] This tension is discussed in Baldwin *et al.* (1992), at 114–24 in relation to adjudication by social security appeal tribunals.

Observing the judges

A central part of the evaluation of small claims procedures in this study involved observing district judges at hearings. It is well known that members of the senior judiciary have been distinctly unenthusiastic in the past about participating in empirical research projects,[7] and the author required the permission of the Senior Presiding Judge for England and Wales before he was allowed to attend small claims hearings or talk to any district judges about them. Once the research was under way, however, the district judges he encountered were without exception extremely accommodating. No judge or litigant raised any objection to the author attending hearings, and all of the judges approached agreed to be interviewed by the writer. One judge turned up at the court in a rather poor state, saying that he had left his sick bed in order to be interviewed. Indeed, the writer was frequently impressed by judges' enthusiasm about participating in the enquiry. Many of them had strong views about small claims, and most were willing to express them candidly, even with a tape recorder turned on.[8]

Over a six month period between November 1993 and May 1994, the writer observed a total of 109 small claims hearings at eighteen county courts in England and Wales, and he interviewed the thirty-three district judges (of whom five were deputy district judges) who had conducted those hearings.[9] This exercise was preceded by a pilot study carried out in the Coventry County Court over a three week period in October and November 1993.[10] In the main fieldwork, judges were observed and interviewed at eighteen county courts in England and

[7] Dramatic examples of judicial resistance to research are to be found in the case studies provided by Ashworth *et al.* (1984); Hood (1992); and Malleson (1996). There have, however, been a few exceptions (Paterson, 1982, for example) where senior members of the judiciary have participated in research. Crown Court judges agreed to complete questionnaires in the study of jury verdicts by Baldwin and McConville (1979). In the early study carried out by Applebey (1978) and that conducted by Touche Ross (1986), 30 county court registrars were interviewed.

[8] Only one judge (in the pilot stage of the study) declined to have the interview with the author tape recorded.

[9] The original intention was to seek interviews with district judges after having observed a number of their hearings. Things did not always go according to plan, however, and three judges were interviewed whose hearings had collapsed for some reason, and these interviews are included in the results. After having requested a meeting with the judge, it would have been impolite, even churlish, not to have conducted the interview simply because hearings had failed for unforeseen reasons to materialize.

[10] Conducting pilot observations and interviews was important in establishing contact with the courts, preparing interview schedules, and in clarifying the procedures to be adopted in the main fieldwork.

TABLE 3.1 *The issue in dispute at the small claims hearings observed*

		%
Consumer goods and services	22	20.2
Quasi-debt recovery	25	22.9
Road accident	16	14.7
Straight debt recovery	22	20.2
Other type of claim	24	22.0
	109	100.0

Wales, which comprised at least two from each of the six Court Circuits.[11] An attempt was made in selecting the sample to include a good cross-section of different types of court. The 109 small claims hearings that were observed covered a wide range of issues, broadly reflecting the mix of cases that one would expect.[12] As Table 1 shows, consumer claims, road accidents, disputes about what were seen as excessive bills from businesses and professionals, and debt recovery cases were all prominent. The distribution is similar to the pattern observed in Table 3 of Chapter 2 at 30.[13]

Almost all observations of hearings were conducted in the district judges' own chambers, and the author sought to remain as unobtrusive as possible by sitting at the back of the room while cases were heard. His original intention was to observe what happened at a distance and to make a careful note of all that transpired. This effort was not always

[11] The number of county courts visited was in part determined by where small claims hearings were scheduled in each Circuit on the particular days that the author was able to visit. Hearings were observed at 18 courts as follows: Northampton, Worcester, Nuneaton, Coventry, Cardiff, Macclesfield, Chester, Warrington, Preston, Manchester, Blackpool, Leeds, York, Scarborough, Portsmouth, Exeter, Edmonton, and Cambridge. The number of cases observed in each Circuit varied from 13 in the South Eastern Circuit to 23 in the Midland and Oxford Circuit.

[12] The sums of money that were at issue in the hearings observed were, however, somewhat higher than found in relation to the examination of the 1,800 court files described in Chapter 2. For instance, almost 40 per cent of claims were for amounts in excess of £500, compared to 33.8 per cent given in Table 4 on 31.

[13] There were more debt recovery cases amongst the cases in hearings that the author attended than in the national sample of 1,800 cases discussed in Chapter 2. One reason for this is that, where only the plaintiff attended the hearing in such cases, so few details were given about the dispute in the court that it is likely that a number of the cases classified as 'straight debt recovery' would have been recorded as 'quasi-debt recovery' cases had more information about the defence been available.

successful because several district judges insisted that the author sit alongside them, even on occasions that he participate at the hearing. It was also often difficult (without running the risk of appearing aloof and unfriendly) to maintain an air of academic detachment. Throughout one particularly lively and good-humoured hearing, for example, the author was required to enter into the spirit of things by standing and holding up a bridesmaid's dress—said by the plaintiff to have been poorly finished—so that comparisons could easily be made with another dress placed on the judge's hat-stand. The author was reminded on such occasions that district judges could be solemn, brusque, and occasionally tetchy, but they were not the sort of people to be pompous or to stand on ceremony.

The objective in observing hearings was, then, primarily descriptive. Since so little research has been conducted in England and Wales on small claims procedures—and the private nature of such proceedings rules out systematic observation of hearings—it was thought worthwhile finding out what actually happens behind the closed doors of the judges' chambers when small claims disputes are being resolved. An attempt was made to examine how far litigants were able to participate in the hearing, how competently they presented their cases, whether they were given a reasonable opportunity to say what they wanted, how legal representatives adapted to the informal nature of proceedings, and how district judges went about playing the interventionist role.

Litigants are frequently reminded by judges when they appear at small claims hearings that, although the setting is intended to be relaxed and informal, it is nonetheless a court. This is easy to forget, not so much because district judges are particularly relaxed in the approach that they adopt, but simply because the judges' chambers rarely feel or look like a courtroom. Many district judges, indeed, make a conscious effort to achieve this effect and make their rooms welcoming to litigants, for instance by putting family photos on display or hanging pictures on the walls. One judge told the author that he gave money every week to an usher so that he could have flowers on his table.

The interviews with the district judges were conducted usually after the author had observed the hearings in the judges' chambers, often in the lunch break over a sandwich. This meant that the judges' views about small claims could be discussed (and occasionally challenged) in the light of the way they had actually conducted the hearings. None of the judges showed much reticence about airing their views about small claims to the author. It has to be conceded, however, that the interviews scarcely followed prescribed textbook procedures. District judges are as a group strikingly self-confident and articulate, and the idea of firing a series of pre-determined questions at them (as it were, from a clipboard) seemed ill-advised, if not faintly absurd. Although the issues raised with each judge were uniform, the general approach was more challenging and discursive than the term 'interview' might imply. It was anticipated that a somewhat confrontational approach would produce more candid and revealing responses than would be the case if a set of standard questions were mechanically put to them.

It is a mistake to assume that, once a claim is made and a defence to it is filed, cases inevitably follow a textbook route culminating in final resolution at a formal hearing. As was noted in Chapter 2, the cases that reach the hearing stage represent only a minority of all those in which a summons is issued and a defence filed with the court. Even when cases are listed for a small claims hearing, a large number do not proceed as such. This problem undermines the efficient administration of the courts, as it means that allocating the appropriate time to deal with a batch of cases is based largely on guesswork as to how many people will turn up on the day. In deciding how long each case is likely to take, district judges make estimates on the basis of the information available to them at the time, and cases are scheduled accordingly. The judges interviewed in this study tended to regard this as a futile exercise, not only because they could not predict which of the parties would turn up but also because they found it extremely difficult to make accurate assessments of the time required for hearings even if cases went ahead as anticipated.[14] The solution adopted to the problem of non-attendance in most county courts is for the court administration to overbook cases on the assumption that only a minority will turn into full hearings. Given the many uncertainties in making these arrangements for listing, it is perhaps surprising that it is unusual for serious difficulties to arise on the day that small claims are listed.

[14] One district judge kept a list of his time estimates specifically for the author's benefit because he wanted to demonstrate what he saw as the absurdities of the exercise. His figures did indeed show how inaccurate such estimates can be. Of the 8 estimates he had made, only one was correct. Of the remainder, one was within 15 minutes; 3 were within 30 minutes; and for the rest the discrepancy was over an hour. One hearing, estimated to last an hour, took three and a half hours. For an amusing and perceptive description of the problems of listing in the Crown Court, see Rock (1993), at 137–41.

In over a third of the 109 hearings included in the present sample, one of the parties (usually the defendant) failed to appear. It was seen in the previous chapter that this is as a rule good news for the party that troubles to attend, since attendance in such circumstances all but guarantees success. In this sample, judgment was awarded to the party that turned up in over 90 per cent of cases.[15] It was interesting to see how widely district judges varied in the extent to which they delved into the details of these claims. Many did no more than ensure in a cursory manner that the plaintiff's claim (or, where relevant, the defence) was reasonably well founded before awarding judgment. A few made no enquiry at all. Because of their brevity and their attenuated purpose, these hearings were in consequence usually concluded within a matter of minutes.[16]

Matters were much less predictable in the seventy-one cases in which both parties turned up. The outcome of these hearings mirrored the results discussed in the previous chapter in relation to the national sample of county court claims. Plaintiffs succeeded with their claims (wholly or in part) in three-quarters of all cases. Defendants who appeared in person, however, secured some relief in almost a half of all claims, either in the form of a reduced award or in a last minute compromise.

There were, as one would expect, wide variations in the length of these hearings. When both parties attended and the matter was not adjourned or settled, 80 per cent of hearings took at least half an hour and 25 per cent lasted over an hour. (It is worth noting, in passing, that small claims are dealt with much more rapidly at hearings that the writer has observed in other countries.[17]) The length of the hearing depends to some extent on the complexity of the issues that are raised by the parties, but it reflects much more fundamentally the approach adopted by the district judge. It is a matter of common observation—and is something that will be discussed at length in this chapter—that

[15] Where the plaintiff alone attended in this sample, judgment was granted in 24 out of 27 cases, although in 2 of these cases for a somewhat lesser amount than the sum claimed. Hearings were adjourned in the other three cases. In the 11 cases in which plaintiffs themselves failed to attend, the claim was dismissed in 6 and the case adjourned in 2 others. In the 3 other cases, the defendant admitted liability and solely disputed the size of the claim.

[16] Over two-thirds of these truncated hearings were completed in less than 10 minutes, and more than a quarter lasted less than 5 minutes.

[17] In observing small claims hearings in other jurisdictions, the author has rarely seen hearings that last much longer than half an hour. In a small claims court in New York City held in the early evening, for example, he observed 8 defended claims dealt with in a 2-hour session.

some judges allow considerable latitude to the parties in developing their arguments, whereas others insist that they address only the pertinent legal issues and do not permit what they regard as irrelevancies.

As with virtually all aspects of small claims hearings, the human dimension is extremely important. Some judges deal with matters briskly; others are far more leisurely, even prolix, in the way they hear cases. In this and in many other respects, there are great variations, and, it is only to be expected that some judges dispose of cases much more quickly than do others. Such differences in judicial approach influence not only the time needed to reach a decision, but also the character and tone of the hearing itself. In considering how small claims are disposed of in the county courts, then, close attention needs to be paid to the different working philosophies of district judges.

Playing the interventionist role

In assessing the efficacy of small claims procedures, it is the district judge's performance as the interventionist judge which must be regarded as the touchstone. Unless the judges are prepared to assist litigants in person, the whole exercise will crumble. As Thomas (1982: 62) observed: 'Where "do-it-yourself" involvement is the norm, the role of the court needs to change fundamentally. . . . The court can no longer remain aloof from the arena of battle when for one—and quite possibly both—of the parties it is probably an entirely unprecedented experience'. Interventionism is not, then, an option for district judges: it is a fundamental requirement if small claims procedures are to work.

It is important to consider the way that the 'interventionist' role was played by judges in the seventy-one hearings which went ahead as planned with both parties in attendance. District judges do not operate in a vacuum, and the way they play the interventionist role is very much influenced by whether both the parties attend and by whether there are legal (or even lay) representatives at the hearing. But the most immediately striking finding to emerge from observing these hearings—and it is one that would surely be readily apparent to any observer—is that there are vast differences in the district judges' interpretation of what it means to be interventionist.[18] Given the

[18] Variations in approach from judge to judge have frequently been the subject of comment and criticism in the past: see particularly the consultation paper issued by the Lord Chancellor's Department (1986); the Report of the Review Body on Civil Justice (1988); and the Woolf Inquiry (1995), at 107–10. See also the discussion in Zander (1989), at 158–60.

flexibility granted to judges to adopt, as Order 19 states, 'any method of procedure which he may consider to be fair and which gives to each party an equal opportunity to have his case presented', it was no surprise to find that district judges attached very different meanings to these words. However, the clear implication of this is that broad generalizations about the way small claims hearings are being conducted are likely to be misleading, since there are few common practices among district judges in how they approach their role.

An early indication of such differences is given even before the hearing starts. It was remarkable that, even where both parties were in attendance, most district judges made no effort to examine the parties' papers before they entered.[19] The papers are for the most part simple enough, and in the main consist of the summons and the defence, requiring no more than a few minutes to read in their entirety. In the larger courts where small claims were timetabled *en bloc* with as many as half a dozen judges hearing cases simultaneously (known in the trade as 'back-to-back' lists or as 'bear gardens'), it would clearly be wasteful for all the judges to read all the papers beforehand. But even when only a single district judge was sitting, few took the time to familiarize themselves with the details of cases before the parties entered.[20] Even when judges did trouble to examine the papers beforehand, it was usually no more than a cursory inspection. The result was that district judges read the papers after the parties had entered in order to discover what the case was about. One district judge explained the way that he tackled this difficulty as follows:

> I must admit that, without pre-reading, you are floundering a bit for the first few minutes. But even when you are explaining the procedure to the parties, you can spend that time looking at the papers for the real issue in the case. You

[19] As already noted, a district judge at each court reads the papers when they are first submitted to the court so as to make an estimate of the time that will be needed for a hearing and, where appropriate, to give directions to the parties. Studying the papers at this stage is of course no alternative to reading them immediately prior to the hearing, since the first reading might have been only superficial and conducted several weeks (if not months) before the day of the hearing by a judge who does not eventually hear the case. Although this issue was not systematically examined in the present study, it was nonetheless clear from talking to district judges that they varied greatly in the care and conscientiousness with which they carried out the exercise.

[20] The writer's attendance may even have led to more district judges reading the papers than would otherwise have been the case. As one district judge, with commendable candour, confided to the author: 'I suppose, if I'm entirely honest, I must admit that I thought today, since you were coming, I ought to read the papers so I wouldn't look a complete Charley!'

get used to the sort of things that people put in, and you can often see that a lot of the paperwork isn't going to help [Interview 1].

Reading the papers after the parties have entered is not satisfactory, and several of the hearings that the author attended started in embarrassed silence as the judge sought to identify the issues in contention. Other judges simply picked up the thread as they went along. In this writer's view, it is an indispensable requirement that a district judge who intends to play a genuinely interventionist role at a hearing be familiar with the details of the case before it commences. This is not, it seems, the prevailing view among district judges, although one particularly conscientious judge set out what he saw as the clear benefits of studying the papers carefully before a hearing:

If you let two people into the room without any preparation, you really couldn't run a proper arbitration hearing. I don't know what other judges do but I personally read the file when it comes before me, and I try to identify the issues at that stage and see if they are properly addressed. If you do that work carefully, the arbitration should be fairly clear and straightforward [Interview 15].

Where a district judge is not familiar with the details of the case, a number of unfortunate consequences may ensue. In the first place, it sometimes emerges early in a hearing that the judge has got hold of the wrong end of the stick, and sooner or later he or she has to be put right by one or other of the parties. Secondly, the parties commonly assume that the judge has studied the details of their respective cases, and it adds to their difficulties where the district judge evidently has no real idea about what they have said in their submissions. Thirdly, it is not helpful to anyone if the judge makes assumptions, particularly where they prove to be unwarranted, from the outset.

A similar point might be made about the judges' introductions to the parties at the start of the hearing. Again, one might consider it as fundamental to the effective performance of the interventionist role that the district judge carefully explains to the parties the purpose of the hearing and the procedures that he or she proposes to adopt. The importance of such introductions applies with particular force where litigants in person are involved. Yet in over two-thirds of the full hearings that the author observed, the judges offered no real explanation to the parties. A few judges spent several minutes explaining matters to the parties at the start of every hearing. In over half of the hearings, however, the judges offered no explanation to the parties at the outset: in a quarter, nothing at all was said beyond a polite 'Good morning'. Some indication of how superficial these introductions can be is given by the following quotations noted at hearings:

Tell me the who, when and where [Case 11].

I intend to be pretty interventionist in getting to the heart of the matter [Case 21].

Yes? [Case 61].

Right, Mr Gregory, it's your start [Case 80].

You're batting first, Mr Townsend [Case 81].

What do you want to say? [Case 88].

You'd better tell me quickly what happened [Case 92].

When questioned about this after the event, the district judges themselves tended to minimize the significance of the different approaches they adopted at hearings and emphasized instead that they must adapt to the particular circumstances of the case and the individual characteristics of the parties before them. But it is easy to overstate this point, and, over and above what were in reality relatively minor adjustments in approach, much more fundamental differences in judicial attitudes and philosophy were readily discernible.

None of this should be taken to imply that the district judges commonly shrink from playing the interventionist role. It emerged clearly in this research that most district judges show evident relish in playing it and indeed in seeing themselves as interventionist. For this reason, it would not be accurate to describe hearings in England and Wales in the way that Ramsay (1990: 27) has described Canadian small claims courts as 'a modified version of the model of higher courts with a sideways nod to the idea of informality'. In most of the hearings observed in the present study, the judicial shift from a traditional, adversarial approach to active interventionism was real enough, and very few district judges showed much hesitation about intervening. It was, furthermore, rare for any of them in interview to express misgivings about doing so. Although some judges undoubtedly played the part more skilfully and sensitively than did others, it can be unequivocally stated there is now widespread acceptance among district judges that it is a desirable, if not a necessary, role for them to assume at hearings of this type.

When examining judicial interventionism, it is relevant to bear in mind that all these judges were experienced lawyers. The vast majority had spent several years as solicitors in private practice before being appointed to the bench, and three of the five deputies included in the sample were in private practice at the time they were interviewed. A third of the sample had been conducting small claims hearings for more than ten years. They may or may not have had brilliant or imaginative legal minds, but most exuded competence and confidence in what they did. They were not, in short, the sort of people to be racked by crises of self-confidence. On the contrary, most district judges approached the interventionist role with strong, sometimes apparently unshakeable, views about how they should go about playing it.[21]

Only two of the thirty-three district judges whom the author observed seemed in basic approach and manner to be too formal and adversarial to be described as interventionist. When interviewed, it became clear that they were no converts to the sentiments contained in Order 19, and the way they approached small claims was probably little different from the way they proceeded in other, more formal kinds of hearing. They insisted, for instance, upon a fixed and rigid procedure, including formal cross-examination by each party.[22] They were unprepared to offer much assistance to litigants as they struggled to oblige, and firmly placed the responsibility upon the parties to adduce their own evidence and prove their cases. It seems, however, that these judges are now a dying breed and that they are being rapidly outnumbered by the enthusiasts.

Having observed over one hundred small claims hearings, the author concluded that district judges are on the whole skilful at putting unrepresented litigants at their ease. Some had evidently given a good deal of thought to how the interventionist role should be played and were quite imaginative in the approaches they adopted. One of the most

[21] An indication of this level of confidence is given in the following remarkable statement by one district judge who was interviewed:

> 'I'm known as a strong judge, but I deal with things in a laid-back way. I radiate confidence and control from the beginning in an informal way. But people are advised not to take liberties with me. So I don't have any difficulties. No, I don't have any difficulties at all [Interview 10].

[22] There were only 3 district judges in the sample who routinely asked for evidence to be given on oath, and a handful who said that they might require evidence on oath in specific circumstances. Although this was an unusual procedure, it seemed to be accepted by the parties without comment and rarely made a difference to the informality or otherwise of the hearing.

enthusiastic judges, for example, made it his practice to invite litigants to stand behind his desk to show him maps or draw a diagram or explain a set of figures, and he encouraged them to move round the room while they explained the significance of exhibits they had brought with them. It was striking how quickly people relaxed and grew in confidence in these circumstances. This is not to say, of course, that district judges permitted litigants to say all they wanted at hearings, and, as will be apparent later, there were a number of judges who had no intention of allowing them to do so. But in terms of providing a forum in which the ordinary lay person can function reasonably effectively, the district judges can be said to score highly.

Examining how district judges go about playing the interventionist role revealed, therefore, a variety of approaches and styles. Given the complexities of the role and the fact that the writer sat with most of them for only half a day, the temptation has been resisted of allocating district judges to hard-and-fast categories. Suffice it to say that, in terms of the approach they adopted at hearings, the author classified the judges into one of four groups which were of roughly equal size.

Going for the jugular

One approach, which was followed in some measure by almost all district judges, though much more single-mindedly by a minority, was to identify at an early stage in the hearing (if not before it started) the central legal issue or issues in a case. The judges varied greatly in the way they did this and in their determination—one might almost say ruthlessness—to stick to those issues at the hearing. In its most extreme manifestation, the judges adopted a robust, almost macho, stance, striving from the outset to get to the crux of the matter in the shortest possible time and limiting the parties to those central issues. Judges of this persuasion tended to employ a variety of metaphors (often of a medical or horticultural nature) to describe their intentions, talking, for example, of getting to the 'root' or the 'heart' of the matter, taking the case by 'the scruff of the neck', 'shaking the tree', or, even more directly, 'going for the jugular'. Two of the most experienced and self-confident judges encountered in the study took a particularly strong line at hearings, and they summarized their thinking as follows:

> In most cases getting to the heart of the matter can be done quickly and easily with experience. It is not difficult to alight on the issue very quickly. You get used to the sort of things that people put in, and somewhere (in either the claim

or the defence) is the clue to the thing that is the nub of it. . . . The parties themselves will go off at a tangent and give details that aren't going to go on the scales at all and are not relevant to the issue if they are not directed. In those cases you see a question that needs to be resolved and asked about and might save going through all the peripheral stuff [Interview 1].

The philosophy in conducting arbitrations is to go straight for the jugular. I take a definite line that arbitrations for the small claims court should be interventionist. With the adversarial approach, you will say to a party, 'Please, Mr Smith, tell me your story.' Then he'll start off by telling you what he had for breakfast. Five hours later we still haven't got the crux of the case. Here I take control of it. I get to the jugular straight away. I get to the facts straight away. My only concern is: what is the point in this case? I'm not concerned with the flowery bits and pieces. I'm concerned with what are facts, what is the problem, what are the facts based upon that problem. That way you get to the solution that much quicker; you save so much time, and I think it puts the parties at ease as well because they haven't got the responsibility of having to conduct the case. They haven't got a clue about that so you have got to take control [Interview 32].

There is undoubtedly a balance that needs to be struck between allowing lay litigants the latitude to roam freely in presenting their evidence and at the same time ensuring that time is not wasted and that cases are decided with reasonable expedition. However difficult and frustrating it may be for a district judge when lay litigants explain their cases in a long-winded and irrelevant way, there is no sure way of knowing until they have done so what is relevant and what is not.

But to return to the author's main concern about the small claims procedure: when judges go for the jugular, it inevitably puts lay litigants at a disadvantage. Without preliminary legal advice, litigants are in a poor position to know what will be the key legal issues on which they should focus. Even when the district judges make explicit at the hearing the legal issues on which they wish the parties to concentrate—and not all judges do so—lay litigants may well be forced to change tack at this late stage and jettison the arguments with which they have come armed because they realize that they have no legal validity. Only those litigants who are sufficiently quick-witted and flexible will be able to satisfy the unexpected legal criteria introduced by the judge. But such mental acuity is probably beyond most litigants. Where the legal issues are not identified by the judge at the hearing, however, the situation is even more difficult for lay litigants, and, in those circumstances, case presentation is likely to be thoroughly hit-and-miss.

Hearing the parties

A number of district judges found the idea of addressing only the central issues at a hearing uncomfortable, and, while acknowledging the importance of identifying the key question in a case so as to keep the hearing within reasonable bounds, they nonetheless granted the parties much greater leeway in developing their arguments in the way that they wished. In other words, they tempered a wholly muscular philosophy by tolerantly listening to what the parties wanted to say, however tangential this might be to the legal points in dispute. While some judges could scarcely disguise their irritation when litigants strayed too far from the pertinent issues at a hearing, others seemed able to listen to their arguments with extraordinary patience and sensitivity.[23]

District judges in this group acknowledged that paying heed to public perceptions of justice was an integral part of their task. For them there was much more involved in this than what others dismissed pejoratively as the cosmetic aspect of public relations. In the following quotation, one of the most thoughtful of the judges interviewed, recognizing the dilemmas that lie at the heart of the judicial role, distinguished carefully between what he saw as the over-robust approach of some of his colleagues and the need to ensure that litigants participate fully at hearings:

I see it as my role to identify the key issues in the case, having read the papers beforehand, while allowing the parties an opportunity to say all that they want to say. But this is a matter of philosophy and I know some of my colleagues differ on this. Some of my colleagues will go straight to the heart of it and say, 'This is what it's about and I want you to tell me about this, this and this.' End of story. That is technically correct and in most cases it would produce the right result. And there is an argument that it is a requirement of justice that things be kept moving to get productivity. At the same time, for the system to work, people have got to believe in it. I have to create a balance, therefore, between making sure that they direct themselves to that which clearly is the heart of the matter and not having them feel rail-roaded into something. So I'm inclined to let them go on a little, but, by being interventionist, I can hopefully nudge

[23] It is significant that, when district judges were asked in interview to identify the main qualities they needed to conduct small claims hearings satisfactorily, almost half spontaneously mentioned patience as the single most important characteristic, and almost all of the remainder described other qualities that were closely related to patience.

them in the right direction—nudge them towards the parts that we want to concentrate on, without their realising that they are being nudged. I want them to go away feeling that I have got what I need to make a decision and they have been allowed to say what they wanted. That is a very difficult balance to strike [Interview 16].

Taking too early a view of a case, particularly on the basis of the written statements of lay people, is fraught with difficulty, and the author saw one district judge in a succession of hearings setting off in the wrong direction, to the evident annoyance of the parties. Unless they strive to do otherwise, judges are prone to build up their own case theory, and, as the hearing proceeds, they may, consciously or unconsciously, interpret the evidence in the light of that theory.[24] One experienced district judge described the judicial tendency to construct case theories as 'hellish dangerous', and he explained:

You can too often miss the case as the parties see it because it is your case you are putting over. I say to the parties at the start in my introduction, 'You assist me to identify the issues because I can't decide them until you tell me what it is you wish me to decide.' That is absolutely right, but what a lot of power it gives me if I then define the wrong issues. I am constantly trying to direct the minds of the parties to the issues that I see as relevant, and I may try to put them off considering issues that they think are important. The danger is that you put them off other points that are uncomfortable and don't fit your view of the case. I may be guilty of elevating irrelevant details as the most fundamental issue in a case. There are points that you don't think of and you have got to be perceptive enough to pick up those points. There is no lawyer here to put you back on the right track if you are following the wrong one. The whole thing could be decided on a total irrelevance. You may get the wrong end of the stick [Interview 13].

Striking a balance between hearing the parties out and restricting them to the legally relevant points is fundamental to the interventionist role. Yet even the district judges who take the view that it is their duty to listen to the arguments that the parties wish to develop give different reasons for doing so. Some argue they need to ensure that they have themselves a proper grasp of the issues, whereas others say they do so

[24] Examining the phenomenon in a sociological context, Christie (1977: 4) makes the point graphically as follows:

> 'Many among us have, as laymen, experienced the sad moments of truth when our lawyers tell us that our best arguments in our fight against our neighbour are without any legal relevance whatsoever and that we for god's sake ought to keep quiet about them in court. Instead they pick out arguments that we might find irrelevant or even wrong to use.'

primarily for the sake of the litigants. It matters to many district judges that litigants leave the court feeling that they have had their say and been listened to, whatever might be the final decision at the hearing. It seems clear, however, that, if citizens' satisfaction with small claims procedures is to be used as one measure of their efficacy, then a judicial concern with ensuring that litigants understand what is happening at the hearing and can participate effectively in it needs to be recognized in both judicial training and in practice.

Passive

As is already apparent from the views cited in this chapter, some district judges conveyed an almost missionary zeal about the way that the interventionist role should be played at small claims hearings. But there were others at the opposite extreme whose hearings (and the author's interview with them afterwards) were singularly low-key affairs. Such differences in levels of enthusiasm and interest pervade small claims hearings and are obvious to any observer. While some judges clearly enjoyed playing an interventionist role—and in some cases seemed delighted to have an academic observer with whom to discuss it—others seemed to care little about it, one way or the other. Although judges in the latter group showed no hesitation in intervening, the hearings they conducted frequently took on (to be blunt) a mundane, even prosaic, character.

Judges in this category interpreted the playing of the interventionist role in effect as simply carrying out interviews with the parties concerned. 'I talk to each of them as I used to talk to my own clients when I was in private practice' is how one of the district judges described the approach he adopted at hearings, and for him the hearing was not unlike the role he would have played as a solicitor when interviewing clients in the office. For these judges, conducting a small claims hearing simply meant asking a few pertinent questions, making a rapid assessment of what had been said, and then bringing matters to a close. Hearings were rather humdrum and unsatisfying experiences for the parties, since their spontaneous contributions were discouraged, if not eliminated. Again they were obliged to meet a series of legal criteria of which they could not reasonably have been expected to have had prior knowledge.

Mediatory

A final group of district judges had their own distinctive interpretation of the interventionist role. They favoured finding a compromise solution to small claims disputes in preference to having a decision judicially imposed, and they conducted hearings with this objective firmly in sight. Even when the parties faced each other at a hearing, some judges adopted a role more akin to that of a mediator than a judge, encouraging the parties to reach their own settlement or agreement.[25] In order to avoid the idea of confrontation, one district judge took pains to ensure that the parties' chairs were arranged in a row in front of him rather than lined up so that they faced each other on opposite sides of the table.[26]

This approach is particularly interesting in the context of the present study, as it illustrates the way that judges may seek, in assisting litigants to reach their own solutions, to moderate the effects that a clinical application of the law might have. Mediated solutions may in consequence reflect more lay conceptions of justice than strict conformity with the law. A good example of this approach arose in one hearing that the writer attended where the plaintiff had sued a young woman who had sold her a puppy in such a poor physical condition that it had died a few weeks later. It soon became clear at the hearing that the plaintiff had sued the wrong person and that the defendant's father was the person who was legally responsible for the sale. However, the district judge took the view that, whatever the law, the defendant was morally responsible and ought to pay something to the plaintiff. Instead of disregarding the law in his decision or encouraging the plaintiff to initiate proceedings again, the judge gave a clear statement to the parties of where he thought the moral responsibility lay and sent them out of the room to discuss what he had said. When they returned, they announced that they had reached the compromise that the judge had himself favoured. The case illustrates the important point that the settlements that occur under the small claims regime may be determined to a much greater extent by social than by legal norms.[27] The

[25] There is now a vast research literature dealing with the respective benefits and drawbacks of court adjudication, settlement, and alternative methods of dispute resolution: for an excellent discussion, see Galanter and Cahill (1994).

[26] In the leaflet dealing with small claims hearings, prepared by the Lord Chancellor's Department, the parties are shown sitting on opposite sides of the judge's table.

[27] Jacob (1992) argues that the concept of 'bargaining in the shadow of the law' developed by Mnookin and Kornhauser (1979: 585–6) may overstate the role that is played by law, and, writing about divorce cases (the legal category to which the concept has been principally applied), he notes:

> 'much of the bargaining over children and support payments occurs with little awareness or concern about law. Expectations about relationships dominate most of the thinking about custody, and agreements are often worked out in private with little apparent law talk'.

writer expressed some scepticism in Chapter 1 about how far the idea of bargaining in 'the shadow of the law' might be applied to small claims hearings, and the relatively infrequent compromised solutions that arise in small claims tend to show how the law is circumvented rather than how it is used to underpin negotiations between the parties. In other words, settlement may be encouraged by district judges specifically in order to avoid applying the law in the first place.[28]

To litigants unfamiliar with the legal system, a court appearance may well be a disagreeable and daunting prospect, and a negotiated compromise (even if on unfavourable terms) may present a considerable temptation. It often does not require much encouragement from a district judge to push the parties in this direction. Although many district judges told the author that they favoured a mediated settlement if it could be achieved, they varied greatly in their readiness to initiate one. The basic orientation of a few judges in dealing with small claims could, however, be characterized as mediatory, and three judges who fell squarely into this group explained their thinking to the writer as follows:

I nearly always tell the parties in my introduction that the best solution is very often one they might arrive at themselves by agreement. I encourage them to spend a few minutes outside, just to see if they can reach a friendly compromise between themselves. I stress that there is no right of appeal and that my decisions are unpredictable and that I am by no means infallible. In quite a high proportion, they do go out saying that there is no harm in having a chat and they come back and say they've reached agreement. I encourage them to do that by telling them that a bird in the hand is worth two in the bush in that they might decide it is better to settle for a smaller sum. I really am trying to bring about a meeting of minds as amicably and as informally as I can. And it's not just a meeting of minds: it's a meeting of pockets as well. A compromise at least avoids the risk of one party losing completely. Some litigants feel that, once they start litigation, there is a compulsion to carry on fighting. All they know about the law probably comes from television programmes and you don't see television programmes about courtroom settlements. So they don't realise that they are not honour-bound to carry on fighting and can agree a draw. I would always respect the decision they reach and I wouldn't try to interfere. I wouldn't go into the rights and wrongs of a settlement. I think that I regard my role as a mediator rather than as an adjudicator [Interview 6].

[28] Other writers have doubted the centrality of law even to lawyers. Sarat and Felstiner (1995: 146) write, for instance, that 'the shadow that [divorce law] casts over lawyer-client negotiations is partial and flickering'. See further Ross (1970); Eisenberg (1976); Macauley (1979); Sarat and Felstiner (1986; 1989); and Griffiths (1986).

I personally try to encourage the parties to settle at arbitrations on the basis that, if they have to come to some agreement, it is their responsibility. It may well be that they know things about the background to their dispute which they are never going to be able to explain to me adequately. So it is better for them to reach a settlement with which they are both satisfied or at least fairly dissatisfied [Interview 19].

I like to encourage the parties to reach their own settlement if I can. I'm of the view that, if the parties can go away from the court feeling happy that they have achieved something from their own perspective, then it is far better than having a decision imposed on them where one at least may be unhappy and possibly both [Interview 33].

Civil procedure is to a large extent geared to settlement, not court adjudication,[29] and it was noted in Chapter 1 that the resolution of small claims represents in this respect something of an exception.[30] But there are subtle pressures at any county court that encourage settlement, even in small claims. The mere fixing of a date for a hearing serves, for example, to focus the minds of the parties on what is at stake. Moreover, the existence of the court in itself fosters compromise, and the court waiting room offers, often for the first time, a neutral arena in which the parties may meet face to face. Some litigants decide to settle their differences even at that late stage.

The author also saw for himself on his visits to county courts that court ushers may themselves prompt settlement discussions between litigants. On occasions, he saw ushers scurrying between the parties in the waiting room before hearings started attempting to initiate last minute discussions between them. One judge told the author that in his court the usher 'operated in effect as the preliminary hearing', and, when the usher in question was asked by the judge to explain her role to the writer, she said that she regularly informed the parties in the waiting room that 'these judges don't like arguments' and invited them to spend a few minutes in a room on their own prior to the hearing to see whether they could reach their own agreement. In another court, the usher said that she routinely reminded the parties in the waiting room that, unless they made an effort to compromise, their cases would be left to the end of the list. Courts are fascinating social institutions,

[29] On this point, see, for instance, Jacob (1987); Glasser and Roberts (1993); and Woolf (1995), at 13–15.

[30] 'In theory, the trial is the model of English civil justice', Sir Jack Jacob (1987: 71) writes, 'but in practice it is the rare exception'.

and much is missed by concentrating solely on what happens on the surface. A mountain of research evidence supports the basic proposition that the informal organization of the courts can often be more significant than the formal. The backstairs discussions and negotiations that take place before court hearings have long been recognized in the academic literature as frequently exerting a more potent effect on the decisions of participants than anything that happens in the formal courtroom.[31] This can sometimes happen in the small claims context, where ushers' blandishments and threats can determine the outcome of the case in court.[32]

The importance of differences in judicial approach

It has been seen that district judges vary greatly in their interpretation of what it means to play an interventionist role in dealing with small claims. The crucial question to consider is whether these differences in judicial approach and style have any bearing upon the outcome of cases. Do district judges reach different decisions simply because their methods vary? This question is extremely difficult to answer since the judges sit alone and are never seen dealing with the same set of facts. District judges themselves tend to play down the significance of individual differences in approach, and, in interviews with the writer, most claimed that the end result would invariably be the same whatever methods they adopted.

But it is not as simple as this implies, and the existence of two critical variables suggests that this reasoning may be flawed. In the first place, the evidence available in small claims is in the usual case very limited, and one of the most striking ways in which district judges differ is in their willingness to dig for more or to make do with what the parties present. Secondly, district judges vary greatly in the extent to which they feel constrained strictly to apply the principles of English law. Both of these factors can have an important bearing upon the decisions that district judges reach in small claims, and it is for these reasons that the writer is sceptical of claims that district judges will reach the same

[31] Negotiations surrounding guilty pleas in the criminal courts provide a striking example: see, for instance, Baldwin and McConville (1977); Baldwin (1985); and McConville *et al.* (1994).

[32] In some county courts, the judges collude in the unwritten practices pursued by court ushers by deliberately running behind the printed times of hearings in order to encourage the parties to settle.

decisions on the facts regardless of the approach they adopt. It seems more likely that the outcome of hearings will reflect in some measure differences in judicial approach. It is important to consider both factors in some detail.

Evidential problems

District judges were divided in their views about how far they should go in insisting that all the relevant evidence is produced at a small claims hearing before they reach a decision. If cases are not to be adjourned—a situation that very few litigants want—the judge hearing the case has to make an effort to extract the evidence from the parties and their witnesses rather than insisting that full documentary evidence and relevant witnesses be produced. But there are formidable difficulties for district judges in seeking to plug gaps in the evidence. In most small claims hearings, the evidence available to the court is extremely limited. In these proceedings, unlike other civil trials, there are no formal pleadings, no discovery or inspection of documents, and no exchange of witness statements. Instead, there is often no more than a simple denial from the defendant in response to the summons and two standard directions saying that the parties must give the names and addresses of their witnesses and serve copies of the documents they intend to use at the hearing.

Since the parties do not receive legal assistance before the hearing takes place unless they themselves specifically seek it, most claims reach the stage of a hearing in only a crude form. Preliminary hearings in small claims are strongly discouraged and are now a rare occurrence at most county courts.[33] And even the minimal directions given to the parties by district judges before the hearing are offered more in a spirit of hope than real expectation that they will be followed. While court staff may assist litigants in completing the forms, they are not allowed to offer them legal advice. There are variations from court to court in the willingness of staff to assist litigants, and, given the intense pressures upon the staff in some courts, many litigants told the author that

[33] District judges are specifically discouraged from holding preliminary hearings under section 6(4) of Order 19, which states that preliminary hearings shall only be held:

> '(a) where [written] directions . . . are not sufficient and special directions can only be given in the presence of the parties, or
> (b) to enable the district judge to dispose of the case where the claim is ill-founded or there is no reasonable defence.'

they found court personnel so harassed that they had decided to turn elsewhere for help.[34] In some of the busier courts, the only practical help that members of the staff feel able to offer is to hand out copies of the small claims leaflets. The leaflets, however, provide no more than general guidance to those who bother to read them.[35]

Few witnesses, still less experts, appear at these hearings, and, if decisions are to be reached at all by the judges, then it is inevitable that they will often take the form of informed guesswork. No one would pretend that the decisions in small claims are carefully considered judgments, based upon a painstaking evaluation of the evidence put before the judge. In no fewer than ninety-one of the 109 hearings included in this study, no witnesses at all were present. Of the witnesses who did appear, only eight could be described as experts. These were four employees of organizations involved in an action, a fellow director of a business, an accountant, a dog breeder, and a car mechanic. In twenty-six other hearings, the parties were accompanied by other people whose role was primarily to offer moral support to the litigants. These people were almost always members of a litigant's family or friends. In some cases, the boundary between supporter, witness, and even lay representative became blurred. As in many other respects, the district judges varied in the part they allowed such people to play at hearings.

To avoid adjourning cases, a robust, not to say rough-and-ready, approach tends to be adopted by district judges. One judge somewhat apologetically warned the author at the start of the day in his court

[34] It is unrealistic in the writer's view to expect county court staff to make themselves available to assist litigants throughout the course of the day. It may, however, be worth considering the alternative of running a 'surgery' with a lawyer in attendance at courts for a few fixed hours in the week. The author saw this approach adopted in the small claims court in Sacramento in California and thought that it had much to commend it.

[35] One writer, who had experienced at first hand what it was like to appear at a small claims hearing, was very critical of the information given to litigants. As she wrote:

> 'At the very least, printed information should be given explaining how a hearing is conducted, who speaks first, when you will be allowed to ask questions, how to ask for help, and how to address others' (Price, 1993: 8).

See also Pedley (1994) for a critical view of the operation of small claims procedures from the litigant's perspective. The main difficulty facing those who provide information to litigants about small claims is that judicial approaches vary so widely that there is no such thing as common practice.

that 'it is certainly not an academic legal exercise'.[36] Many district judges themselves assume the role of expert at hearings, having realized that it is almost as important for them to know about car and DIY manuals as it is to be familiar with the law books. Most district judges are no doubt perfectly competent in applying straightforward legal principles to routine small claims, but they differ widely in their abilities (and indeed their inclinations) to ask the pertinent questions for one side or the other and to fill in gaps in the evidence where there is, say, a dispute involving the quality of the work carried out by a car mechanic, plumber, or builder.

The methods that district judges are obliged to adopt in reaching decisions are not, therefore, ones that would please the legal purist, since much of the evidence to which they might seek to apply legal principles is simply not produced at the hearing. Because litigants do not want cases to be adjourned (and only sixteen cases in the present sample were adjourned), district judges strive to do the best they can with whatever evidence is available to them. As the following comments suggest, the prevailing attitude among the judges is a determinedly pragmatic one.

> The greatest difficulty we face in most arbitrations is getting through to the parties that they need evidence in support of their case. So often in arbitrations the parties come along and expect that you will merely hear their grievance and make an award on the basis of the grievance [Interview 2].

> Frequently people come to court without all the papers despite a direction on the Notice of Hearing. When this happens we do our best and get on with it. I just decide the case on the evidence that is before me. I don't adjourn cases apart from in very exceptional circumstances [Interview 3].

> You do the best you can with what you've got. Up to £1,000, that's fair enough. I sometimes say to litigants, 'I'll do the best I can'. In effect, I'm saying to the parties, 'Look, you've got a sledgehammer here: you've not got a scalpel and I'm going to use my sledgehammer. That's tough but that's it.

[36] This point was dramatically underlined later that day at one of the hearings where the judge deliberately allowed a fierce argument to develop between two businessmen who had fallen out with each other. Although the judge let the dispute continue for a lengthy period, he interrupted it rather abruptly and immediately announced his decision. As he explained to the author later, the documentary evidence provided by the parties was very thin, and it was extremely difficult to tell which of the parties was telling the truth. He said that the acrimonious exchanges at the hearing were, therefore, useful in shedding some light on the issues in contention.

You've paid your money, you've got your result, good, bad, or otherwise.' It's the best I can do with what I've got [Interview 7].

The problem with arbitrations is that you have to make decisions with improperly prepared cases, usually having heard one or both parties who are not advocates and don't always address the issues. You are very conscious that, while you are trying to be fair to both parties, you haven't always been able to get the full picture [Interview 15].

There must be a dividing line where you simply have to say that you haven't got the evidence and would be guessing—and no more than guessing—and I think that's wrong. The contra-indication is that the litigants themselves would almost prefer you to guess and get rid of the thing than come back later. The cases that I would always adjourn are where the evidence is of a non-technical nature and one party has simply not brought the evidence. They say that somebody could tell you about that but he's not here. I am very ready to adjourn in that situation because we don't nowadays very often have a pre-trial review. This means that the litigants in person don't quite know what evidence to bring, and, if you have a feeling that the evidence is there and that you ought to hear it, I would usually adjourn the case. I know that some of my brethren and sisters take a different view and say that, if they haven't brought the evidence, it's just bad luck. I'm not happy with that although, again, I think it may be that the litigants would prefer to get the thing over [Interview 22].

The problem with arbitration is that you are dependent on the documentation that the parties have presented and you know from experience that both parties are going to be dependent upon your questioning rather than their own. It is true that lawyers may confuse things, but it is also true that the truth may be obscured by the information that the court might not have which you might need . . . . I don't think there is very much you can do about it. If we are going to have arbitrations and litigants in person conducting the case, then I think it's going to be very much down to us at the end of the day in doing the best we can [Interview 28].

You need a basis of evidence to decide cases upon. Often the parties are pressing you to make a decision, and in those circumstances it's probably best to make the decision, though emphasising to them that you can only really do it on the basis of the somewhat limited evidence available to you. Where you would need to enter the realm of total speculation, an adjournment may be called for [Interview 31].

Arbitrations are a form of instant justice. It may be an inferior standard of justice, because you don't have the strict rules that apply, and you don't normally get all the documents which might go to prove one party's case or disprove the other. Frequently, therefore, one is dealing in hearings where the case for either side is ill-prepared and ill-documented. Had more thought been applied to it and had there been structured rules, then more would come out of the hearing [Interview 33].

The picture that emerged in this research was, then, of district judges struggling to reach decisions on the basis of the thoroughly inadequate evidence that was frequently at their disposal. The attitudes of the judges varied as to how far they should themselves assume responsibility in seeking to remedy evidential deficiencies in a litigant's case. It was apparent that some judges were much more tolerant than were others of such limitations and more prepared to fill in the gaps themselves. Decisions were in consequence likely to be affected by the approach that district judges adopted at the hearing.

Applying the law

Even more striking than the variations in approach in overcoming evidential difficulties were the district judges' attitudes towards the law. While it is a recurrent theme in this book that the operation of the law sets a critical limitation on the way that lay litigants can participate in informal legal procedures, it is important to recognize that the district judges themselves expressed very different views about how far they felt obliged to apply the rules of English law in resolving small claims. An appeal in small claims is possible on the grounds of a judicial error in law, yet, were such an error to have occurred, it is extremely doubtful that a lay litigant without legal assistance would know (and perhaps even care) about it. And the district judges' oral statements of their reasons for the decision given to litigants at the conclusion of hearings rarely included any detailed explanation of the way that the relevant law had been applied.

In the interviews the author conducted with district judges, he was surprised to discover that it was only a minority who took the view that it was their unequivocal duty strictly to apply legal principles in reaching decisions in dealing with small claims. In other words, a majority felt that they could disregard the law in making decisions if in their view the law would produce an unjust outcome.[37] Rightly or wrongly, many judges felt that, when they were dealing with small claims, it was more appropriate to seek solutions that would provide a standard of

[37] There are parallels that might be drawn here with the debate about jury 'equity': see, for example, Note, *Yale Law Journal* (1974).

justice that would be understood and accepted as fair by the parties, even if this meant disregarding the law.

As has been argued in earlier chapters of this book, it is frequently apparent in observing small claims hearings that the arguments on which lay litigants rely have no real basis in law. One task confronting district judges is, therefore, to translate or reconstitute these everyday disputes into a legal framework, the rules of which may be entirely unfamiliar, even alien, to lay people. Yngvesson and Mather (1983) referred to the role of judges and other adjudicators as 'agents of dispute transformation', arguing that this is their most important function. This authority to recast lay people's disputes into a legal framework gives lawyers and judges a potent authority. But there were many district judges within the present sample who, in different ways and to varying degrees, saw a wider responsibility upon them to 'do justice', even if it meant disregarding the law in certain cases. Some, indeed, took the view that the application of the law needed to be tempered by their own values and their own sense of justice.

It may be helpful to give an illustration of the kind of tension that exists for judges between applying the law and seeking to do justice. The author observed one acrimonious hearing in which the plaintiff, who was a local money-lender with a reputation for inveigling people into signing contracts for loans at very high rates of interest, had sued an elderly woman for non-payment of a debt. After the hearing, the district judge confided to the author that, although the relevant law was clear, he had refused to allow an unscrupulous plaintiff to 'get away with it' and exploit the ignorance of the defendant who had foolishly signed the contract. It should be added that the author, who had considerable sympathy for the defendant and none whatever for the plaintiff, could not help agreeing with the district judge's decision, even though it owed more to common standards of morality and decency than to the law. However, another district judge carefully described the way he would approach the same moral dilemma:

> This conflict frequently causes me unease. The prime instance that faces you all the time is contracts which have been entered into for the hiring of goods or machinery, usually from leasing companies who employ high-powered salesmen who know all the tricks but also know all the Consumer Credit Act and know what they should do. It's quite clear that people have been conned—in inverted commas—to take things on that they should never take on. But it's a legal con. Now moral justice should say they should never have to pay, but legal justice says that they should if it's all done properly in accordance with law.

That's when you get the heart searching. I would say that in those circumstances I investigate every legal detail very carefully, and, if I can find a way of legally getting round that, I will feel very happy in doing it [Interview 16].

District judges hold different views, then, of the role of law in small claims and of the objectives to be pursued at a small claims hearing. Before considering the possible dangers that may arise in freely disregarding legal principles, it is instructive to consider the range of views expressed by judges about whether the law should assume primacy in resolving small claims. In discussing with the district judges what seemed to the writer a straightforward point, it was very interesting to see how confidently judges expressed opposed views about it. In the following quotations, the judges are divided into two groups—those who adopted a traditional view of their obligation clinically to apply the law and those who said that they felt no such obligation.

The traditional legal view

You have to apply the law. That has got to be the focus of what you are doing. You may well have sympathy for people but, if they are wholly wrong in law, then they cannot recover as a matter of law what they are seeking to recover. Whatever personal feelings one may have, you have to cast them aside [Interview 8].

I don't subscribe to the theory of palm tree justice. It's rubbish. I desperately try to follow, where appropriate, the rules because without that underpinning then we are actually operating in a very uncontrolled and dangerous way. The fact that you are a district judge doesn't give your opinion any greater validity than anyone else's opinion. I don't think we can ignore the law. I feel that it is terribly important because it gets too freelance otherwise and we are not freelancers [Interview 13].

There is a tension between following the law and making decisions that I can live with, but I've always got to follow the law. I can do a Denning. I can bend the law. If I think there's scope, I can interpret the law. But the law has to come first. I am first and foremost a lawyer. The parties that come before me know that they have got to abide by English law. So there is a tension—sometimes an emotional tension—but one's professional training and ability as a lawyer teach you to override that. I might be unhappy about an outcome but still content that I've made the right decision [Interview 15].

The whole purpose is to apply the rules of English law, although you have to be flexible as far as procedure is concerned. You are not to depart from the law. If the law is quite clear on a particular point, then it must be applied. The leeway really comes as to procedure. If, for instance, a contract has been drawn up which is quite legal (regardless of any moral dimension), you can't get away from that [Interview 24].

You don't need to feel straight-jacketed by the law, but obviously one tries to achieve justice according to proper legal principles. I think you've got to do that otherwise we are not being true to what we are supposed to be doing. It also makes it very difficult for people such as lawyers, Citizens Advice Bureaux and the other advice agencies to advise litigants if they think that all they are going to get is palm tree justice. You've got to have a reasonable legal framework within which to operate, otherwise it would be difficult in many ways [Interview 31].

I'm not in the habit of making up my own laws to suit what I consider to be the justice in the parties' case [Interview 33].

The non-legal view

We are seeking to do fairness and not let formal rules of law or evidence stand in the way. One of the beauties of arbitrations is that you don't need to feel that you are straight-jacketed by the law if you think the law is pushing you in the wrong direction. It can be disregarded in the interests of flexibility. There will be a very few occasions—and I may be criticised by some people for saying that we should put the law on one side—when the strict legal position would in fact result in unfairness. I hope that more district judges will come to my point of view, but I think there may be as many, unfortunately, who would stick with the strict letter of the law. They have been brought up as lawyers and it's difficult for them to wear this other hat to that extent. I think that some judges would find it very difficult to set an awkward legal rule on one side and do fairness in that situation [Interview 1].

If the problem is complicated by legal considerations but the parties are not looking at it in that way, then I will not let the law get in the way. I would try to look at it in the same way as the parties. If, on the other hand, the plaintiff takes up a legal position of his own, then I have a problem because that plaintiff is relying upon that legal issue. He obviously knows the issue and you can't just say, 'Let's just ignore that, shall we?' When neither of the parties is taking up any legal issue, then you can seek to do justice in a general sense and you can look at the issues in the way that they want you to sort them out. If you can look at the issues in the way that the parties look at them and there is no critical legal issue raised by them, then I would be minded to disregard the law. If, according to a legal rule, the plaintiff is entitled to succeed, then you have to be very careful before you turn a blind eye to it. That is always a problem. Where lawyers are present, it is not possible for me always to do justice in that way. The lawyers act as a restraint upon me. If litigants are represented by lawyers, it is difficult for me to say, 'We are all lawyers here, but we are going to disregard what the law says', or rather that 'We are going to stretch the law a little to see that justice is done rather than allow artificial points to determine the issue' [Interview 4].

There is always a temptation to try to twist the evidence and the law to meet what you think is the justice of the case. I wouldn't say that I have always avoided that temptation! It's repugnant if you feel that someone is being bloody-minded and unreasonable throughout but, nevertheless, he is right in law. There are some judges who take a legalistic view and others who are much more fluid as far as the law is concerned. I like to think that I am in the latter category [Interview 6].

You have to decide whether the case will stand up to the normal law and, if it doesn't, you have to decide what you are going to do. Are you going to allow an injustice to prevail? Or are you going to move to adopt the justice of the matter? For myself I prefer to adopt the justice in the matter. Sometimes it is more important to apply common sense (and palm tree justice) rather than strictly applying the law which may lead to dissatisfaction all round [Interview 10].

The more common sense one has and the less one feels absolutely bound by the fact that things are written in pillars of stone, the better. One is dealing with two lay people who are, at the end of the day, going to be looking at things from a common sense point of view, rather than a from a legal point of view. I think that common sense has to bear a large part in any decision you make [Interview 20].

People talk about whether we apply common sense or law. I'll apply common sense if I don't think there is any law. If I'm aware of the law (or what I believe is the law, whether I am right or wrong in my belief), I'll endeavour to apply it. But I think common sense is all important in many of the cases we hear. A number of my colleagues would be able to tell you the exact paragraph of the relevant statute or the page in *County Court Practice*, but I'm in the other category who tend to look at the problem and think what is the common sense answer to it. And then I ask myself whether there is any law on the matter. . . . I don't try to burden litigants in person in arbitration cases on the law. I personally wouldn't put a deep knowledge of the law high on the list of qualities that a district judge needs in conducting arbitrations satisfactorily. Usually the parties prefer the judge to deal with the case on its merits regardless of what the law says [Interview 23].

No apology is made for quoting from the interviews with district judges at such length because they go to the very heart of the judicial task. Although one should not exaggerate the frequency with which district judges reach decisions at small claims hearings which are at odds with the law—in most cases, law and justice are probably conveniently aligned—nevertheless the different stances that district judges adopt on the primacy of law are so fundamental that they are mirrored in many subtle ways in the approaches they adopt at hearings.

The term 'arbitration' is used almost universally by the cognoscenti when talking about small claims hearings. The writer is himself uneasy about its use, and he has tried as far as possible to avoid using it in this book. The term can be misleading and may in itself serve to encourage district judges to regard small claims hearings as essentially non-judicial in character. It is this writer's opinion that use of the word 'arbitrator' creates the misleading impression that the primary responsibility of the judge is to resolve disputes rather than adjudicate on a legal basis. 'It is the use of that form of words', one district judge perceptively observed to the author, 'which has enabled those judges who feel that they wish to free themselves of the constraints of the law and the judicial process to act accordingly.' This point was borne out by another judge who, arguing strongly in favour of the adoption of a non-legal approach, observed that judges should regard finding 'a fair solution' as their first responsibility. 'It is obviously true', he continued, 'that an arbitrator is in a different position from a judge: he is "arbitrating" and in a sense the word "arbitrary" gives a clue.'

Whether it is desirable and necessary for the everyday disputes of lay people to be translated into legal disputes is not an empirical question. For what it is worth, the author takes the view that, while the district judges who seek to resolve small claims by reference to their own understandings of 'justice' no doubt do so for laudable motives, it can be dangerous to allow free rein to the judges' value systems in determining the outcome of small claims. Such latitude fosters inconsistency, capriciousness, uncertainty, even prejudice, in decision-making, and may serve to undermine, not strengthen, the substantive legal rights of individuals. It is as if the individual district judge, rather than Parliament, determines the relevant law to be applied in each case.[38] Although the idea that district judges should be free to apply common sense notions of justice to everyday disputes has a superficial appeal

[38] Although litigants have a right of appeal in small claims where the district judge has made an error of law, this does not seem to be a consideration which bears heavily upon district judges in dealing with small claims. One district judge, who in interview argued more vehemently than any other judge in favour of his right to disregard the law when he felt it appropriate to do so (and actually did so in one of the hearings that the author attended), stated that he had never had a decision in small claims tested on appeal in over 10 years on the bench.

(for instance, because it introduces some sense of community equity into decisions), it nonetheless carries certain dangers. Since it is district judges to whom the small claims jurisdiction has been allocated in this country (and not lay magistrates, *pro bono* lawyers, local elders, or lay adjudicators as in some others[39]), it is safe to assume that the resolution of disputes within a legal framework was what was intended when the small claims procedure was introduced.[40]

However, it is hazardous to make confident, critical evaluations of the wide differences in judicial style observed in this study since there are so few rules or set procedures laid down in small claims. The outcome of most small claims is probably determined by the facts rather than by the law and, for the reasons already given, the former may provide such a precarious basis for decision-making that strictly applying the letter of the law will be in many circumstances a luxury that the district judges are scarcely in a position to indulge. It should nonetheless be acknowledged that, while flexibility is doubtless desirable in dealing with small claims, it can create great difficulty and uncertainty for lay litigants and their advisers.

The role of lawyers at small claims hearings

Since one of the original purposes in devising a special small claims procedure was to encourage unrepresented litigants to make use of the courts, it is rather odd that lawyers continue to make regular appearances at these hearings, and in county courts in some parts of England, it is not uncommon even for counsel to appear. It is odder still that the individuals and organizations (particularly consumer organizations) who might be regarded as the champions of individual freedoms have been amongst the first to advocate the apparently illiberal step

[39] See, for instance, the interesting discussion in Frame (1990) of the use of referees without legal training in small claims hearings in New Zealand. Lord Woolf (1995: 145) favoured similar moves, and he recommends that greater use be made of 'external arbitrators' (including solicitors, surveyors, engineers, patent agents, and members of other professions) to assume a new function of 'civil magistrates'. He envisaged that they would assume a number of functions, including acting as adjudicators in small claims.

[40] The author's preliminary findings on variations among district judges in applying the substantive law were submitted to the Woolf Inquiry (1995) and were discussed at some length in his interim report. Lord Woolf concluded that it is 'questionable whether such differences are acceptable even in a jurisdiction limited to £1,000' (*ibid.*: 109), and he discussed a number of ways in which greater consistency might be achieved.

of banning legal representatives from the small claims arena. It is worth examining how this paradox has come about.

It should be recognized that the advent of the interventionist judge, with the corresponding relaxation in the strict rules of evidence and procedure, has made the role of lawyers at small claims hearings at once uncertain and uncomfortable. While legal representation is permitted at small claims hearings in England and Wales,[41] the 'no costs' regime that applies and the non-availability of legal aid for small claims hearings mean that the parties themselves must bear the cost. Legal representation is in that sense discouraged. Lay representatives, though permitted at small claims hearings since 1992, appeared at only five hearings out of the 109 observed.[42]

Where lawyers are present, the character of a small claims hearing is likely to change and a rather dramatic clash of cultures can frequently be observed.[43] Intended to be informal and inquisitorial in character, small claims hearings are not designed to operate with lawyers who want to be adversarial. It has already been seen that the district judges experienced difficulties in adjusting to playing an informal, interventionist role, but many legal representatives have undoubtedly found it a much greater shock. As the author noted in observing hearings in this study, few legal representatives made much of an effort to adapt to the spirit of the small claims regime.[44] The lawyers who appear at small claims hearings have generally received no training whatever in small claims procedures, and, unless used to appearing at informal hearings of this kind, they tend to be unfamiliar with the role played by an interventionist judge. They may well find the hearing a strange and unsettling experience, and feel as a result that they are at a consider-

[41] Legal representation is not permitted in all countries. On this, see the discussion of procedures in Singapore by Ho Peng Kee (1988); in Quebec by Ramsay (1990); in Australia by Yin and Cranston (1990) and Ingleby (1993); and in New Zealand by Frame (1990). See generally National Consumer Council (1989), at 289–94. Weller *et al.* (1990: 11) noted that eight US states prohibited lawyers at small claims hearings, and they reported that there was a growing trend in that direction.

[42] Before the new rules were introduced in 1991, lay representatives had no statutory right to appear at small claims hearings, and did so only with the permission of the judge in the case: see Applebey (1992). The operation of the provision relating to lay representatives is being monitored by the Lord Chancellor's Department.

[43] The same phenomenon has been noted in relation to other kinds of tribunal hearing where proceedings are expected to be inquisitorial: see, for example, Genn and Genn (1989: 158–170) and Baldwin *et al.* (1992: 114–23).

[44] Some interesting points about the solicitor's role at small claims hearings (including differing perspectives on the admissibility of hearsay evidence) are made by Greenslade (1996).

able disadvantage. For their part, district judges tend to view the presence of legal representatives as something of an impediment to their playing a full interventionist role: they may even regard the lawyer's presence as defeating the whole object of the exercise. It was also evident at hearings that many legal representatives were unprepared for relaxed and flexible procedures, and regarded the advent of the interventionist judge with little sympathy, still less enthusiasm.[45] They sometimes discovered, to their obvious irritation, that they were in effect side-lined by the district judge who wanted to talk direct to their clients and had no intention of allowing them to engage in prolonged or formal examination of the parties. Some no doubt felt that the interventionist judge unfairly limited their effectiveness in playing the kind of role for which they had been trained, and were indeed being paid.

Legal representatives featured in just under a quarter of the 109 hearings that were observed, three times as often on behalf of plaintiffs as for defendants.[46] To an outside observer, these hearings were often curious affairs in that the lawyers occupied an ambivalent position. Unless the judge was very forceful or else deliberately decided to marginalize the lawyer, some concession in procedure had to be made to accommodate representatives. The result was often a rather awkward compromise between adversarial and inquisitorial styles as the judge allowed the lawyers to conduct their part of the proceedings according to one set of principles while the rest of the hearing proceeded according to a quite different set.

District judges tend to dislike ambiguities of this kind, and, in interviews with the author, few of them expressed much enthusiasm about the presence of lawyers at small claims hearings. Although only five judges said that they would favour banning lawyers altogether, most of the rest were lukewarm about having legal representatives at small claims hearings. There were, however, wide differences of attitude and practice in the extent to which judges were prepared to make accommodations to the presence of lawyers. Observing the way that district

[45] The debate about the Lord Chancellor's proposal to include certain personal injury claims in the small claims regime showed that practising lawyers had no great fondness for small claims procedures. On the fire that this proposal drew from the legal profession, see *Law Society's Gazette* (3 November 1993 and 10 November 1993) and *New Law Journal* (21 January 1994 and 28 January 1994).

[46] There was only one case in this sample in which both of the parties were legally represented at a hearing.

TABLE 3.2 *District judges' views about the presence of legal representatives at small claims hearings*

		%
DJs say they make little or no adjustment to legal representatives—lawyers in effect marginalized	6	18.2
DJs say they make a more substantial accommodation to lawyers though preserve interventionist role	16	48.5
DJs say they abandon the interventionist role though would help out an incompetent lawyer	6	18.2
DJs say they abandon the interventionist role and let the lawyers take over	5	15.1
	33	100.0

judges conducted hearings showed that some more or less allowed the lawyers to take over and assumed a back seat themselves; others saw it as their own responsibility to ensure that all the evidence was brought out and played an interventionist role even when it meant helping out an incompetent lawyer; yet others treated lawyers as an irrelevance, even a nuisance, and conducted the hearing as if they were not there.[47]

It would, however, be misleading to suggest that district judges fell into neat or watertight categories in their reactions to having lawyers at hearings. The calibre of the lawyers who appear at small claims hearings varies greatly, and some fit in much better with the prevailing ethos than do others. Where the lawyer is prepared to adapt to the spirit of these hearings, the judge may well respond accordingly. Table 2 shows how the district judges interviewed said they reacted to the presence of legal representatives at small claims hearings.

[47] There are legal limits in the extent to which district judges are free to ignore lawyers. The Court of Appeal, in *Chilton* v. *Saga Holidays plc* [1986] 1 All ER 841 (a case in which a registrar had refused to allow the solicitor for the defendants to cross-examine the plaintiffs), took the view that it was contrary to the rules of natural justice and unauthorized by the County Court Rules not to allow cross-examination of witnesses giving evidence. The Master of the Rolls said in that case that it was fundamental that 'each party shall be entitled to tender their own evidence and that the other party shall be entitled to ask questions designed to probe the accuracy or otherwise, or the completeness or otherwise, of the evidence which has been given'. This judgment has been criticized by some commentators as a reversion to adversarial trial principles and therefore as limiting the value of small claims procedures: see Jacob (1986) and Smith (1986). See also Greenslade (1996) for an interesting discussion of how district judges should regard the judgment in the light of subsequent changes to the County Court Rules.

Whilst not falling into exact or discrete groups, it was nevertheless apparent that district judges' attitudes towards representatives reflected to a considerable degree the basic approaches they adopted at hearings. For instance, those judges who took a strident line in restricting the scope of argument to the key legal issues were much less likely to be kindly disposed to the excesses of lawyers, whereas those who allowed greater latitude to the parties tended to be more sympathetic towards legal representatives. The place of lawyers at small claims hearings is so central to debates about future expansion of the small claims jurisdiction that it is worth considering in some detail what the district judges said about it.

Marginalizing the lawyers

Table 2 shows that there were six district judges who said that they deliberately cut the lawyers out of small claims hearings. They told the author that lawyers were allowed to occupy at best a minor, subsidiary place at the hearings they conducted. These judges tended to see the presence of lawyers as an obstacle in conducting hearings in the way they favoured. They in effect circumvented the lawyers and insisted that the litigants answered for themselves. On occasions, there were unseemly clashes at the hearing as some lawyers expressed their disquiet about the limited part they were being allowed to play. A few had to struggle at the hearing for their voices to be heard at all and were relegated to little more than a hand-holding role. The following quotations from interviews give an idea of judges' strength of feeling on the point:

> Local solicitors are very good in understanding that they should take a rather second place and that the arbitrator is going to listen to each litigant in person if possible. Solicitors are usually content to let the arbitrator ask the story or version of events from each litigant in turn. The solicitor might in that situation be a bit embarrassed because he knows he is not going to play a full part. I try to persuade the solicitor, in as nice a way as I can, that I would rather hear the story direct from the client first and then the solicitor can ask any supplementary questions that I've not covered. If I've carefully tried to cover everything, then I don't leave him much scope. The worst thing for the arbitrator to do is to keep his head down and just keep writing and letting the solicitor run it, because you'll find yourself in a similar position to a court case. To be honest, I think that the solicitors are superfluous. You form your opinion from the parties' evidence and the solicitors are not going to persuade you otherwise.

I think it would serve the system better if lawyers were not involved at all [Interview 1].

I usually tell the lawyers to shut up and hear the parties. I tell them that their client can tell me perfectly well what it's all about and I don't want to hear it three times. More often than not, the lawyers are a nuisance at arbitration hearings. They have been taught how to do advocacy on the courses they've taken and they get terribly flummoxed when you stop them. I think the textbook approach is completely inappropriate in these hearings [Interview 7].

I chop the lawyers out—totally, I'm afraid. I can't stand them in arbitrations! I say to lawyers, 'I hope you don't mind but I do find in these cases that it is easier for me to talk to the litigant direct.' I would let the lawyer add anything at the end but I would do the questioning myself. Basically I keep the lawyers out, marginalise them as much as one can, because I honestly think that they don't have a role to play in here except in very exceptional circumstances. The lawyers want to run the hearing on an adversarial basis and get very irritated with me when I question their client, rather than them asking the convenient questions of their client. I would go as far as to get rid of lawyers from arbitration hearings. They have absolutely no role to play [Interview 13].

To marginalize legal representatives, many of whom are themselves forceful and assertive characters, requires a high level of self-confidence, not to say toughness, on the part of the district judge. More of the judges in the sample chose to follow a less confrontational course and modified their approach when legal representatives were present. Sometimes this meant a reversion to adversarial trial procedures.

Making room for lawyers whilst trying to preserve an interventionist role

Table 2 indicates that almost half the district judges sought to achieve a balance at small claims hearings between allowing the lawyers to represent their clients in the way they wished and running the hearing in an informal and interventionist manner. The author's observations at hearings showed, however, that this was at best an uneasy compromise. Unless the lawyers in question were themselves prepared to adjust to the demands of an inquisitorial hearing—and few seemed able or willing to do so—proceedings were almost invariably disjointed and contained strange formal interludes in an otherwise informal drama. A few quotations will help illustrate how the judges, who said that they strive to make substantial accommodations to the presence of legal representatives, described the way they approach the dilemma that inevitably confronts them:

Lawyers tend to make it a little more formal in the sense that you have to allow them to conduct their client's case or defence. It's more like a court case. The lawyers can still play their role but I will still ask questions directly to their clients, backwards and forwards, and raise things as I normally would in an arbitration hearing. At the end of the day, the method of conducting the arbitration is still within my control, whether lawyers are present or not . . . I don't like lawyers at arbitration hearings at all because I think it creates a different type of hearing. Very often they don't know what is going on, and invariably I have to deal with the case as if the solicitor is not present. When the lawyer is incompetent, I feel obliged to assist the litigant to make sure that the matter is properly dealt with and that the issues are properly brought out [Interview 4].

I must in fairness to the lawyers give them a chance to present their clients' case in the way they want to. We have to return to the adversarial approach. I will then redress the balance by asking those questions that they have carefully not asked and which the other side don't know how to ask but which are essential to get at the truth of the matter. In arbitrations one is not going to say that he or she with the strongest case (or the best mouthpiece) is going to get the result. One is trying to get at the truth. I won't allow adversarial lawyers to get in the way. As far as the hearing is concerned, it is by and large better without lawyers [Interview 10].

'Many people think they will be at a disadvantage if the other side has a lawyer. Obviously I will do my best to ensure that they are not at a disadvantage. One generally assumes that the lawyer knows what he is doing and there is a danger, if I chip in every few minutes and don't allow him to make the points that he wants to make, that he will say at the end of the day that I haven't conducted the arbitration fairly. They may interpret my interventions as hostility towards their case . . . . It depends on whether the lawyer conducts it as if it is a full-blown trial or whether they treat it like an arbitration and just ask a few relevant and pertinent questions. You saw an example this morning of a lawyer treating it as a formal court hearing. Even if that had been a full-blown trial, I still would regard the painstaking way in which it was all done as being rather pedantic and laboured. He didn't try to get to the heart of the matter but took up each and every point, however unimportant. You obviously have to step into the fray more when one of the parties is represented than where both are [Interview 23].

Conducting an arbitration with lawyers is frustrating because there are very many times when I want to take control but I can't. I nevertheless guide them along the lines I think are appropriate and if they miss something I jump in. My hands are tied very much when I have lawyers present. It prolongs the whole hearing. But quite frankly I don't want representation at arbitrations. It hinders me. It gets in my way. We don't need it at all. I see no role for representation at arbitrations at all [Interview 32].

As a number of judges acknowledged in interviews, the presence of legal representatives often created an awkward mixture of adversarial and inquisitorial approaches. (One district judge even referred to them as 'bastardized' hearings.) The judge's control of a part of the hearing was in effect relinquished to the lawyers. Many judges regarded lawyers as presenting something of an obstacle to their capacity to fulfil a fully interventionist function. Legal representatives tended in consequence to be tolerated at hearings, rather like unwelcome guests.

Abandoning the interventionist role

A third of the district judges who were interviewed said that they felt obliged to abandon the interventionist approach when confronted by lawyers, although most were referring here to the very rare situation in small claims where both parties were represented. In the much more usual case, where only one of the parties has a lawyer, all district judges said that they would make some effort to redress the balance on behalf of the unrepresented party. As is apparent from the results presented in Table 2, some district judges decided to run the hearings on strict adversarial lines, making no allowance at all for the level of competence of the lawyers involved; others said that they would be willing if need be to bale out an incompetent lawyer. The following quotes illustrate the range of views expressed:

I find that if there are lawyers arguing it, I just shut up. That's their job and I let them get on with it. I wouldn't play any interventionist role. It makes no difference to me whether they are well represented or badly represented: I feel no obligation to redress the balance. That's not my job. I wouldn't do a thing except make notes. If the parties are paying for a lawyer, it's up to the lawyers to present the case as they think fit [Interview 9].

I play a very non-interventionist role. As a judge I keep quiet. I just literally turn to the advocates and say, 'Yes, Mr Smith . . .'. If they make a cock-up, that's their worry. If I think of a point in the case, I wait until they finish their evidence. If they are long-winded, I would try to speed things up. I can't prevent lawyers being here but I'd prefer they weren't [Interview 14].

The lawyers want to run the case as though it were a trial. I wouldn't stop them because they would be more at ease doing it that way. When I was younger, occasionally, to my shame, I conveyed to the lawyers that they were a bit superfluous by putting a lot of questions myself. But I wouldn't do that now. If the parties have elected to use solicitors, I would let them conduct it in a way that they feel most at ease in conducting it. If one of the parties were poorly represented, I would feel an obligation to redress the balance, but I would hope not to do it too obviously. If the lawyer was poor, I would wait until all the evidence was over and then say that there are one or two questions that I would like to ask. I think that is a delicate situation actually because the other party could say that, if the advocate isn't good enough, they should win. There are cases where lawyers get in the way. That's not to say that I don't welcome them. I'm often very pleased to see them because it does help to get the arguments properly marshalled. In many cases it doesn't make a lot of difference [Interview 22].

It makes a big difference when there is a solicitor representing one side or the other. You tend to conduct it in their way and let them carry on. Where the parties are represented by lawyers, then there is not a lot of difference between an arbitration and an ordinary court hearing [Interview 23].

Where there are lawyers, I stand strictly out of it and let them get on with it. There would not be that much difference from a hearing in open court because, once they've chosen to instruct lawyers, then it ceases to be the really informal arbitration to put the layman at his ease. But I think that, for these arbitrations, it is unfair to instruct a lawyer. It defeats the purpose of the small claims court. It's not playing the game. Where a lawyer is incompetent, I leave them to their own devices. If they can't get their tackle in order, that's their fault. Don't forget they're being paid for it. I wouldn't do anything to bale the lawyer out. They have got to learn if they are going to come and represent people at any level. That's their job [Interview 25].

Where extreme fluidity in the rules and flexibility of procedures are the order of the day, it is not surprising that there are wide differences in the attitude of district judges towards the presence of lawyers. Faced with the dilemma between playing the part of the inquisitorial judge and allowing lawyers to represent their clients as they themselves choose, many judges opt for the latter and the proceedings tend in consequence to take on much more of an adversarial character.

The need for legal representation at small claims hearings

Whether legal representatives can be said to have a worthwhile role at small claims hearings remains among the many unresolved dilemmas in the evolving theory of judicial interventionism. The most powerful arguments against the inquisitorial judge are based upon the possibilities of conflict between the roles of adjudicator and representative. It is claimed that no adjudicator, however conscientious, can be expected to engage in the kind of imaginative presentation of arguments or vigorous cross-examination that a competent legal representative would. An adjudicator, in other words, cannot act as a champion of the litigant's cause, nor even as a genuine advocate. In their study of representation at different kinds of tribunal, Genn and Genn (1989: 248) concluded that:

> while simplicity in initiating proceedings, informality in surroundings, and procedural flexibility are valuable qualities worthy of preservation, they should not be used as a justification for denying the contribution that representation makes to tribunal decision-making processes, nor the need of appellants to have their cases advocated on their behalf.

Although there is in England an almost instinctive attachment to the principle that individuals have a right to be represented at legal tribunals, it is not self-evident that this principle should apply in all situations. Most people would concede that the significance of the case (as reflected in the money and issues in contention) is relevant in deciding whether representation is called for or not. In relation to small claims, where neither the livelihood nor liberty of litigants is seriously threatened, it is difficult to make out a strong moral case for representation, at least if it is to be state-funded. And since representation is likely to reinforce existing social and economic imbalances between the parties rather than reverse them (because the more powerful individuals and organizations are better placed to afford to employ lawyers), the moral line is all the more difficult to draw. It has even been viewed by many commentators as a virtue of the small claims system that the presence of lawyers is actually discouraged.[48]

The question whether litigants would be unduly handicapped if small claims hearings were to be made lawyer-free has scarcely been addressed in England and Wales. Many litigants who read the leaflets on small claims procedures conclude that it is not worth their while paying for a lawyer, and they may well feel misled and disadvantaged when they turn up to the hearing and find that their opponent is

[48] The National Consumer Council (1979) strongly advocated the banning of lawyers from small claims hearings, arguing that, once lawyers started to appear regularly, litigants would feel that they could not proceed without them. It also asserted that the presence of lawyers tends to make procedures 'more formal, more forbidding, slower and altogether less geared to the individual'. The Council backtracked from this position in its report 10 years later, although it regarded it as 'a fault of the present system that lawyers appear too often' (*ibid.*: 293).

represented. Although it was noted in the previous chapter that the presence of lawyers has a statistically significant effect on the outcome of hearings—making victory about 10 per cent more likely than otherwise—it is not difficult to explain away a difference of this magnitude. It might well be, for example, that people are more likely to engage lawyers when they have a strong case or where there is more money at stake. And these litigants are themselves much more likely to turn up to the hearing—something already noted as strongly associated with success with a small claim. While the author has strong views about the need for litigants to have access to competent legal advice before activating legal processes, it did not seem to him that the presence of lawyers at the hearings themselves had any great bearing on the outcome.

The lack of impact made by lawyers is explained in some degree by the calibre of representation at hearings, and, since parties who wish to be represented have to pay for a lawyer out of their own pocket, it is perhaps almost inevitable that it is primarily lawyers at the junior end of the profession who appear at small claims hearings. Many of the legal representatives are not qualified solicitors at all but clerks and legal executives.[49] Standards of representation are variable, and the performance of some of the lawyers observed in this study was so ineffectual that it could have done little to advance their clients' cause. Although unfailingly courteous to legal representatives at hearings, many district judges in interview expressed thoroughly disparaging comments about the legal representatives who appeared before them. An indication of the low esteem in which many representatives were held by the judges was given in the descriptions of them as, for instance, 'the nearest thing to the tea-boy or tea-girl', 'the blind leading the blind', and even 'the secretary's daughter or the cleaner's daughter or God knows what'.

There is, then, a wide spectrum of views amongst district judges about the appropriate role to be played by legal representatives at small claims hearings and about the concessions that ought to be made to them. There is no right answer to the question that lay litigants reasonably ask: how important is it to be legally represented at a small claims hearing? The equivocal official response to this question has

[49] The widespread use of unqualified staff has also been noted in other contexts, particularly in relation to the provision of advice and representation in criminal cases: see, for example, McConville *et al.* (1994).

already been noted. While it depends to a degree upon the competence of the lawyer concerned, the unhelpful answer to the question is that it depends much more fundamentally upon the district judge before whom the case is listed.

Conclusion

There are surely limits to how far the rough-and-ready approach adopted by district judges in dealing with small claims can safely be taken. As far as the production of evidence is concerned, for example, it is not satisfactory in this writer's view to allow the parties to prepare their cases in whatever way they think appropriate and to ask district judges to make the best of it at hearings. If endless adjournments (and the cost and inconvenience they cause to the parties and to the courts) are to be avoided, then attention needs to be paid at an early stage in proceedings to ensure that cases are adequately prepared and, where they are not, to give appropriate directions so that deficiencies can be rectified. This tends at present to be done in only a cursory way by district judges in many courts. Yet it is this author's view that the preliminary scrutiny of the case papers can have an important bearing upon the efficacy and fairness of small claims procedures.

If the case papers were carefully vetted by a district judge well in advance of the hearing date, then much time, inconvenience, and nervous energy could be saved at later stages in the process. A district judge could, for instance, check that the plaintiff was suing the right party, or indicate the relevant documents or articles that would need to be produced at the hearing, or else ensure that the case had no implications for non-parties (as where, for example, a landlord is suing one of a number of tenants for a service charge). District judges hold different views about the desirability of holding preliminary hearings, and few judges nowadays hold them in small claims. But it may be that some thought will need to be given to resurrecting them now that the small claims limit has been raised to £3,000 and seems set to go much higher. This said, it has to be conceded that over-elaboration of procedures at an early stage rapidly comes to defeat the object of the exercise. Striking the right balance between attaining an adequacy of legal and evidential refinement and encouraging the effective participation of lay people lies at the heart of the small claims dilemma.

In the usual case, judicial involvement in small claims at the pre-hearing stage is confined to a perfunctory reading of the case papers in order to estimate the amount of time that will be needed to hear the case and to issue standard directions to the parties. Yet small claims cry out for more affirmative judicial intervention at an early stage to ensure that relevant evidence is produced at the hearing. In practice, the operation of small claims procedures is, by common judicial assent, a hit-and-miss business, and, if progress could be made in ensuring at least that the parties bring the relevant evidence (and, where appropriate, the relevant witnesses) to the hearing, then the difficulties faced by district judges would be considerably eased.

When one turns to the hearings themselves, the experience of presenting a legal case is likely to be foreign to the lay person. This applies no matter how relaxed the procedures or how sympathetic the judge who hears the case. Although the performance of many lay litigants at small claims hearings is impressive, they inevitably have to confront the hurdle of the law itself, and this represents a major handicap, the more so when they face a legally represented opponent. Litigants are sometimes taken aback when they find they are up against a lawyer and complain that the court leaflets had led them to understand that it would be an informal hearing with litigants dealing direct with a district judge. While the author does not see the need for legal representatives at hearings as particularly pressing, he nevertheless regards access to preliminary advice as critical. To encourage litigants in person to make use of the small claims procedure—and indeed to expand its scope—without making corresponding provision for them to have access to prior legal advice is likely to lead to frustration and disenchantment when matters are finally determined by a court.

The varied methods adopted by district judges inevitably diminish one's enthusiasm for the small claims procedure. While there now seems little resistance amongst judges to adopting an interventionist role at small claims hearings—indeed, many district judges relish having a free hand in deciding how to play it—it is inevitable that, without adequate guidance, they will conduct small claims hearings in diverse ways according to their own values and working philosophies. Some judges see the purpose of the small claims procedure simply as a form of law enforcement, enabling disputes to be resolved in a predictable and orderly manner according to the letter of the law; others see the county courts as providing a forum in which lay people can be guided towards their own solutions and compromises in which the law may even be disregarded; and others talk more ambitiously about small claims procedures increasing citizens' access to justice. As was discussed in the introductory chapter of this book, these views find resonances in the academic writing on small claims.

No one wants the district judges who hear small claims to adopt rigid and uniform procedures for the sake of it. The beauty of the small claims procedure lies in its flexible and 'human' character. But the freedom allowed under Order 19 does not mean that anything goes. In the view of this writer, it is to be regretted that nothing much is done at present to monitor what happens at small claims hearings in the county courts and that little effort is made to ensure that the standards applied by district judges are satisfactory.[50] Much would be gained by seeking to ensure that at least they follow the same ground rules. It may be that the time has come to consider the introduction of some form of judicial appraisal system along the lines adopted in certain other jurisdictions. Whilst unpopular amongst the senior judiciary,[51] it is an idea that received the powerful support of the Royal Commission on Criminal Justice (1993: 141).[52] The Commission argued that it was not convinced that adequate monitoring arrangements for judges were in place, and said that it found it 'surprising that full-time judges seldom if ever observe trials conducted by their colleagues'. It accordingly recommended that a formal system of performance appraisal be introduced for the judiciary and that resident judges 'attend trials so that they can assess the performance of judges in their courts'.[53] These observations carry particular weight when applied to small claims hearings.

One obstacle that stands in the way of achieving a greater measure

[50] There are signs that things may be changing in this respect. The very fact that the Lord Chancellor's Department allowed this study of small claims to be conducted and itself funded a significant part of it is perhaps indicative of changing attitudes. At the time of writing, the Association of District Judges, under the leadership of its President, District Judge Richard Greenslade (a member of the Woolf Inquiry team), is considering the introduction of a Code of Conduct for its members.

[51] The former Lord Chief Justice, Lord Taylor, expressed the following view (cited by Rozenberg, 1994: 119–20) on the subject:

> 'To introduce formal performance appraisal such as may be appropriate in industry or the civil service would clearly endanger the fundamental independence of individual judges, not only from the executive but also from each other.'

[52] See Royal Commission on Criminal Justice (1993), at 137–41. The idea of a judicial appraisal system has also been canvassed by Pannick (1988: 97); JUSTICE (1992); and Rozenberg (1994), at 117–21.

[53] It seems to be accepted on all sides that such appraisals would be carried out, at least initially, by fellow judges rather than by members of the court administration or any other body.

of consistency in the approach adopted by district judges is their isolation. Most carry out their work in a sheltered and private manner, in many courts insulated even from contact with fellow judges. There is no supervision of practices, no inspection, and no come-back if things go awry.[54] The principle that litigants might present their own cases in court has been referred to in this book as 'Do-It-Yourself' justice. It is important to note, however, that there is more than a hint of DIY about the judges' approach too. District judges in England and Wales have been given little, if any, guidance or training over the years in how they might play the interventionist role.[55] In the early days, it was left entirely to individual judges to evolve their own style and their own approach. They had to learn the job essentially by doing it. Although training courses, incorporating the small claims procedure, have been provided in more recent years for newly appointed district judges and deputies by the Judicial Studies Board, it is still the case that a majority of district judges have never received any training at all in how to conduct a small claims hearing.[56] No fewer than nineteen of the judges interviewed in this study (57.6 per cent) said that they had received no training in how to conduct a small claims hearing, although two-thirds of them thought there was no need for any either.

In his interim report on the reform of civil justice, Lord Woolf (1995) argued that much more extensive guidance and training should be provided for judges in playing the interventionist role to achieve greater consistency in procedure and in applying the substantive law. Lord Woolf (1995: 110) made the point that there is also 'a need for guidance as to best practice', and in his final report in 1996 he gave some information about the progress that is being made to that end.[57] In

[54] As one district judge put it in interview:

> 'It can be a very lonely job and, if you are not careful, you can develop idiosyncratic habits. I sometimes listen to my colleagues from some of the remoter regions of the country telling me what they do, and I think, "My God! Let's hope the Appeal Court never finds out about that!" Some judges who have sat for many, many years do develop some very strange habits.'

[55] Indeed, before 1979, when the Judicial Studies Board was set up, judges in England and Wales received no training in how to play the interventionist role or anything else. Since then, times have significantly changed although the attention paid in judicial training to a subject like small claims has been extremely limited, if it has been covered at all. On training offered by the Judicial Studies Board, see further Sir Thomas Legg (1996).

[56] Following the recommendation made by Lord Woolf (1995), progress has been made by the Judicial Studies Board in providing training in handling small claims: see Woolf (1996), at 98–9.

[57] Woolf (1996), at 98.

this writer's view, the promulgation of a code of practice for district judges would be more likely to reduce inconsistencies amongst judges (and at lower cost) than would enhanced training programmes. A working party was set up late in 1995, under the chairmanship of His Honour Judge Sumner, to produce a guide to good practice. At the time of writing, the working party's draft is apparently nearing completion.

District judges sit as emperors in relatively small dominions, and most have no more than a hazy idea of how colleagues even in the same court building operate, still less how judges in courts elsewhere in the country function. The individual district judge rules supreme, for the most part answerable to no one. The judges sit alone and, in some of the smaller courts, have only the court staff for company.[58] There is no one who might comment on the way they conduct small claims hearings.[59] Since few lawyers or other representatives attend hearings, competence as a district judge remains an essentially private matter. Several commented in interview that the only observers who ever attended small claims hearings were deputies in the course of training.[60] A few even remarked that having an academic observer present was a novel (and not an altogether unwelcome) experience for them.

It is important to recognize, then, that diversity in approach is a natural consequence of the flexibility in procedure allowed under Order 19. But it means that litigants' experiences of the small claims procedure are bound to be coloured by the fortuitous circumstance of the identity of the particular district judge who hears their case. Litigants' perceptions of small claims are likely to be heavily dependent upon whether their cases are heard by a district judge in, say, Cambridge or Northampton, Chester or Preston. And, since it is frequently striking how widely judges differ in approach even when sitting in adjacent rooms in the same court building, litigants' experiences will be very different according to the particular courtroom in those towns in which their case happens to be listed. It is fascinating, therefore, to consider what the other main group of participants in small claims—the litigants—make of the experience. This is the subject of the next chapter.

[58] The life of a district judge can be a solitary one and, although he or she might meet a colleague for a sandwich at lunchtime, many spend the lunch hour doing paperwork and choose to eat their own sandwiches alone in chambers. In most of the courts visited in this study, no communal dining facilities were provided for judges.

[59] There is, however, a national Association and local Circuit Associations when district judges meet from time to time to discuss common problems.

[60] All deputies are now required to observe the hearings of full-time district judges as part of their training.

4 Litigants' Perceptions of Small Claims

It is tempting to regard what litigants say about small claims as the acid test of these procedures. If small claims hearings are conducted to the general satisfaction of the parties, should we worry overmuch about how district judges go about reaching their decisions? One might argue that the whole point of devising special procedures in the county courts has been to assist lay people to present their own cases at hearings and to encourage them to make greater use of the courts. Although this reasoning is attractive, even seductive, the point can nonetheless be overstated. Indeed, it is a central argument in this book that the preparation and presentation of legal cases in small claims carry certain dangers—dangers, moreover, that lay people cannot be expected to recognize and avoid. This means that, while the small claims procedure may have been devised with the interests of lay litigants in mind, they may not always be in a strong position to evaluate its fairness. This is not to say, however, that the litigant's perspective does not provide an important yardstick by which to assess the operation of informal legal procedures like small claims. If it were found, for instance, that the parties were frequently disgruntled because they could not understand what happened at hearings or thought that they were unable to present their case adequately or else felt rail-roaded into submission by judges, some considerable rethinking of underlying principles would be required.

While there are signs that litigants' views of court procedures are beginning to be taken seriously in official circles in England and Wales (and the Lord Chancellor's Department now carries out large-scale court user surveys[1]), the voices of litigants themselves have been strangely silent in the literature of judicial administration.[2] This is

[1] The Court Service is required under the Courts Charter to 'carry out regular surveys of court users to find out how we can continue to improve the standards to make sure they meet your needs'. Thousands of court users are included in these surveys, and the Lord Chancellor's Department published the results of a national survey in March 1995: on this, see Sir Thomas Legg (1996) and Morgan (1996). In some small claims courts in the United States, the parties have for years been invited to complete users' questionnaires (of the kind commonly found in hotel rooms) and to comment on the standard of service they have received.

[2] There is only a sparse literature on the way that litigants make use of the courts: on this, see the discussion in Genn (1995), at 395–6. In much of the writing about litigants in person, the focus is upon the problems that they pose for the courts rather than the other way round: see particularly JUSTICE (1971); Bawdon (1994); Woolf (1995), at 119; Otton (1995); and McConnell (1995).

odd because the courts have frequently been criticized in the same literature for their tendency to operate for the convenience of court personnel, especially judges, rather than for the convenience of the parties. As Church (1990: 7) has argued:

> Most courts . . . are organized for the convenience of judges, of court staff, and of lawyers; usually in that order. If the convenience of the public is considered at all, it comes well behind these courthouse 'regulars' . . . . Yet no consumer-oriented establishment could set its priorities in this way . . . . With the exception of the prison service and perhaps a few unrepentant social welfare organizations, I know of no organizations. . . which appear to be quite as cavalier about their clientele as are the courts of the English speaking world.

This author is convinced that, while there may be clear limitations in accepting at face value what litigants say about the legal processes they experience, their perspective is nonetheless one that must be taken seriously. In evaluating informal legal processes in the civil courts, it would be of little comfort to know that, say, adjudicators, policy-makers or court staff regarded them highly if the litigants themselves were dissatisfied. It is right and proper, therefore, that we should treat litigants as central in any evaluation of small claims, and, in the present investigation, finding out what they made of their experiences was viewed as critical.

The litigants interviewed

Litigants do not by any means represent a single homogeneous group, and it is in consequence hazardous to indulge in extravagant generalization about their responses to legal processes. They comprise a wide spectrum of characters and circumstances—plaintiffs and defendants; business users and individuals; males and females; young and old; represented and unrepresented parties; professionals as well as those making their first (and probably only) appearance in a court. They also differ greatly in terms of personality, background, intelligence, experience, expectations, and self-confidence. For some people, appearance at a small claims hearing is a single and awesome experience in which they have an enormous emotional stake; for others, it is routine and familiar and its outcome little more than a matter of professional pride.

A determined effort was made in this study to find out what litigants involved in disputes dealt with under the small claims procedure thought of the experience. By far the greatest expenditure of time (and therefore of money) in the whole project was devoted to this exercise. A small army of research assistants was recruited, and for several weeks they travelled the country to interview small claims litigants in a number of county courts.[3] The interviewing was done between January and September 1994, and, in all, 262 litigants in sixteen county courts in England and Wales were interviewed about their experiences.[4] The author is not aware of small claims litigants having been interviewed on a comparable scale in the past,[5] and, since all the interviews were tape recorded, a great deal of qualitative material about the experiences of the litigants concerned was obtained from the exercise. An attempt will be made in this chapter to understand how an appearance at a small claims hearing in a county court is regarded, and, as with the district judges in the previous chapter, the objective will be to allow the litigants to describe the experience in their own words.

A few limitations, relating primarily to sampling and interview procedures, should be acknowledged at the outset. It is, for a start, extremely difficult to obtain a representative sample of litigants across a number of courts, not least because a large proportion of them fail to turn up to hearings. Since almost all litigants were interviewed within the precincts of the court,[6] the substantial numbers who failed to attend were not contacted. And it is not easy to decide when is the right time to interview litigants. In this study, they were interviewed immediately after the hearing. Yet speaking to them at that stage—as it were, just after the heat of battle—presents its own problems. Passions may still be running high, and assessments of the fairness of the procedures adopted at the hearing may be clouded as a result. In a few extreme cases, indeed, respondents felt such outrage because their

[3] Almost a third of the interviews were also conducted by the author or by Mrs Sue Deebank (a qualified solicitor who was employed on the project). Although most of the research assistants worked on the study for only a few weeks, great emphasis was placed upon their training and supervision. Supervision was greatly facilitated by having all interviews tape recorded.

[4] A broad mix of county courts of different sizes was selected in consultation with officials in the Lord Chancellor's Department. As in other parts of this study, at least 2 county courts in each of the 6 Circuits in England and Wales were selected for inclusion in the sample. Interviews with litigants were conducted at the following courts: Northampton, Worcester, Cardiff, Chester, Macclesfield, Warrington, Manchester, Preston, Blackpool, Leeds, York, Scarborough, Portsmouth, Exeter, Edmonton, and Cambridge.

[5] The National Audit Office (1996) conducted a study of litigants involved in 3,000 small claims cases in 7 county courts. This survey was, however, based upon a postal questionnaire, and the response rate for litigants, particularly defendants, was low.

[6] A room was provided at most of the courts so that interviews could be conducted in private.

claims had been unsuccessful that their views about the conduct of the hearing itself were of limited utility in assessing the fairness of court procedures. It is likely that litigants' views of their experiences of this kind will change over time, and the exercise reported in Chapter 5, in which successful plaintiffs were re-interviewed six months after the original court hearing to find out about their experiences in enforcing the judgment, enabled the author to consider shifts of view with the passage of time.

Certain practical difficulties were also encountered in carrying out the interviews with litigants. Although an attempt was made to interview all litigants whose cases were heard on selected days in a particular court,[7] many people slipped through the net, especially when more than one district judge was hearing small claims on that day. It is worth trying to picture the scene at county courts on the days on which small claims are being heard. Even in the busiest courts, small claims are not as a rule heard on more than one day each week.[8] The hearings are not usually scheduled as appointments, with litigants turning up to court as they might arrive to keep an appointment with a doctor or a dentist. Instead, a number of litigants are invited to attend at the same time. This is a much more convenient arrangement for the courts because a main problem facing the court administration is that, since many parties do not trouble to attend, hearings do not go ahead as planned but are concluded within a matter of minutes. Special arrangements are, therefore, made at many courts so that cases can be heard with reasonable efficiency and expedition. This means inviting blocks of litigants to attend at the same time, and, in some courts, two or more district judges deal with small claims simultaneously. This allows the listings officer to overbook the lists, confident that, out of a large number of claims, many will not proceed as full hearings. The larger courts hear small claims 'back to back' when cases are 'block-listed' for hearing. The busiest courts run what

[7] Although an attempt was made in organizing visits to the courts to pick those days on which a number of small claims were scheduled to be heard, several visits had to be made to most courts to secure a reasonable number of interviews. Since the courts varied considerably in size and workload, this meant that the bulk of the interviews was conducted at the larger courts. The author is extremely grateful to the court staff in each of the county courts concerned for their willingness to facilitate this part of the study.

[8] At the smaller courts, there may be no more than a single day each month on which small claims hearings are held, and it is likely that only one judge will hear those cases. With the increase in the small claims limit from £1,000 to £3,000, this situation may change in the future.

are dramatically known as 'bear gardens', when as many as half a dozen district judges may be dealing with small claims at the same time. When this happens, lists can be considerably overbooked without much risk that claims will not be dealt with on the day for which they are scheduled. The main disadvantage is that many litigants will be inconvenienced, and some may be kept waiting for lengthy periods before their cases are heard. Worse, it may not always be possible for all cases listed on a particular day to be heard, and some litigants will have to return to court on another occasion.

The timetabling arrangements adopted by the courts aggravated the difficulties experienced by interviewers in this study, because there was a limit to the number of interviews that could be conducted at any one time. Even though the author was fortunate in being able to recruit a dozen research assistants (mainly law graduates) to work on this part of the study between July and September 1994, so that more than one person could attend each court on a particular day, it was simply not possible to interview everyone who passed through the courts on the days on which the researchers attended. The best that could realistically be achieved was to interview as many of the litigants appearing in each court on any day as was possible. As far as practicable, the interviewers made contact with litigants in the waiting room at the court before the hearing commenced and explained the purpose of the research.[9] But many litigants were subsequently missed simply because, at the time their hearings finished, the interviewers were engaged elsewhere. Notwithstanding these and other difficulties that the interviewers faced, as many as 85 per cent of the litigants initially approached at the courts were eventually interviewed. Only about a third of the remaining 15 per cent actually refused: most of the non-respondents were people who were missed at the court.

The primary purpose of the interviews was to obtain litigants' perceptions of their experiences from the time they first decided to proceed to the court until the final determination in court.[10] An effort

[9] A few of the people who agreed at that stage to be interviewed said that they could not spare the time to talk to the interviewer at the conclusion of the hearing. Where the researcher had taken a telephone number, contact was made with them by telephone the following day.

[10] All small claims are heard in private and permission had to be obtained by the author from the Senior Presiding Judge for England and Wales before he could attend hearings. It was not possible, therefore, for the interviewers themselves to be present at hearings. Considerable efforts were, however, made by the researchers to enlist the assistance of court ushers so that the relevant court files could be scrutinized and the issues in the case established before interviews with litigants were conducted.

had to be made in the interviews to steer clear of the judge's decision (since respondents' views on that subject tended to be heavily coloured by self-interest) and to focus upon the hearing itself. Although this proved a tricky, even at times an artificial, exercise, it was not as a rule difficult to find out what litigants thought about the court procedures they had experienced. In some cases, it was only possible to talk about the way the hearing was conducted by first giving respondents the opportunity to sound off about what they thought of the district judge in question.

After a brief period in which pilot interviews in the Coventry County Court were conducted,[11] a schedule of questions was drawn up which was used throughout the main fieldwork. Although the principal issues covered in interviews were the same for all groups, the questions had to be adapted according to whether the respondent was a plaintiff or a defendant, a lay litigant or a regular court user. The issues raised in the interviews were, however, common to all groups of litigants and related to whether they had experienced any difficulties with the claim before the hearing; whether they had sought advice about their claim and from whom; how far the court procedure squared with their expectations; whether they understood the proceedings and felt they had had a fair opportunity to present their case fully; whether the district judge succeeded in putting them at their ease, and if they would be encouraged, as a result of their experiences, to proceed with a small claim in the future. Since few litigants wished to remain at the court after the hearing, interviews were for the most part of short duration. Some took no more than ten minutes, although a few lasted much longer. The aim was to keep them succinct and to the point. All the interviews were tape recorded—and not a single person declined to be recorded—and this meant that less time was needed in conducting them than might otherwise have been necessary because there was no need to make notes of what was being said. More important, the tape recording yielded a much richer and more accurate rendition of what litigants said than a written record could have provided.

Although there was occasional hesitancy at the outset, the recording of interviews nonetheless made for a more relaxed and natural encoun-

[11] The pilot work was conducted at the end of 1993. This work proved useful not only in formulating the appropriate questions to be put to respondents, but also in ensuring that the research assistants conducted the interviews in accordance with the author's instructions and fully understood the purpose of the questions. A number of potentially serious difficulties and misunderstandings were ironed out at that stage.

ter than would have been possible had the interviewer been obliged to make a written record of what was being said. Some of the litigants expressed disappointment about what had happened in the court, others were irate or aggrieved about it. But most were willing enough to talk about their experiences. On the whole, these small claims litigants did not prove difficult to interview, since most had a keen interest in the subject under discussion, and it was only in a few cases that serious difficulties were encountered in establishing rapport with them. A few were very verbose or voluble, occasionally to a degree that was not entirely to the interviewer's liking. (In one case, an interviewer, who was a rather diffident young man, was seriously put out when the woman he was interviewing insisted on breast-feeding her baby while he put the questions to her.)

The sample consisted of 162 plaintiffs and 100 defendants, of whom sixty-five and fifty-three respectively were private individuals as opposed to those appearing on behalf of commercial and business concerns. It was reassuring to note a high level of congruence between the characteristics of this sample and the national sample of county court claims described in Chapter 2. In most respects, the two samples matched closely, with roughly the same proportions of plaintiffs and defendants involved in each kind of action. There were some variations between the two distributions, but the similarities were far more striking than these minor differences. Again it was found that small firms appeared as either plaintiff or defendant in about two-thirds of hearings. Despite any vagaries of the sampling procedures adopted, it can, therefore, be claimed that in most respects the interview sample of litigants closely approximated a nationally representative one. It is a sample that covered all types of litigants, with roughly equal numbers from each of the six Court Circuits covered in the study.[12]

Who comes out ahead at small claims hearings?

In Chapter 2, an attempt was made to assess the extent to which business and commercial interests emerged as the beneficiaries of the small claims procedure. No overall patterns or associations were found. Using the material drawn from the interviews, this question could be

[12] Of the 262 interviews conducted, 41 were conducted in county courts in the Midland and Oxford Circuit; 40 in the Wales and Chester Circuit; 47 in the Northern Circuit; 41 in the North Eastern Circuit; 50 in the Western Circuit; and 43 in the South East Circuit.

examined further by assessing whether litigants' perceptions of the fairness of the legal processes squared with the findings derived from the straight statistical analysis. The views of the individual litigants were compared with those of business users in relation to a number of the criteria described earlier, such as whether litigants felt they were given a good opportunity to say what they wanted, whether they had a fair hearing, whether they had complaints about the procedures adopted, and whether they would be encouraged in the future to use small claims procedures.

These comparison showed that, although most respondents voiced no serious complaints about the way their cases had been dealt with, it was nevertheless more often commercial litigants than individuals who featured amongst the minority who felt seriously disgruntled about the hearing. This phenomenon was more evident in relation to so-called consumer cases, particularly where an individual consumer sued a business concern in relation to the sale of alleged shoddy goods.[13] A number of professionals (especially solicitors and accountants) and the representatives of small business concerns complained that district judges leant over too far to protect consumers' interests. It is worth pausing to consider a few examples of what business litigants said on the subject.[14]

The plaintiff alleged that the alterations that a seamstress at a shop had made to a dress were botched. The defendant shop-keeper was interviewed after the district judge had found in favour of the plaintiff, and she said:

> I expected exactly what happened. I go to these court hearings knowing thoroughly that the person taking us to court is going to win because the J.P. [*sic*] is always—always—quietly representing them, unbeknowingly actually representing them. You sat there, you heard everything—it was quite obvious that we had done what we could for that lady. A girl on a machine had spent a good hour and a half on that dress without any cost to this woman. What more could we have done? 99 per cent of my friends are in business and they've all gone through the same experience. None of them come out a winner. There doesn't seem to be any protection for the actual shop-keeper. He was all on her side. He felt sorry for her—'the poor woman!'—the customer. They are not always right. . . . They think that the customer is always the damaged person,

[13] For further discussion of consumers' use of small claims, see Baldwin (1996).

[14] In a few of the quotations from interviews used in this chapter, incidental details have been altered to preserve the anonymity of respondents and district judges.

that they are the ones who have been harmed. They don't think about you, how you run your business [Case 84].

The owner of a small garage expressed the following views about the outcome of a case in which the district judge decided that the parts he had fitted to a car were defective as the plaintiff had claimed:

You could say whatever you wanted to say at the hearing, but, you see, I'm here for the garage and it's all for the consumer now. It's all one-sided. For most purposes, you'll lose anyway before you even turn up. I couldn't believe that we would lose today. If it had been two private people, then we would have had the decision. But it isn't so good against the private individual when he's taking us to court. I was told, 'You've no chance in the court even though everything is in black and white, written down.' I could say what I wanted but you felt like you were losing anyway. I think that's only because it was a company against a private individual [Case 88].

An accountant had sued for unpaid fees, but the defendant was successful in his argument that the work the accountant had done was not satisfactory. The accountant said:

I think the procedure is fair and very good for litigants in person. It's just that it's difficult for accountants because it is so expensive to attend hearings. If I'm charging up my time at £100 an hour, I can't afford to be spending hours and hours in the court. With great respect to the judge, it's really rough justice. It's impossible in the time available for a district judge to get right to the bottom of a case and investigate all the complaint fully. So he did the best he could, I suppose. He didn't look at the file, for example, which he would have needed to have done if he were to investigate the matter properly. It was a summary remedy. You can't expect a Rolls Royce treatment when there is only a few hundred pounds involved [Case 131].

The district judge accepted the plaintiff's complaint that a fax machine she had bought from the defendant was not working as she expected. The defendant responded:

If you had looked at the paperwork, I think you would have agreed with me. We are a reasonable company. We have been in business for ten years. I went to every length during the transaction and in the various visits by my staff to give Mr K. every opportunity to complete the transaction correctly. But he seemed to be making further obstacles each time . . . I thought the judge was against me from the start in the way that he presented the questions and the way I was having to defend what was said. His questions to the other party were very, very minimal. . . . In business we have to have somewhere we can take disputes to, and I wouldn't want to suggest that anyone eliminate that possibility. But I was disappointed about the outcome this time. In business life today, you have to cover your back all the time. You can never be sure at the end of the day, but I was surprised about the outcome in this case. I know for a fact, though, that other companies treat their customers much worse than I do [Case 175].

It would be misleading to overstate the extent to which business litigants were discontented at the end of hearings, since a substantial majority of all types of litigants expressed overall satisfaction with the way that their cases had been dealt with. It was, however, a more common perception among business litigants that district judges, in playing an interventionist role, favoured individuals over litigants who appeared on behalf of commercial organizations. The potency of the 'consumer movement', supported by well organized pressure groups, was cited by some of the representatives of the small businesses in the sample as producing a situation in which district judges have come to be more sympathetically disposed towards the consumer at the expense of business interests—indeed, they would say at the expense of justice.

This was a surprising thing to hear and runs counter to much of the received wisdom surrounding small claims procedures which has been discussed in earlier chapters of this book. If weight is attached to these perceptions, it can be concluded that the picture that has often been painted in the academic literature on small claims—that the individual litigant is likely to get a raw deal, with traders and businesses easily able to exploit the informality of small claims procedures to their own advantage[15]—is not supported by the findings of this study. While it would be hazardous to draw sweeping inferences from these views, the frequent expression of such sentiments by those traditionally assumed to be unduly favoured by the operation of small claims procedures suggests at least that it would not be accurate to regard the operation of these small claims procedures as being in any sense 'anti-consumer'.

One explanation for this somewhat surprising finding is that litigants who appeared on behalf of business and commercial concerns were not as a rule 'regulars' or even particularly familiar with the court setting and the court routines. In reality, the business litigants shared more similarities than differences with individual litigants. Fewer than one in five of the business litigants interviewed could be regarded as professionals or court 'regulars' in the sense that they made frequent use of the court and were familiar with small claims procedures. (The excep-

[15] See, in particular, Yngvesson and Hennessey (1975) and Weller *et al.* (1990).

tions tended to be members of firms of solicitors, accountants, and estate agents who appeared on their own behalf as plaintiffs seeking to recover unpaid fees.) Nor were those from commercial concerns more likely to bring a legal representative to the hearing than were individual litigants. Excluding the representatives of firms of solicitors, only 10 per cent of litigants were legally represented at hearings, and this proportion was, surprisingly, even lower among commercial than individual litigants.[16] Furthermore, 57 per cent of all the litigants interviewed said that they had never appeared in a county court case before, and this applied to 40 per cent of those appearing on behalf of commercial organizations. Most of the people appearing at small claims hearings (whether they were private individuals or the representatives of business and commercial concerns) were, then, litigants in person. As there are so many similarities between the two groups, fine distinctions will not be drawn between them in most of the ensuing discussion.[17] This is done primarily in the interests of the simplicity in presenting the results, although the type of litigant will be specified in the extracts that are cited from interviews.

Anticipating the court appearance

The litigants interviewed in this study were to a remarkable degree an uncomplaining group. Legal commentators commonly make assumptions about what litigants want when they pursue an action in the courts. But in truth we know very little about their wishes. It is often assumed, for instance, that litigants will object strongly if there are lengthy delays before their cases are heard, or if they have to travel long distances to hearings, or if the courts sit at inconvenient times, or if they are left in the dark about what is expected of them. Yet the truth is often more prosaic and more mundane. It seems, for instance, that most litigants are prepared to comply without much complaint with the demands of the court administration, and, while they are acutely sensitive to impatience, condescension, and lack of courtesy on the part of judges and court staff, they appear to tolerate personal inconve-

[16] The examination of the 1,800 county court files discussed in Chapter 2 also showed that rates of legal and lay representation, both for individual litigants and commercial concerns, were low.

[17] This procedure was adopted notwithstanding the strictures of Whelan (1990, at 111–18) who warns against the aggregation of sub-groups of litigants in analyses of this kind.

nience with commendable fortitude. They may have to wait months on end for their case to be heard, but it may well be the unexplained two-hour delay before the hearing starts or poor sign-posting in the court building that really upset them.

It is important, therefore, to try to examine the operation of small claims procedures through the eyes of the litigants themselves, because false assumptions can be easily made about what they need and want from legal processes. Assumptions are often made, for instance, about how far people will be prepared to travel to hearings.[18] Although we do not know how many people are put off from pursuing actions because of the inconvenience of the journey to the court, or how many people fail to attend hearings for the same reason, it is nonetheless interesting that only one in six of the litigants in the present sample complained because they had had a difficult journey to reach the court.[19] Two-thirds said that getting to the hearing had not been a problem for them. For almost three-quarters, it had involved only a relatively short car journey, and one in seven lived or worked within walking distance of the court.

Apart from the small number of court 'regulars', for whom presenting a case in court was part and parcel of their professional duties, few of those who were interviewed could be said to have relished the prospect of an appearance at a small claims hearing. Despite the reassuring tone and clarity of the leaflets about small claims procedures that have been prepared by the Lord Chancellor's Department, few plaintiffs or defendants had much idea about what lay in store when their cases reached the court. One litigant, writing about her own experience of appearing at a small claims hearing, echoed the perception of many of the litigants interviewed in this study when she referred to 'a ball and chain of ignorance' that she felt she was dragging.[20] A similarly grim appraisal was made by many litigants in the present study, and as one defendant revealingly expressed it, 'the layman is undoubtedly going to feel nervous, whether he has something to fear or not'.

Much more is involved here than mere nervousness, however. It is also a question of people, unaccustomed to speaking in a public place,

[18] Concern is increasingly being expressed about the closure of county courts and the consequent inconvenience occasioned to the parties: see Gilvarry (1995), for instance.

[19] Less than a fifth of the sample said that the journey had taken over an hour. For over a third, it had taken no more than 20 minutes.

[20] Price (1993), 8.

anticipating what will be expected of them—having to talk in a formal setting, having to cope with accusations that may be made against them, and having to argue their own corner. In consequence, many court users, especially if they are there for the first time, approach the court with considerable trepidation. These findings lend support to the observation of Merry (1990: 142) who, in her study of courts in New England, noted that a court appearance was frequently viewed by first time court users as 'awesome and fearful' and that 'naïve court users often feel scared about appearing in court, afraid of talking, and anxious simply about being in a courthouse'. It is in large part the perception of what is likely to be involved that is important, and, even where the reality proves to be less threatening, the anticipation of formality—or of 'being on trial' as some litigants would have it—is a daunting prospect for many people.

Although small claims hearings are intended to be informal, with district judges helping unrepresented litigants to present their cases, it is very easy to overlook the fact that a court appearance, of whatever kind, can be a stressful, sometimes a frightening, event to those who are unfamiliar with the court setting. Some indication of how distressing, even traumatic, the thought of an appearance at a small claims hearing might be is given in the following quotation from an interview with one defendant, who was involved in what seemed at the time to this writer a routine road traffic case. She described her feelings after the event as follows:

> I feel drained. All of the worry has made me feel drained, I'm telling you. It has been a terrible time. Even for someone like me, going into something like this when you know you are not wrong is terribly draining. . . . But at least now I can have some sleep and the mental anguish is gone. I may have lost and I've got to find the money from somewhere, but at least I won't feel drained about all this any more [Individual defendant, Case 252].

The implication of this is clear: if there is a genuine wish to increase citizens' access to civil justice and to ensure that ordinary people make greater use of the small claims procedure, then it will not be achieved simply by developing and extending an informal judicial approach in order to make county courts more 'accessible' or 'user-friendly'. Moves to make legal procedures sensitive to the needs of the general public will not in themselves do much to encourage people to make use of the courts. The more critical factor that inhibits those with legal difficulties from activating small claims procedures is the unfavourable public image of the courts themselves. No matter how much times may have changed and no matter how relaxed and informal judicial procedures may have become, it is this factor that seems to deter potential litigants and to make them disinclined to look to the courts as the appropriate arena in which to resolve their disputes. Much more needs to be done by the courts, therefore, to overcome what is undoubtedly a serious image problem.

Failure to turn up to the hearing

Litigants are frequently surprised to find on the day of the hearing that the other party has failed to appear. (Some even assume that they are compelled to attend and that they would be in contempt of court to do otherwise.) The leaflets that have been prepared by the Lord Chancellor's Department in fact make no mention of this common occurrence and give no indication of what is likely to happen in these circumstances. Yet as many as ninety-seven (37 per cent) of the litigants interviewed in the present sample found that the other party had failed to attend. As already noted in earlier chapters, however, the non-attendance of their opponent usually turned out to be very much to the advantage of the vast majority of these litigants. They discovered not only that it obviated the need for a court hearing but also that the district judge was very likely to find in their favour. In most of these cases, the hearing was concluded in less than ten minutes and was seen by the litigants concerned as little more than a friendly discussion with the judge.

Since one of the central ideas behind the adoption of streamlined small claims procedures is that issues will be resolved on the day and that the decision will be final, most district judges are loath to adjourn cases simply because one of the parties has not bothered to turn up to the hearing. In this sample, adjournments occurred in under 10 per cent of cases in which only one of the parties attended. Litigants as a rule found instead that the district judges, having quickly assured themselves that a valid case had been made out on paper, terminated proceedings. As noted in the previous chapter, a few district judges made scarcely any examination of the issues at all in these circumstances. After having answered a few simple questions, most litigants emerged from the experience victorious, well satisfied, and not a little relieved. 'It was game, set and match when the other party didn't attend' is how one respondent aptly described it. Only four absent parties (two plaintiffs and two defendants) were successful. In these truncated hearings, there was no forensic battle with the accompanying acrimony and stress that many litigants in person particularly dreaded.

Claims that are dealt with in the absence of one of the parties are frequently overlooked in discussions of small claims procedures because the focus is naturally upon full hearings in which both parties participate. Yet the non-appearance of parties occurs so frequently that, in listing cases to be heard on a particular day, court officials actually operate on the assumption that a sizeable proportion of litigants will not attend. Since non-attendance is endemic in hearings of this kind and something for which lay litigants are as a rule unprepared, it is worth pausing to consider what a few of them had to say on the subject:

Having overcome the initial disappointment of the defendant not appearing, then it's a pleasant experience. It was very informal. We were chatting over the relative merits of the case and he gave me some guidance for the future. You can't ask for more than that [Plaintiff from a large firm, Case 46].

It was undefended, so that makes it easier. It was mostly straightforward—it wasn't difficult. It was like talking to you. More comfortable than a normal courtroom situation [Individual plaintiff, Case 91].

I was surprised first of all because the defendant didn't turn up, and secondly as to how brief the proceedings were. The judge accepted my verbal explanation and documentary evidence and awarded the decision on that basis. It was very brief. He explained the criteria by which he had reached his decision and what was involved. It wasn't really a hearing at all [Individual plaintiff, Case 105].

The judge was very good. I didn't have to say anything because it's been thrown out. I got a shock. I thought I would have a load of, you know, law sort of thing. But there was nothing. It was straightforward talk [Individual defendant, Case 106].

It was better than we expected. He [the defendant] didn't turn up and the judge just listened to our evidence and passed judgment on our evidence alone. We were expecting an adjournment. If he'd have come along, we'd have had to do it face to face with the guy—our landlord—who was ripping us off. I was quite nervous. He's a judge, you know. You hear all these things about the legal system; you just hope that it's going to go your way. Obviously we know we're in the right. It's just a matter of proving it and whether he believes that. We're honest people and this guy isn't. . . . I think we'd have had to put our case fully if the other guy had turned up. But the judge already knew what our side of the argument was and so we didn't really have to present much today. He just asked us one or two things and we had to clarify a few points. So it wasn't really much of a presentation. It was very easy and relaxed [Individual defendant, Case 107].

I found it slightly faster than I expected—seeing as the defendant didn't turn up. It was very annoying. It's one of the factors I wasn't aware of beforehand—whether you legally had to turn up, whether there was a legal compunction, and if I didn't turn up whether I would be in contempt of court. I wasn't sure whether that was the case or not. So I assumed that you had to turn up. It's very frustrating having taken the time and effort to find that they can't even be bothered to appear. . . . As it turned out, it wasn't necessary to present my case. I'd prepared the basics and was prepared to argue them if needs be. But there was no counter argument to it [Plaintiff from a small firm, Case 140].

The defendant didn't turn up. The judge went through the bare facts of the case, gave judgment and it was all over in less than ten minutes. Basically the judge just asked me about three questions which needed one word answers, and that was that [Defendant from a small firm, Case 151].

It was very good. I didn't need to present my case because he [the judge] was already on my side. It was just a question of looking at the papers really and he accepted the facts. I didn't really have a case to present [Plaintiff from a public organization, Case 175].

I was quite relieved because the other people didn't turn up and put their defence. It was fairly informal, I would say. He [the judge] made us feel at ease. He didn't start spurting out any technical details or anything like that [Individual defendant, Case 250].

In the interviews, litigants commonly described hearings of this kind as 'non-events'. While relief was often expressed because the anxiety, unpleasantness, even embarrassment, of a confrontation with the other party had been avoided, a few litigants, particularly those representing small businesses, felt frustrated, as they had looked to the hearing as an opportunity to resolve longstanding differences with their adversaries and felt cheated of their day in court. Some plaintiffs even viewed their victory in court in these circumstances as hollow and as an ominous sign that difficulties in enforcing the judgment would be encountered later. As we shall see in Chapter 5, such fears were often well justified.

The non-appearance of the other party is not the only thing for which lay litigants are ill-prepared, however. Uncertainties and misconceptions about what an appearance at the hearing will entail are rife amongst lay litigants, and in the main only those with prior experience of the courts had much idea of what to expect. Such uncertainties were only partly dispelled by the taking of preliminary advice. Indeed, only a minority of litigants availed themselves of such advice, or at least did so in a systematic fashion. And even when advice was given, it gave only a partial idea of the nature of the procedures that would be encountered. Advisers are in some difficulty in this respect because, as noted in the previous chapter, district judges vary so widely in the way they conduct small claims hearings that it is in practice not possible to describe to a prospective litigant what will happen at a typical hearing. Excluding the professionals for whom advice is unnecessary, less than 40 per cent of litigants said that they had consulted a solicitor about the case.[21] Fewer than one in ten said that they had approached a voluntary advice agency such as a Citizens Advice Bureau or a local authority department like Trading Standards. Fewer still said that they had obtained guidance from staff at the court itself beyond collecting the small claims leaflets.[22] These results, therefore, confirm the paradox noted by Whelan (1990: 118) that 'by far the most frequently used sources of help, in a procedure designed to be accessible without the use of a solicitor, are solicitors'.

A majority of litigants either took no advice at all or else relied upon informal sources of advice like neighbours, friends, or family. Of those who took advice, however, 87 per cent said that they had found it useful. A majority of litigants whose cases make it as far as the county courts go it alone, and it is in that sense appropriate to refer to most claims dealt with under the small claims procedure as examples of Do-It-Yourself justice. In a few extreme cases, litigants reach the court with reams of notes having spent many hours in the local library, researching the legal texts, before they complete the summons. But these are the exceptions. Most litigants trust to luck and common sense, prepare their own cases as best they can, and arrive at court armed with little

[21] In the study conducted by the National Audit Office (1996), less than a quarter of litigants reported receiving assistance from a solicitor.

[22] The Civil Justice Review (1988), however, argued that:

> '[Individual litigants'] primary source of information and guidance is the staff of the court, who should be available to advise any litigant on the remedies open to him in relation to a particular claim, the procedure for pursuing those remedies and the precise manner in which court forms should be completed' (para. 363).

In the academic literature on small claims, the point is often made that the assistance provided to litigants by members of the court staff is crucial to the success of the small claims enterprise: see, for instance, Weller *et al.* (1984); Whelan (1990), at 232; Yin and Cranston (1990); and Frame (1990).

more than a strong conviction that right is on their side. Professional advisers, para-legals, and voluntary workers play only a minor role in most small claims, and this is particularly so at hearings.

As legal advice is not widely sought and members of the court staff are expressly forbidden to provide it themselves,[23] it might be thought that the Lord Chancellor's Department's explanatory leaflets about small claims procedures would plug the gap of ignorance. But this is far from being the case. Seven leaflets have been published, each one dealing with a discrete stage of the process. As the writer himself observed, staff in some county courts struggled to provide litigants with a complete set, and (excluding the professionals for whom the leaflets were not designed) well over a third of litigants in this sample said that they had never seen any of them. As this was a sample of people whose cases had reached the stage of a court hearing, this strongly suggests that the extent to which the leaflets have raised public awareness of the existence of the small claims procedure and more generally facilitated access to civil justice has been extremely limited.[24]

There are other problems with the court documentation. As happens in other jurisdictions, the court literature tends to be overwhelmingly oriented towards plaintiffs, not defendants.[25] Furthermore, it is hit-and-miss whether the leaflets find their way into the right hands because they are not sent out automatically with the court papers and are given only to those litigants who specifically request them.[26] This is

[23] The staff in some small claims courts in the United States are permitted to offer legal advice to litigants, even to the extent of telling plaintiffs whether they have a case in law: see Weller *et al.* (1984). In this country, however, the leaflets provided to litigants by the Lord Chancellor's Department explicitly state:

> 'Remember that court staff are not solicitors. They cannot give legal advice or answer questions like: Am I claiming from the right person? Do I have a good claim? How much money should I claim?'

[24] The same was noted in the study conducted by the National Audit Office (1996): see 13–14.

[25] Advice offered by court staff is also likely to benefit plaintiffs much more than defendants: see Weller *et al.* (1984), at 72–3. Cain (1986: 129) goes further and argues that 'the court . . . exists, and always has done, to serve the purposes of plaintiffs'.

[26] Some small claims courts in the United States make a point of enclosing copies of explanatory booklets when the court papers are sent to the parties. This means that at these courts there is no need for anyone to request them. This is still, however, far from being standard practice even in the United States. The present author agrees with the recommendation of Weller *et al.* (1990: 13) that 'information booklets which detail key elements of preparing for trial . . . be automatically distributed to each plaintiff who files a complaint and mailed to every defendant along with the complaint'.

to be regretted since over 60 per cent of litigants who managed to get hold of the county court leaflets said that they had found them useful. The value of the leaflets tended to be seen by litigants less in terms of providing information and guidance about how the hearing would proceed than in assisting them in the completion of the court forms.[27] There were, however, many complaints about the fragmented presentation of information in seven separate leaflets. ('Umpteen bits and pieces' is how one plaintiff described them.) Despite the criticisms levelled at the seventy-two-page booklet (Birks, 1984) that was the fore-runner to the leaflets,[28] there may after all be something to be said for including all relevant information for litigants in a single document.

Most litigants arrive at the county court, then, with little idea of what lies ahead. For some, misconceptions are fuelled by what they have seen in television dramas. They find themselves being ushered into the district judge's chambers, often a relatively small, pleasantly appointed, and surprisingly intimate setting. As noted in Chapter 3, the judges' chambers simply do not feel like courts. The early impressions of the informality of the occasion strike many lay litigants forcibly and generally come as a welcome relief to them.[29] The following quotations from interviews are a few typical examples of these first impressions:

I was expecting a more formal court room with a shield on the wall [Individual plaintiff, Case 8].

There was no intimidation which is the problem which you can have when the magic word 'courts' is mentioned, where one expects a chap in a wig and a load of other ancillaries around [Plaintiff from a large firm, Case 14].

[27] This is not to imply that litigants commonly said that completing the summons created difficulty for them. Only 8 litigants interviewed said that they had experienced serious problems filling in the relevant sections. See also the study conducted by the National Audit Office (1996: 15) in which few of the litigants contacted reported that they had experienced difficulty completing the court forms.

[28] See White (1985), at 145, and Whelan (1990), at 124–7.

[29] Given the wide variations in the ways that judges conduct small claims hearings, it was not surprising that some litigants found the proceedings more formal than they had anticipated. This occurred particularly when they discovered that their opponent was legally represented. As one plaintiff put it to the author, 'My idea of "informal" is obviously totally different to the legal profession's idea of "informal"'. As several researchers have noted, informality is a slippery concept and to a large extent in the eye of the beholder: see, for example, Dickens *et al.* (1985: 183–200); Genn and Genn (1989: 219–41); and Baldwin *et al.* (1992: 111–23).

I didn't expect it to be all sitting round a table, all casual, the judge just there talking, laid back, no slanging match, nothing like that, quite relaxing actually. It was nice [Defendant from a small firm, Case 67].

It was more informal than I thought it would be. It was more like a meeting at work than being in court [Individual defendant, Case 85].

It was simply a question of sitting down and speaking person to person without any intermediaries, without any intimidating legal jargon and without any formal procedure [Individual plaintiff, Case 123].

Basically it's just a room. It's not a like a courtroom. It's just an office, tables and books, and the judge is just in a normal suit rather than, you know, what you expect when you see the television [Plaintiff from a small firm, Case 128].

It was relatively informal and a complete shock to me. It felt rather like being in a headmaster's study [Plaintiff, Individual trader, Case 169].

It's better than a court, because we're sitting opposite each other, better than sitting in a court [Individual defendant, Case 251].

Many litigants were, then, pleasantly surprised to discover that the setting in which their cases were to be determined was nothing like the formal courtroom they had anticipated. But what did they make of the procedures that were adopted? Were they satisfied by the way their claims were dealt with? Did they feel able to participate in what was taking place? Did they think that they had been given a fair hearing? As noted in Chapter 1, a theme that runs through much of the academic literature is that it is the economically powerful (especially when they are regular or professional users of the courts) who are best placed to benefit from the operation of legal processes, even when the formality of those procedures is relaxed. According to this view, those who lack economic muscle are likely to be at a disadvantage unless the court itself assumes an active role in balancing the scales. Since one of the main objectives in encouraging district judges to play an interventionist role at small claims hearings is to do precisely that, it was a central part of this study to ascertain how litigants viewed the district judges' role at hearings.

It has already been seen that most small claims litigants, whether they were private individuals or those appearing on behalf of business and commercial concerns, were inexperienced and unfamiliar with the court setting. High levels of anxiety about appearing in court were easily discerned even after the event. While district judges were on the whole adept at putting people at ease (and the relaxed approach that most adopted at hearings prompted frequent expressions of apprecia-

TABLE 4.1 *Whether litigants were put off or encouraged by the experience of appearing at a small claims hearing*

		%
Not put off—happy about using the procedure in the future	201	76.7
Not put off but would use the procedure with some reluctance in the future	36	13.7
Ambivalent—uncertain about whether s/he would use the procedure in the future	2	0.8
Put off—unlikely to use the procedure in the future	14	5.3
Seriously put off—would definitely not use the procedure in the future	7	2.7
No view expressed on the matter	2	0.8
	262	100.0

tion from the parties), the prevailing view nonetheless was that a court appearance was a thoroughly nerve-racking experience.

A variety of measures was used to assess litigant satisfaction. The measures included whether they said that they were able to follow court proceedings; whether they felt able to understand the proceedings; whether they were given a reasonable chance to put their case; and whether they felt that they were put at ease by the district judge and were favourably disposed towards the approach that he or she adopted. It quickly became clear in the interviews with most litigants that, no matter how apprehensive and nervous they were beforehand, they had been able to grasp what was happening at the hearing and to participate effectively in it. Win or lose, litigants expressed high levels of general satisfaction, and less than a fifth remained unhappy or disgruntled after the event.[30] One useful indicator of the generally high level of satisfaction is found in the expressed willingness to use the procedure again in the future. Table 1 shows that few litigants had been seriously put off by their experiences.[31]

[30] The postal survey of small claims litigants carried out by the National Audit Office (1996), at 35–7 also showed high levels of litigant satisfaction.

[31] A similar result was obtained in the study commissioned by the Lord Chancellor's Department and conducted by Touche Ross Management Consultants (Lord Chancellor's Department, 1986). In that study, 81 per cent of plaintiffs said that they would be likely to use the small claims procedure again in the future. Somewhat less favourable expressions were noted in the main Scottish study where only 60 per cent of individual litigants said that they would be willing to use the small claims procedure again: Scottish Office Central Research Unit (1991).

The picture to emerge from these interviews was, therefore, that most litigants were well pleased about what happened at the hearing. Moreover, favourable responses were found amongst litigants in all groups—plaintiffs and defendants, winners and losers, those from business and commercial concerns as well as private individuals. Criticisms of the way district judges conducted hearings were voiced by only a minority. The author's own observation at small claims hearings strongly suggested that most district judges strive to tackle the issues conscientiously, and, although some judges can be decidedly tetchy on occasions with legal representatives, it is unusual to encounter one who is curt or high-handed with a litigant. Being able to sit around a table in a relaxed and informal setting to resolve the matter was particularly welcomed. The following are fairly typical quotations from the interviews that were conducted, and they give some idea of the general tenor of litigants' comments about hearings:

It was fairly easy to understand what was going on. The arbitrator went to considerable lengths to speak, you know, in non-lawyer talk (or whatever you want to call it) and to keep it so that I knew what was happening and why he was making the decision that he was. I felt that the arbitrator took account of the fact that I was obviously unaware of the procedure and probably I didn't really get my point out as I would have wanted to. But he did seem to pick up the point from what I was saying, so I was fairly impressed by that [Individual defendant, Case 15].

The actual procedure at the hearing was fine—no problems at all. We had a very able, intelligent man who was able to understand the situation and give his opinion. I thought he was wrong but he was able to give his opinion [Defendant from a small firm, Case 18].

It was very informal. You just sit down and talk like I'm talking to you now. It was just normal talk. There was no taking the oath or waiting your turn to speak. It was just a normal conversation with the gentleman. I felt very comfortable [Defendant, Individual trader, Case 38].

It was very easy to understand. Really easy. There's no technical words to do with courts and things that I didn't understand. Just plain old English. That was all. It was like sitting talking to you now [Individual defendant, Case 49].

I thought it would be a bit more traumatic than it was. I thought it would be a bit 'courtish'. I didn't realise it would just be a room like that. I expected there would be boxes and seats. The judge was quite good really. He was reasonably understanding. He was pretty good at explaining everything. He let us each have our say . . . . I was quite relieved because I really thought it would be worse than what it was. It was quite nice really, not nice, but you know what I mean—a lot better than I expected. It wasn't a bad experience at all [Individual plaintiff, Case 82].

It was much more relaxed and informal than I expected. I expected at least the judge to be very stern with both parties. I served on a jury and all the formality of that compared with the informality of the court here is amazing. I used to take the kids from the school to the court to see what was going on. That made us all shake even though we hadn't done anything. This was far less intimidating. The judge was a human being with his visual aids and things like that which all help to take the edge off any formality. Rather than the bewigged judge sat up there, I was very impressed by the man himself. Very, very impressed [Individual defendant, Case 87].

It was pretty straightforward. There was no legal jargon and the judge just sat there and let you put your case. He was very much in charge and informal at the same time. It was much more relaxed and informal than I'd expected [Plaintiff from a large public organization, Case 145].

I didn't know it would be as informal as it was. But it was very good. I was treated marvellously well. It was plain English plain speaking—none of this 'party of the third part' or 'my learned friend'. It was just, 'Sit down, Mr T. . ., tell me what happened.' It was like going to a doctor. No hassle because it was just sitting down talking to the man. I went in and the man was dressed in a suit, and looked very smart. No wig, no nothing. He was just like an ordinary gentleman [Individual plaintiff, Case 186].

I was quite happy. I was able to follow it. The judge was brilliant. He put us at ease in about two minutes and laid down the ground rules, and then I didn't feel so uncomfortable. I feel highly satisfied. He had a lot of sympathy. I had every opportunity to present my case and was given a very fair hearing [Individual defendant, Case 206].

I found it very reasonable and it was all quite informal—just sitting round a table and talking. It's not like being in court. It was relaxed and in no way did I feel I was under any pressure [Individual plaintiff, Case 209].

It was quite laid back actually. It wasn't as dramatic as I thought it was going to be. It was less complex and intimidating. I wasn't expecting it to be so informal and laid back. I'd been on jury service and that was totally different. I was expecting it to be something similar to that, without a jury [Individual plaintiff, Case 247].

Litigants' perceptions of the extent to which they understood what happened at the hearing may reflect a certain wishful thinking, in that people may claim to understand more than they really do. Yet the generally favourable picture to emerge from the interviews with the parties was largely borne out by the author's own observations at small claims hearings. Although litigants vary enormously in terms of personality, confidence, articulacy, experience, competence, preparedness, and the like, there were only half a dozen who were noticeably floundering and out of their depth in these surroundings.[32] There were rather more litigants who on the day allowed their passions to get the better of them and who perhaps realized in retrospect that they had failed to do themselves full justice. Some were evidently very nervous and ill at ease at the start, particularly where the other side was represented, but most visibly relaxed as the hearing got under way. This is not to say that all litigants advanced their cause in the most effective manner, but, in the estimation of this writer, most litigants performed competently enough.

The basic purpose in devising small claims procedures is to facilitate the presentation of claims by lay people without resort to lawyers, and this is reinforced by the 'no costs' rule which operates in small claims in England and Wales. The 'no costs' rule serves both to assure lay litigants that they will not face a huge bill if their claim is unsuccessful and to discourage the use of lawyers.[33] Although it has been repeatedly observed in this book that litigants who do not take legal advice before the hearing are inevitably disadvantaged by their ignorance of the law, different considerations apply when one considers the involvement of lawyers at small claims hearings, not least because few district judges are enthusiastic about the legal representation. But what do litigants themselves think about the need for representation? This sample is particularly useful for this purpose since the parties were interviewed immediately after the hearing. With the benefit of hindsight, did those who turned up to the hearing without representation think that they would have been better off with a lawyer? Or were lawyers seen as redundant? Did those with representation regard it as necessary? Table 2 sets out their answers to these questions.

Table 2 shows that, when interviewed after the event, over 80 per

[32] High levels of litigant competence were also noted in the study of small claims conducted in Northern Ireland in which the authors observed that 'once individuals overcome their initial nervousness they are usually capable of presenting their own case': see General Consumer Council for Northern Ireland (1992), at 33.

[33] Whelan (1990: 221) raises the question whether the 'no costs' rule might be misconceived since it may operate so as to discourage representation only by some parties, particularly individuals.

TABLE 4.2 *Who needs representation at hearings?*

		%
Unrepresented: said they managed perfectly well without representation	159	71.0
Unrepresented: said they managed fairly well without representation	3	1.3
Unrepresented: said they managed fairly well but would have preferred representation	34	15.2
Unrepresented: said they did not manage well and would have preferred representation	6	2.7
Represented: said they could not have managed without representation	3	1.3
Represented: think they could have managed without but preferred to have been represented	17	7.6
Represented: think they would have done better without representation	2	0.9
Not relevant—a professional/regular court user	38	–
	262	100.0

cent of those who had been unrepresented at the hearing said that they had managed well enough on their own. Although most of the twenty-two litigants who had legal representation were pleased that they had had it, only three thought that they could not have managed without it. It is, therefore, only on rare occasions that litigants' perceptions of the value of representation are contradicted by what happens at the hearing. As is apparent in the following quotes, the great majority of litigants interviewed in this study said that they were content to present their cases themselves:

I was happy enough to do it myself. I could only tell the truth as I saw it. For me to have to explain it to a solicitor and for him to do it and make money out of it was not what I wanted. I just wanted to tell it as I saw it [Individual defendant, Case 2].

I hoped, stupidly or innocently, that the facts would speak for themselves. Basically if we were legally represented, we would only be feeding these facts to a solicitor. In whatever terms he chose to phrase these things, they would still be the facts [Individual plaintiff, Case 4].

To be honest, a solicitor can only look at a file. We knew what happened. We felt we could probably put the case forward better than a solicitor in this instance. It's just two people in a room arguing over a table [Plaintiff from a large firm, Case 14].

I was perfectly happy to represent myself. I was master of the facts because I did all the work and I'm the best person to give answers to the judge and/or the defendant [Plaintiff individual trader, Case 29].

I'm happy to do it myself because you have to tell a solicitor and he has to tell the judge. Why don't you just tell him yourself? That's how I look at it [Plaintiff individual trader, Case 32].

There is no question at all that I can present my own case better myself. It's much easier than having a lawyer. You can have a more frank discussion. It doesn't get lost in legalese and frankly two lawyers really can't get down to the nitty-gritty, the real issues and do it justice [Plaintiff from a small firm, Case 37].

I couldn't afford to get somebody here to represent me, and, even if I had had the option offered me of, shall we say, the 'community' providing me with a solicitor, it would have been money thrown away. The case was so innocuous anyway [Individual defendant, Case 52].

For something like that, I don't think it would have come out any different. Even if you had George Carman, it wouldn't have made any difference [Individual defendant, Case 55].

It was very useful to be represented. I would have been unsure of what the procedures were. I wouldn't have known what was relevant and what wasn't relevant, whether I would have been wasting the judge's time in what I was saying if I hadn't had legal representation [Individual plaintiff, Case 66].

I was happy to do it myself because I thought I was in the right. I still do. So I didn't feel I needed to bring anybody in [Individual defendant, Case 74].

I wouldn't have dreamed of coming without a representative because it's a new experience for me. Within the meeting, I could have handled anything that was said because it was not very formal. As it turned out, it was all right. It was useful [being represented] because there were court procedures that I didn't know about. I felt I needed someone with that court experience when I started this thing going. So it made me feel better [Individual plaintiff, Case 89].

I can put my case over as I want, not with the legal jargon. I'm a worker, and that's what it's about, work [Individual defendant, Case 106].

It would have been nice to have someone with me. I was up against a firm of accountants—two partners who were highly qualified and used to making legal arguments [Individual plaintiff, Case 108].

I was happy to do it myself. I was involved from the very beginning so I knew all the facts, and I remember the conversations, and I wrote the letters, and I know what is meant by the letters, and I know what I read into the replies [Individual plaintiff, Case 111].

I think it would have been better [to be represented]. You just go in with no back-up. I mean, I'm nobody, am I? It may be better with somebody who's quite authoritative. It's mildly intimidating because you see somebody who's like the boss in charge—the judge. And I'm just the average person on the street, aren't I? If I'd had with me somebody with authority, maybe I'd have carried a bit more weight. I felt at a disadvantage because it was quite intimidating [Plaintiff individual trader, Case 148].

No, I wouldn't have preferred a solicitor because what I told the judge was the truth and everything was there. The facts were there and I could do it just as easy as a solicitor. When it's something so straightforward, it's easy [Plaintiff from a large firm, Case 156].

I think it is better if you do it yourself because you know the full ins and outs of the case. You have all the thoughts on it, so I think it is best if it is done personally [Plaintiff from a small firm, Case 160].

I think that the layman is better coming on as a man off the street, even if it is a person like me. The judge will make allowances for him. I think that the man on the street is much better in coming along and saying,. 'I am a simple man on the Clapham omnibus' [Plaintiff from a small firm, Case 198].

I was happy to do it myself. There's nobody else who really knows what happened, is there? It's only what I tell them. So it's easier for me to put my story across in my own words [Individual plaintiff, Case 204].

I would prefer to do it myself. I think it jeopardises your own chances if you have professional advice. The informality disappears. As a lay person, I was able to make mistakes without being shot down. I felt highly satisfied with the arrangement [Individual defendant, Case 206].

Someone else representing me would not have been able to give my point of view. They would have given what I had said from their point of you [Plaintiff from a small firm, Case 226].

I think you can tell the truth more yourself than by going through a second person, because you know what's in your mind and you want to say what's in your mind. You may not think they've handled the case correctly at the end of the day. If you do it yourself and if it goes against you, you've only got yourself to blame [Plaintiff from a small firm, Case 235].

I was perfectly happy to do it myself because I know I'm right [Individual defendant, Case 237].

If the difference between winning and losing had been having a solicitor, I still would not have had a solicitor purely because the amount of money involved was so small and it was just a matter of principle [Individual defendant, Case 240].

I wouldn't want anyone to represent me, because I don't see the point. It's a factual dispute, where he says, 'You did this' and I say, 'I didn't.' Why do I need someone to say that? [Individual defendant, Case 260].

Litigants' perspectives on the need for representation have been quoted at considerable length because they illustrate the strength of their feeling on this important subject. Whether litigants need representation at these hearings is an issue that is central to the debates about the desirability of extending the small claims jurisdiction. It can be confidently concluded that, as far as litigants themselves are concerned, most strongly favour presenting their own cases and few prefer the option of entrusting (as they frequently see it) the matter to a representative. The point made by Sarat and Felstiner (1986: 125) that 'clients know their histories and goals, lawyers must learn about them' was parallelled by the comments expressed by many litigants in this study, and is indeed reflected in many of the above quotations. There is, it seems, considerable resistance on the part of lay litigants to involving lawyers in their disputes unless they are obliged to do so. Furthermore, when they find themselves confronting a lawyer, unrepresented parties tend to view it as putting them at a serious and unfair disadvantage. Even when litigants regarded lawyers as potentially useful, many concluded that, because of the relatively small sums at issue and the fact that legal aid is not available for representation at small claims hearings, it was simply uneconomic to pay for a solicitor. The writer remains firmly of the view that, provided they receive advice beforehand about the legal merits of their case, the great majority of litigants are well able to represent themselves at small claims hearings,[34] and, in his view, few would be seriously put out by a prohibition on representation at such hearings.

The active participation of litigants in the resolution of their own

[34] See above 113–14. There has been a great deal of debate over the years about the extent to which legal representation is likely to improve rates of success before different kinds of tribunal: see particularly Genn and Genn (1989). Weller *et al.* (1990: 11–12), in a study of American small claims courts, drew a subtle distinction about the benefits of representation:

> 'Our data support the existence of a clear bias in the system where attorneys at trial were involved, but the bias was not that which had been assumed previously. The bias was not in favour of represented plaintiffs, but rather against unrepresented defendants. Unrepresented defendants did equally poorly whether facing a represented or an unrepresented plaintiff'.

disputes carries considerable social, economic, and political appeal. It is hard to challenge, particularly when it is what the participants themselves appear to favour.[35] There is, however, a qualification that needs to be made. To return to the point made on several occasions in earlier parts of this book: for the unwary, there is a trap, and it is a trap which underlines one of the inherent contradictions in the small claims model itself, relating to the translation of disputes into a legal framework. The limitation of Do-It-Yourself justice is that lay litigants cannot be expected to view their disputes in a legal context or to know how they should go about proving their case. The point was made by McGuire and Macdonald (1995: 14) who argued that 'All judges see their active participation as a way to render the problem presented to the parties into a legally cognizable dispute. Their primary mission is to interpret the law to the parties, not to interpret the parties to the law'.

Courts, as Merry (1990: 10) puts it, 'establish the discourse within which a problem is framed and its solution identified'.[36] This problem becomes plain at the outset at many small claims hearings. When left to their own devices, lay litigants commonly arrive at the court empty-handed. A few are armed with copious notes in order to present their arguments to the judge, but not many bring relevant documents or witnesses who might support their position. The overwhelming judicial response in this situation is a pragmatic one, and only exceptionally are the district judges prepared to adjourn a hearing so that documents can be retrieved or witnesses located. But a determination to reach a decision on the day masks the important point about the operation of small claims procedures: notwithstanding the idiosyncrasies of individual judges, some of whom may adopt an approach that owes more to common sense than to the law,[37] lay litigants will be obliged in most situations to prove their case within a legal framework.

Many litigants fail fully to appreciate that, although they feel an acute sense of injustice about their claim and are in no doubt whatever about the moral rectitude of their position, it is still necessary for them

[35] A survey, based upon over 8,000 adults in England and Wales, published by the National Consumer Council (1995) and jointly conducted with the BBC, showed that most lay people preferred their legal problems to be dealt with by informal means (particularly if this involved a mediated settlement in which they could actively participate) rather than formal court adjudication.

[36] On this point, see also Mather and Yngvesson (1981); Sander (1985); Cain (1986); Sarat and Felstiner (1988); and Rock (1993), at 30–40.

[37] See 00–00.

to establish that it has legal validity. This requirement is not by any means a simple or straightforward task or one that can be conveniently conveyed to lay people in a few simple leaflets. Indeed, the leaflets will prove to be useless in helping litigants to determine the legal merits of their case. As Weller *et al.* (1990: 13) noted in their examination of American small claims courts, 'even the most elaborate booklet . . . contained nothing which would assist a litigant in determining whether he had a case worth filing or what evidence he should bring to trial'. The same applies to the flimsy leaflets which are provided by English county courts. This means that, even though lay people may appear to function competently at hearings, it is unrealistic to expect them to know how they should go about proving their case. Putting the point into a sociological context, O'Barr and Conley (1985: 662) argued that:

> the opportunity to tell a story in everyday terms to an authoritative decision maker enhances litigant satisfaction with small claims courts, but this ability and the resulting satisfaction may have a hidden cost . . . [in that] many accounts of disputed events that are entirely adequate by the standards of ordinary conversation prove to be legally inadequate.

The upshot is that the obligation upon judges to view disputes in a legal context and to conduct hearings accordingly seriously disadvantages lay litigants and can leave them feeling disappointed, if not baffled. 'Is it any wonder', asks Cranston (1986: 131), 'that many clients do not understand, or more importantly, fail in court when the matter has been transformed beyond their recognition?' Lay litigants frequently feel that at the hearing they have not been allowed to say all they wanted or at least to say it in the way that they wanted.[38] This is a point that is played down in the official literature in which matters tend to be viewed from a common sense rather than from a legal perspective. Some of the other published advice is actually misleading on the point.[39]

[38] As was seen in Chapter 3, fitting into a procedure that may seem alien is not a problem that affects only lay people. Legal representatives may also experience difficulty in adapting to the small claims regime. Nor is such unfamiliarity confined to small claims hearings: for a discussion of the same phenomenon in relation to social security adjudication, see Baldwin *et al.* (1992).

[39] In one of the most useful manuals on small claims available for purchase, the Law Pack, *Do-it-yourself. . . Small Claims*, advises litigants, for example, 'Write out what you are going to say as a speech and then stick to it' (at 31). Not many district judges are, however, prepared to allow litigants such latitude.

In resolving everyday disputes, district judges are, therefore, obliged to translate litigants' problems into a legal framework, and this framework is likely to be one with which lay people are unfamiliar. Common sense may be a poor guide in these circumstances, and there is frequently a disparity between litigants' notions of justice and justice according to law. It means that litigants are sometimes confused and perplexed because the district judge asks them, when they present their evidence, to concentrate on certain key legal issues (which may seem to lay people to have little real relevance to their grievances) rather than explaining the situation in their own terms. When district judges talk, as many of them do, of their predisposition to 'go for the jugular', by focusing directly, if not exclusively, on the legal issues at the nub of the case,[40] the effect on lay litigants, who may see matters in very different terms, is easily underestimated. Litigants usually have, as Sarat and Felstiner (1986: 125) noted, 'different agendas, expectations, and senses of justice' from lawyers and judges, and they 'possess different information and have different needs to fulfil'. This difficulty sets a critical limitation on the operation of simplified procedures like small claims. It is worth pausing to consider how it was perceived and articulated by some of the litigants in this study:

It just seemed to me that you weren't able to express yourself as you wanted to. I wouldn't say I misunderstood it but it was just a bit backwards . . . It seems like tunnel vision. The magistrate [*sic*] says that you've got to do this. You don't seem able to read your notes as you wrote them down [Individual trader plaintiff, Case 1].

I'm very disappointed. Basically I thought it was a waste of time. There is obviously a way of presenting things to a judge, and I think it should be explained to people going to arbitration that they should take a lesson in law before they go . . . . I thought the arbitration was going to be someone looking fairly at the rights and wrongs of the case. But that was not how it appeared to be . . . . The judge was jumping all over me when I was trying to explain points in layman's terms, not from a solicitor's point of view. He was doing absolutely the opposite of what I expected from the leaflets [Defendant from a small firm, Case 16].

The judge wanted to know things and we were trying to tell him things which were irrelevant to what he wanted to know. We were telling him things about the plaintiff which he wasn't interested in. He just wanted to know the black

[40] See the discussion at 58–60.

and white parts which were relevant to him [Defendant from a small firm, Case 113].

The judge put me at my ease, but I would have liked it if I could have had a bit more opportunity, if a point came up, to deal with it there and then. The judge kept saying, 'Don't ask him about that now'. That happened three or four times [Individual plaintiff, Case 129].

It seemed to me that the judge dwelt on items which were not the substance of the case—things that may be legally important, but in reality are trivia [Individual defendant, Case 134].

You get very nervous. You don't say things you want to say, and then the judge says, 'It's your turn to ask questions', and your mind goes completely blank. I tried to say things at the time, but he said, 'No, this is not the time for this.' The judge was very, very nice, but, from a layman's point of view, you've got a train of thought and you want to continue with it. But if that's not relevant. . . . [Individual plaintiff, Case 185].

With this case, the whole thing hinged on a point of law that we, as amateurs, weren't aware of. So it didn't matter what the rights or the wrongs of the matter were. It's the point of law that was the thing. The very first time we've come up against this point of law was when it was pointed out to us this morning. Once the point of law was raised, there was no argument against it. It was covered by law and that was it. The judge didn't question my honesty. He simply said generally, 'You're a nice sort of chap, but the trouble is that you didn't realise that this point of law existed and therefore I have no choice but to find against you.' That's all right. We learn by experience [Individual plaintiff, Case 209].

The judge obviously has rules but there wasn't enough leeway, and he would sort of say, 'Stop that, you are not supposed to be answering that.' So it was all stilted. If it had been a sort of question and answer, it would have been a whole lot easier. It is all very quick and you think, 'I must ask such a question' and of course it goes out of your mind. It all went wrong because we couldn't present our case as we wanted to [Individual plaintiff, Case 213].

I had provided myself with a written summary of the accounts which would have taken about a quarter of an hour to read. The judge wouldn't let me read that out, and he just went straight into it. I think his approach was rather abrupt. I was asked a few questions which I wasn't prepared to answer at that time because I thought that they would have been answered during my statements. I think that he picked up on what he probably calls a point of law which I had disagreed with [Individual plaintiff, Case 216].

I was prepared to present the evidence, but it seemed as though the judge was just asking questions. Obviously he is trained to find out the relevant details and I didn't actually have to present anything. All we ended up doing was just answering questions which threw me a little bit when I was prepared to go through the whole thing. But we didn't really get the chance to do that. I was quite prepared to go through it all and I had two piles of papers, one the proof and one dealing with what actually happened. But the judge was going through and skipping about from part to part which left me thrown [Individual plaintiff, Case 217].

The judge said, 'These are the areas I would like you to highlight—the possible areas for you to look at.' It was quite obvious to me that, if you went off at a tangent, it would count against you [Plaintiff from a small firm, Case 226].

Small claims hearings present, then, a curious paradox: while they appear on the surface to offer an appropriately informal and relaxed setting in which straightforward legal disputes can be resolved, they do not work well when there are unstated legal criteria that must be satisfied. Meeting these criteria for lay litigants is inevitably hit-and-miss, and it may be quite fortuitous when the arguments they advance at hearings prove to have legal validity. The point that emerges strongly is that, if litigants are to perform adequately in the small claims arena, they require some familiarity with the rules of the game in advance of the hearing. What this means in practice is that litigants must receive advice beforehand about the validity of any claim (or a defence to a claim) if the principle of lay people presenting their own cases is to work.[41] And a scrupulously fair hearing before an interventionist judge is not a satisfactory alternative to that.

Conclusion

The small claims regime represents the cheap and cheerful end of the judicial market—the bargain basement of English civil justice. Talking to large numbers of small claims litigants reveals that the vast majority accept the rough-and-ready legal procedures they encounter at hearings without question and without complaint. They are not on the whole perturbed, therefore, if legal processes do not provide a refined brand of justice, in the sense that 'refinement' would be defined by

[41] A similar conclusion was reached in the interim report of the Working Party, under the chairmanship of Lord Justice Otton (1995), which examined the difficulties confronting litigants in person in the Royal Courts of Justice.

lawyers. Almost all litigants who make it as far as the court are prepared actively to participate in the hearing, and for the most part they do so without the intervention of legal representatives. It seems that what most litigants want first and foremost from a court hearing—and this applied to professional, business, and lay litigants alike—is a speedy and final resolution of their disputes achieved by means of a straightforward process that they perceive to be fair. A similar result emerged from the main Scottish study of small claims procedures (Scottish Office, Central Research Unit, 1991: 67) where it was noted that 'individuals respond as much to procedural justice and how they are treated by key actors in the process as they do to whether they win or lose'. Victory is sweet, but defeat is more palatable when it follows a process perceived to be fair. But any lack of fairness is generally felt almost as keenly by litigants as the failure to win their cases.[42]

This is not to say of course that, because the small claims procedure can be said to provide most litigants with a standard of justice that they find satisfactory or acceptable, that is all that matters. The underlying dilemma in small claims remains unresolved: how can litigants in person be expected to satisfy legal criteria of which they may have no former knowledge? And how can they be assisted in preparing and presenting a legal case? Allowing lay people to proceed to a court hearing on the basis of common sense principles is bound to lead frequently to disappointment and frustration. But it is surely also of the utmost importance that litigants' experience of bargain basement justice should be that it is impartial and fair, whatever other difficulties might need to be confronted.

It should not be overlooked in this discussion that litigants are very conscious of the treatment they receive from court staff as well as from judges. Many turn to court officials for help not only on the day of the hearing, but before things reach that stage. (A few also seek assistance about enforcement mechanisms months after the hearing.) Although prepared to tolerate with remarkable fortitude personal inconvenience at the hands of the court administration, the litigants interviewed in this study nonetheless voiced complaints about the long periods they were obliged to wait, about uncomfortable surroundings, about the

[42] There has been a good deal of writing and research in the United States on the question of procedural fairness: see in particular Thibaut and Walker (1975); Lind and Tyler (1988); Tyler (1988); and Lind *et al.* (1990). See also the perceptive discussion in Armstrong (1995), at 100–3.

cursory treatment they received from harassed officials, about poor sign-posting inside the courts, about difficulties in getting hold of relevant information, and about inadequacies in the explanations of procedures they were given. While such complaints might be dismissed as minor or as merely the 'public relations' aspects of court administration, they are of undoubted importance to small claims litigants. Despite a Courts Charter and the greater efforts that are now being made by court staff in many county courts, there is clearly room for improvement.

In principle, if not always in practice, the small claims arena offers lay litigants several significant qualities that they welcome. In no order of priority, the main attractions tend to be the low cost in initiating the process, personal participation in the resolution of the dispute, the absence of lawyers and the attendant formality, simplicity of procedures, a pragmatic and direct judicial approach, courtesy and politeness of judges and court staff, an expeditious outcome, and finality of result. If the results presented in this chapter are any guide, the small claims regime in England and Wales can be said to score pretty highly on these measures.

5 The Enforcement of Small Claims Judgments

This book ends on a somewhat sour note. While the study that has been described in these pages has shown that small claims procedures in England and Wales operate in the main to the satisfaction of the participants, the same cannot be said of the enforcement of judgments. If, after judgment, the defendant does not pay the plaintiff within the time period specified by the court, the plaintiff may seek to enforce the judgment by requesting that the court take action against the defendant. Many plaintiffs have such bad experiences at this stage that it causes them to re-appraise the value of pursuing small claims in the first place. Indeed, a number become so jaundiced and disillusioned as a result of their failure to enforce the court's judgment that they say that they would not contemplate using the small claims procedure again in the future. These attitudes stand in such sharp contrast to the largely positive views of litigants discussed in the previous chapter that it is clearly important to ascertain what is going wrong to produce this change of heart.

When interviewed at the end of court hearings, successful plaintiffs frequently expressed relief and satisfaction that the matter had at last been concluded. It did not occur to more than a handful of them at that stage that serious difficulties might still lie ahead in securing payment from the defendant. Their assumption was that, since the district judge had found in their favour, that was an end of the matter. But the subsequent experiences of many plaintiffs showed that this view was unduly sanguine. It would in fact have been more realistic for plaintiffs to regard the hearing as merely marking the end of round one in what might well prove to be a prolonged, acrimonious, and ultimately fruitless, contest. The sad truth is that only a minority of defendants pay up at that stage. This is without doubt a depressing conclusion, since it suggests that legal and judicial processes, even when sensitively structured to meet the needs of lay people, count for little if no satisfactory mechanisms exist to ensure that court judgments are enforced.

It is surprising that very little attention has been paid to the question of civil judgments, still less with the enforcement of judgments in small claims. 'From the point of view of legal and social theory', Sir Jack Jacob observes, 'the enforcement process is in a kind of backwater, seldom examined or studied' (1987: 188). Not much empirical research has been conducted on the subject either[1] and the little that has been done suggests a rather disturbing picture. The findings of the present study confirm the grimness of the situation. Before describing these results, it is worth considering briefly what is known about the way that enforcement procedures operate in this country.

The *Judicial Statistics* indicate that well over a million enforcement proceedings were initiated in the county courts in England and Wales in 1995. The *Judicial Statistics* include a couple of pages on the frequency with which the different enforcement methods are used, but they show nothing at all about the outcome of such measures. Some limited information is collected at the county courts on whether plaintiffs institute proceedings to enforce a court order, but again this sheds little light on the success of enforcement procedures.[2] Even when one examines the special cards on which information about enforcement is recorded at the county courts, one finds out little about the outcome of measures that have been taken. Instead, the information collected at the courts often seems to reveal more about the low priority that is accorded by many county courts to enforcement than about the efficacy of the enforcement mechanisms themselves. At some courts, it is evident that much of the material collected is partial, inaccurate, and untrustworthy. In contrast to the concerns about court hearings, clearly seen in the attitude of court administration and judges, interest in enforcement seems often to be no more than half-hearted and superficial. This serves to confirm the impression gained by many plaintiffs that the courts lose interest in their claims once they

[1] A number of studies have, however, been conducted into the way that creditors pursue those who owe them money. Several of these studies are discussed by Phipps (1990).

[2] Cotterrell *et al.* (1986) have argued that the case cards are of limited utility to the courts since they are arranged serially by plaint number, not by individual debtor. This means that there is no link between cases involving the same debtor even in the same court. They also make the perceptive point that:

> 'the fact that the timing and method of enforcement are left to the initiative of individual creditors, each of whom is ignorant of the enforcement steps being taken by the others, results in a multiplicity of enforcement processes which militates against orderly payment of debts and imposes severe strains on debtors and their families' (at 96).

have been heard. This is in a sense paradoxical since it is at odds with the popular description of the county courts as operating in essence as debt-collection agencies.[3]

This lack of official interest is to a large extent mirrored in the academic literature. It was seen earlier that small claims procedures have been neglected by researchers in England, and the point can be made even more strongly about the enforcement of judgments. One might again draw a telling contrast with the research and writing in the United States. Although there is now a sizeable North American research literature dealing, for instance, with the respective merits of consensual as opposed to adjudicative procedures and their relation to compliance with the outcome,[4] there is no parallel in the academic writing in England and Wales. There has been only a handful of English studies concerned with the enforcement of county court judgments,[5] and many of these have been small-scale exercises which are now rather dated. The conclusion drawn by Cain in 1983 that plaintiffs' low success rates in enforcing judgment in the county courts were 'startling indeed' (at 129) nevertheless does nothing to engender much optimism.

A fascinating piece of research concerned with the enforcement of county court judgments in consumer debts was conducted by Professor Roy Goode and his colleagues at Queen Mary College, London, in the 1980s.[6] This study focused on the success of 'warrants of execution' (colloquially known as 'sending the bailiffs in') in enforcing judgment debts in the county court. The research showed that as many as three-quarters of plaintiffs seeking payment for judgments for debt were obliged to take some enforcement action and that warrants of execution were issued in no less than 67 per cent of judgments in the sample.[7] But such warrants failed to produce full payment in almost 60 per cent of cases. Furthermore, the research showed that the greater the sum that was owed, the less likely it was to be paid. Indeed, most of the respondents contacted by the researchers said that they did not even expect payment to be made in full. It is nonetheless interesting to

[3] See Cain (1986) for further elaboration of this paradox.

[4] See particularly McEwan and Maiman (1982, 1984); Vidmar (1987); and Galanter and Cahill (1994), at 1377–8.

[5] See Cain (1983, 1986); Cotterrell *et al.* (1986); Touche Ross (1986); Phipps (1990); and National Audit Office (1996).

[6] See Cotterrell *et al.* (1986) and Phipps (1990).

[7] Phipps (1990) draws some useful comparisons with a similar study conducted by the management consultants, Touche Ross (1986), for the Review Body on Civil Justice.

note that the main explanation given by the researchers for the low rate of success of the bailiffs was not, as many people assume, the natural cunning of defendants in evading payment, but rather the insufficiency of goods on which to levy and difficulties in tracing the defendants in question.[8]

This observation, however, provides no more than a glimmer of hope, and the generally dismal picture relating both to the low rate of payment of court judgments and to the general ineffectiveness of enforcement mechanisms themselves was confirmed more recently by the extensive study conducted by the National Audit Office (1996) which provided useful information on enforcement procedures in the county court. This important survey, based upon a postal survey of several hundreds of litigants, presented disquieting findings about what happens at this stage. It revealed, for instance, that, while 58 per cent of successful plaintiffs recovered all or part of the money from defendants, two-fifths of them had had to take steps to enforce the court's judgment. But only about a third of those who said they had taken such action—again mainly by resort to the court bailiff system—managed to recover even a part of their claim.[9]

One needs to treat the study carried out by the National Audit Office with some caution, since postal surveys present notorious methodological and other problems. What respondents write in reply to questionnaires has to be taken on trust, even though there is no guarantee that they have properly understood the questions. Response rates in postal surveys of this kind also tend to be low, and one cannot assume that those who return questionnaires are representative of the sample as a whole. Only 46 per cent of the plaintiffs contacted in the National Audit Office survey responded (and no more than 12 per cent

[8] Phipps (1990: 241) gives some idea of the scale of these difficulties in the following passage:

> 'These results imply, that if the correct address is supplied to the Court, and the debtor has goods which theoretically are worth levying, the procedure is successful in achieving payment without actually removing the goods for sale. Only five per cent . . . of the warrants failed because of some action by the debtor such as refusing entry to the bailiff, or applying to suspend the warrant'.

[9] Some interesting figures were given in the report on the relative success of different methods of enforcement. These figures showed that, in just over two-thirds of the cases in which bailiffs had been involved, no money at all was recovered from defendants. Some of the other methods appeared to meet with somewhat greater success, but the number of plaintiffs (not given in the report) must have been very small in some of the sub-categories.

of defendants), underlining the need for caution in interpreting the results. Taking the results on their face value—as the authors of the report appear to do—the survey nevertheless gives some indication of the severe problems that confront plaintiffs when they seek to enforce county court judgments.

Talking to plaintiffs about enforcement

In the course of visiting a number of county courts around the country and talking to officials, district judges, and other court personnel, the author encountered a range of views about what does (and should) happen after the court hearing. But these views tended to be based much more upon impression and wishful thinking than upon firm evidence. The information provided by the National Audit Office (1996) about enforcement procedures is in important respects illuminating, particularly in shedding light on the effectiveness of the different methods of enforcement, but the survey was exclusively statistical in character and provided no real insight into the ways that plaintiffs confronted the question of enforcement. The survey concentrated, moreover, on court-based methods of enforcement, and included no information on other kinds of action (including the use of private debt collections firms) that plaintiffs may take, even though the latter may be used no less frequently and perhaps with greater effect than the former. In the study reported in this chapter, plaintiffs were contacted several months after their court appearance in order to find out what had happened after they had left the court and awaited payment of the money that was owed to them. By carrying out follow-up interviews with plaintiffs who had been successful in the court, it was possible to ask some searching questions about the ways they tackled the problems of enforcement and what they did about defendants who had defaulted.

So what happens when plaintiffs seek to obtain the payments to which the court has deemed them to be entitled and what is going wrong with the procedures available to them when defendants fail to pay up? Out of the sample of small claims litigants, the interviews with whom were discussed in the previous chapter, there were 111 plaintiffs who had been successful, wholly or in part, at hearings.[10] An attempt

[10] The analysis of enforcement procedures excluded the following types of action: first, claims initiated by insurance companies against other insurance companies (not individuals) in which liability in road accidents was being determined; secondly, cases in which the parties themselves had settled in advance of the hearing; and, thirdly, the small number of cases in which defendants had made successful counterclaims.

was made to contact these people six months after they had been interviewed at the county courts in order to find out whether they had received payment. Some people had changed addresses in the meantime or were for other reasons untraceable, but ninety-four plaintiffs (84.7 per cent) were eventually contacted and interviewed.[11]

It was beyond the resources available to the author to travel the country to speak to the plaintiffs in question, and they were instead interviewed over the telephone. When initially interviewed at the court, successful plaintiffs were asked whether it would be possible to contact them at a later date, and telephone numbers were requested from them. The interviews relating to enforcement, all of which were recorded, were short, straightforward, and easily conducted by telephone. Information was sought on whether payment had been made by the defendant, whether difficulties had been encountered, whether advice had been sought about enforcement, and whether any action had been taken.

The results of these interviews proved disturbing. Six months after the event, only half of successful plaintiffs said that they had received full payment from the defendant without having to take further legal and other measures. A substantial proportion had received no payment at all. And even where full payment had been made, in over a third of cases it had been received outside the period stipulated by the court, thereby causing additional anxiety to many plaintiffs. With less than a third of the plaintiffs in the sample receiving full payment on time, the inescapable conclusion is that enforcement poses major problems for the small claims regime. The results also suggest that, even when enforcement procedures are activated, they do not function well. In many instances, they are wholly ineffectual. Table 1 gives some idea of the frustrations that a majority of plaintiffs described in these interviews.

The interviews revealed no obvious or clearcut differences between types of plaintiff in terms of their success in securing payment. Commercial and other types of organization were no more successful than were individuals in securing payment. Indeed, large public organizations (particularly local authorities chasing arrears of various kinds) seemed to have less success in securing payment than other kinds of plaintiff, although the numbers of cases in this sub-group were too

[11] Of the 94 interviews conducted, 58 were carried out by the author and 36 by Mrs Sue Deebank.

TABLE 5.1 *Whether payment made after six months*

		%
Payment received in full and on time	30	31.9
Payment received in full but outside period indicated by the court	17	18.1
Over 50% of payment received	5	5.3
Over 10% up to 50% received	5	5.3
Nominal amount paid—10% or less	4	4.3
No payment whatever received—plaintiff still actively pursuing the matter	17	18.1
No payment whatever received—now abandoned	16	17.0
No interview conducted	17	—
	111	100.0

small to allow firm conclusions to be drawn.[12] Nor did any discernible patterns emerge in the kinds of defendant who defaulted. Individuals, as opposed to commercial concerns, were somewhat more likely to feature amongst those defendants who defaulted than would have been expected from their numbers in the overall sample. But the fact that 45 per cent of those who had not paid up were businesses suggests that inability to pay is unlikely to be the main explanation for non-payment in many cases.

It has been noted in earlier chapters that it is usually good news for parties when the other side fails to turn up to the hearing since its absence all but guarantees victory in court. It may not be such good news later on, however, since there is a close (and statistically significant) relationship between defendants' failure to attend the hearing and their disinclination to pay up later when judgment is awarded against them.[13] Whereas only 18 per cent of defendants who had troubled to attend had paid none of the amount that was owed within the six months following the court hearing, this proportion rose to 54.5 per cent in the case of defendants who had failed to turn up to the hearing. Looking at this comparison in another way, 57.8 per cent of the defendants who had not made payment within six months had

[12] It is noteworthy that the study of the recovery of judgment debts conducted by Cotterrell *et al.* (1986) also showed very low rates of debt recovery by local authorities.

[13] The same tendency was reported in relation to small claims courts in the United States by Weller and Ruhnka (1979), at 35.

failed to appear at the original hearing. This compared to 48.5 per cent of the defendants who had paid.[14]

A striking illustration of the benefit of having the defendant present occurred in one case that the author observed in the Exeter County Court. At the end of the hearing, while the judge was announcing his decision in favour of the plaintiff, the defendant produced his cheque book with a flourish, wrote out a cheque, and handed it to the plaintiff on the spot. The difficulties facing plaintiffs would be considerably eased were district judges to encourage defendants to do this. But no district judges did so, perhaps because they saw it as none of their business. Very few judges made any reference at all to enforcement at hearings, beyond offering an occasional word of advice to plaintiffs where a defendant had failed to attend the hearing.

Having subjected themselves to the inconvenience and stress of a court appearance, plaintiffs commonly assume, when they find that the defendant has defaulted, that it is then for the court to take steps to ensure that payment is made. They are, therefore, frequently disappointed when they discover weeks later from court staff that it is their own responsibility, not the court's, to pursue the defendant. 'The court provides the facilities and legal framework for enforcement but it is up to the individual as to how he proceeds' is how Applebey (1994: 118) summarizes the position. The simple truth is that the civil courts, in England and Wales as in many other countries, show surprisingly little interest in the collection and enforcement of judgments—a situation that has on occasion been the subject of critical comment. Describing the position in the United States, Weller *et al.* (1984: 74) note, for instance:

> Typically, . . . collection is the one part of the small claims process that courts are least interested in. Many judges believed that the job of the court ended once they had pronounced their judgment. In contrast to the criminal side of the judicial system, . . . the civil side of the court (including small claims) leaves the responsibility of collecting judgments to the winning party.

It is worth pausing to consider what plaintiffs themselves make of this lack of involvement—one might say lack of interest—in enforcement on the part of the county courts. Many are astonished and disappointed to find that they have to take the initiative in matters

[14] Given the small numbers in these sub-groups, the differences in this latter comparison did not reach a level of statistical significance and may therefore have been the result of chance variations.

of enforcement and that they are very much on their own at this stage. They are even more disturbed to discover that the court is largely impotent in the face of a defendant who is knowledgeable, cunning, or unscrupulous enough merely to ignore its judgments. Plaintiffs' respect for legal processes may well diminish as a result of these discoveries, and many described in the interviews how they had come to regard their resort to the county court as a way of resolving their differences with the defendant as a waste of time. This indicates a real change of heart on the part of many litigants. 'Getting the judgment is the easy part: it's after the court hearing that it gets difficult' is how one plaintiff aptly put it to the author. Another made the same point when he said, 'Winning the case is no problem if you are owed money: it's just getting paid that is difficult.' The same theme was reiterated by several other plaintiffs in this sample. Some idea of the acute sense of frustration and disillusionment felt by many plaintiffs at this stage in proceedings was given in the following quotes from the interviews:

In my opinion, the whole procedure is a waste of time unless you know the person has money or unless they've got a job where you can attach his earnings, or unless you know they've got a house or something . . . . It's not a procedure that we would go through again because you don't get anywhere with it really. You may as well not bother. I think the court process is totally against the person that the bill is owed to, like ourselves. It just doesn't work . . . . To my mind, it's all a waste of time. If you are trying to raise the money to keep your business afloat, you might as well forget it. You'd have to find another way outside the court to do it [Small business plaintiff, Case 10].

I think it is a total parasitic waste of time. I think after my experience in this case, I would be unlikely to use [the small claims procedure] again. I think it benefits those people who avoid their responsibilities. I think the system is loaded in favour of people who don't conduct themselves properly. I think it favours the villain rather than the victim [Small business plaintiff, Case 15].

We've used bailiffs in other cases and the success rate with court bailiffs is zero. It's a total waste of money. It's throwing money away. Court bailiffs are the worst of the lot . . . . My overall opinion hasn't changed on account of what's happened. The court system is a debtor's paradise, and anyone who knows the system can use it to suit themselves and get away with it . . . . In my experience, the courts take themselves very seriously, so when you're in court the district judge will tell you if you're saying too much and he expects to be obeyed. But once he's given his judgment and once it leaves the court, the whole thing goes to pot. There's no way of enforcing the judgment. We've got two or three cases now where we're debating whether it's worthwhile following them through [Small business plaintiff, Case 35].

I am disillusioned. What really scandalised me was the fact that the judge had agreed with me that these people had stolen money from me, but she was not in a position to enforce payment . . . . In general, I think it is a very unwieldy procedure and I think a lot of people who get involved in it are very disillusioned as I was myself. My disillusionment arose because of the ineffectiveness of the court in enforcing payment rather than the procedure itself. Absolutely. The procedure itself was fine. Inasmuch as having a judgment against them is inconvenient to a company, that was fine. The company probably was being punished for what they had done, but that still wasn't giving me any satisfaction. So, from that point of view, I was rather disillusioned: there was no mechanism of enforcement. My impression was that, once I had been successful in court, that would be an end to the matter. You have to do everything on your own initiative if you are to secure payment [Individual plaintiff, Case 45].

We are still chasing this one up. To be honest, for a small business like ours, it's not really worth going to all this trouble for such a small amount. The paperwork I've done on it in the past six months is really a waste of time . . . . When we received nothing, we arranged for the oral examination of this gentleman, and, when we got the date through from the court, I attended the court but he had moved address and the court never advised us. That is all additional expense for the company I work for. It was a wasted journey. I was then given another date and he was unable to meet, then another date, and then the last date was last week. So we've had three or four dates. I didn't go to the court last week because the court wrote to me and said that apparently the defendant was unable to meet. Although we will continue to go ahead with this case, my view of the courts is that they are an absolute load of rubbish. The courts are not strong enough and the defendants know how far to push us [Small business plaintiff, Case 47].

I rang him up three times and there were two or three other letters sent to him in between, just to cover what was said on the telephone. The court maintained that they were not in a position to be able to help us, to be able to advise us. They gave us the options of what to do. I think one of them was to freeze his company's assets. But I believe there are three or four different steps that you can take which they pointed out to me. So I said, 'Which one shall I take?' They said that basically it was up to me and they couldn't advise . . . . They told us what I could do but none of the things that they suggested was any good to me. What would be the point of freezing his company's assets unless there were sufficient funds in there to pay me? Making him sell his house was a bit radical for £700 [Individual plaintiff, Case 50].

I'd think twice about using it [the small claims procedure] again because I don't think the collection methods are good enough. They are OK in obtaining judgment. They are fine up to that point. But if judgment doesn't mean anything, are we wasting our time and our money? . . . I have no confidence in the bailiffs actually collecting any money. Most of the people I speak to say that [defendants] tell the bailiffs that they haven't got any money. And the bailiffs say, 'OK' and off they go, and nothing happens [Small business plaintiff, Case 54].

This guy didn't even bother turning up to the small claims hearing. When the judge ruled in my favour, I thought, 'I'll just go round and get the money off him.' I thought that would be the end of it. It was probably a bit naïve of me really. . . . As far as I am concerned, I've written it off now. I wouldn't want to put myself out any further to get the money. Certainly in time, it has cost me more than it was worth . . . . I just wouldn't bother because it costs me far more . . . . But the lack of sleep about it, worrying about it was just far in excess of what it was worth . . . . I was a bit disappointed because, although the court was involved and they have said that the chap must pay, they don't actually make any effort to follow it further. That is very disheartening, I think. I have had to learn the hard way that enforcement is something you have to do on your own [Small business plaintiff, Case 57].

I suppose we're reasonably satisfied in that we got the money. It's difficult to be critical but, in terms of the way the system works—you go to court, you get judgment and effectively it's just no good. If the guy doesn't want to pay, then unless you're prepared to pursue him to bankruptcy and all the costs that are included in that, he can more or less just stick two fingers up at you. As far as the court is concerned, we were treated quite properly, quite fairly. I've no complaints about that. It's just the enforcement afterwards which is very hit-and-miss. It has taken at least four months for us to get paid [Small business plaintiff, Case 64].

I've written to the court to say that the woman has done absolutely nothing. The court sent the bailiffs in supposedly over a month ago and we've still heard nothing. It's been a shambles to say the least. I can't say that I am best pleased. I'm still waiting to hear from the court about what will happen . . . . I'm not thinking yet of abandoning it. I still intend to carry on with it but I haven't had a single penny yet. I'm not pleased about it to say the least . . . . She has been lying and cheating and deceiving all away along the line and it is just carrying on. When you get someone like that who sticks to their guns and ignores the court judgment and won't budge on it, then you get problems like this occurring. I just think it is strange that a court of law can say something and then it is ignored, but I don't know how far you can take it. Another punishment should then be dished out . . . . You just feel that the whole thing is a waste of time. There's no effort to enforce. We are disgusted that it has gone to court. A court of law has said, 'You must pay' and it's still ignored. If that was drink-driving or something, it's all enforced. But the small claims seems different. She has just ignored every letter, every phone call and then it ends up going to court, but the court's judgment can still be ignored. There doesn't seem to be any way of enforcing the law. What does it take for them to enforce it? It just feels as if she has got away with it. I thought at the time of the court hearing that I would never go through all that again and what has happened since does put you off. I'm out of pocket and I've still paid for the shoddy goods. I'll never get that back . . . . It does put you off. For such a small amount, it is surprising how difficult it is to get the money [Individual plaintiff, Case 94].

Although it's supposed to be done for the layman, there are still procedures that are not very easily understood . . . . There is a lack of information again as far as enforcement is concerned. It's not very clear about how you go about extracting the money from the other party. Do you have to go back to the court? Do you write to them and wait for the other party to pay you? The other party doesn't seem to have to worry if they don't pay. There should at least be more information about what you are letting yourself in for in the first place [Individual plaintiff, Case 110].

As is apparent in the above quotations, many of those who experienced difficulty at the enforcement stage commented that the legal procedures seemed tilted in favour of those defendants who understood the workings of the system and who were prepared to manipulate it to their own benefit.[15] It has to be conceded that there is some truth in this position. Many plaintiffs complain, when they discover at the start of proceedings that the hearing is to be held in the defendant's local court not in their own, that this unfairly favours the defendant. Their grouses on this score are often reinforced at the enforcement stage. While there are doubtless a number of defendants who are simply unable to pay the sums that are owed, it remains the case that any defendant who is prepared to brazen things out and who knows how to avoid the predatory eyes of the bailiffs can evade payment without too much difficulty.

The main danger to defendants who adopt this position probably comes not from any sanction that a court might impose but from the consequences of having a county court judgment—a CCJ as it is known in the trade—recorded against their name in the Register of

[15] As one plaintiff put it to the author: 'These people know it all. They know all the loopholes. They are the professionals at it.' Such sentiments, which were not solicited in the questions, were echoed in many of the other interviews.

County Court Judgments. This Register is frequently used by credit and loan companies to assess the creditworthiness of people who want to borrow money, and anyone who has a CCJ recorded against them may find themselves seriously inconvenienced.[16] The *Judicial Statistics* showed that in 1995 there were almost 47,000 searches of the Register,[17] mainly conducted by post by banks, building societies, and credit companies. Defendants' names and addresses are entered on the Register and, unless the judgment is set aside, reversed, or paid in full, they remain on it for six years. For a small fee, plaintiffs can also check the Register to see whether the defendant has other debts outstanding and decide whether it is worthwhile continuing to pursue the claim. Since the sums of money at stake in these small claims are not on the whole large, however, aggrieved parties may with some justification feel that it is not worth their while to risk expending further time, money, and emotional energy in the pursuit of what seems increasingly to be a lost cause.

There are of course various legal steps that plaintiffs can take when payment of the judgment is not forthcoming,[18] although the small claims leaflets themselves make little reference to the likelihood that plaintiffs will need to initiate some enforcement action, even if they are successful with the claim. One of the small claims leaflets merely informs plaintiffs that they can get a leaflet about enforcement from the county court office if the defendant does not pay up. It also warns that 'If you decide to ask the court to do any of the things the booklet suggests, you will have to pay another fee', and there is a further leaflet, called 'Fees you will have to pay to issue or enforce your claim', which sets out, in off-putting detail, the charges that the court will impose for each enforcement measure. At the time of writing, plaintiffs are charged at least £40 if they wish to issue one of a variety of enforcement orders in the county courts. It is worth noting in passing that such

[16] In the report of the National Audit Office (1996), certain criticisms were made of the county court forms which, the authors said, did not make it clear to defendants what action they needed to take to avoid being entered on the Register. The authors of the report argued that 'if more explicit information were provided on the consequences of not replying to a summons—and having judgment entered by default—more defendants would probably respond and disputes could be resolved earlier' (at 16). The Court Service, in devising the new form of summons to be used after January 1996, took this point on board.

[17] Table 4.15 in the *Judicial Statistics Annual Report 1995* (Cm 3290, 1996).

[18] Some details of the range of mechanisms available to plaintiffs seeking to enforce county court judgments are given in the *Judicial Statistics Annual Report 1995* (Cm 3290, 1996), at 42–5; Jacobs (1987), at 192–210; and Applebey (1994), at 118–35.

fees for enforcing court judgments are not charged in all countries, and in those jurisdictions where the courts themselves take a more active role in enforcement than is the case in England and Wales, they seem often to be waived.

Court staff are not allowed to offer advice to plaintiffs about their claims, although they are permitted to give them guidance about the procedures they will need to follow. The same situation applies when it comes to deciding upon the most appropriate option to choose in enforcing the judgment. The relevant leaflet explicitly states that court staff 'will not be able to tell you which method of enforcement to choose. It is up to you to decide which one is most likely to get you your money.' Plaintiffs are in that sense again left on their own in making this decision, and the information provided by the Lord Chancellor's Department merely explains the various options that are open to them. The leaflet that sets out the information about the enforcement possibilities ('I have a judgment but the defendant hasn't paid') refers plaintiffs to yet more leaflets offering detailed information about what is involved in pursuing the different options.[19] It is, however, extremely difficult in a short and simple leaflet to provide more than very general guidance to plaintiffs on the most appropriate option for them to choose. The enforcement leaflet, for instance, merely states:

> Choose the one which is most likely to get you your money. For example, if the defendant is unemployed or self employed, you would be wasting your time and money asking for an attachment of earnings order. But if the defendant has money in a bank account a garnishee order might be suitable.

In the light of the general nature of the official guidance that is on offer, it is no surprise that many plaintiffs complain that they have very little idea of the right steps to take in enforcing the court's judgment and that they are obliged to go it alone in enforcing the court's judgment, with the court curiously reticent about offering them assistance. One consequence is, as Jacob (1987: 189) notes, that 'the selection of the mode of enforcement is generally made at random and somewhat in the dark'. This is another aspect of the problems that arise with Do-It-Yourself justice to which reference has frequently been

[19] The titles of the relevant leaflets are 'How do I ask for a warrant of execution?', 'How do I ask for an attachment of earnings order?', 'How do I ask for a garnishee or charging order?', and 'How do I ask for an oral examination?'

made in earlier chapters of this book. The result is needlessly to handicap the litigants concerned.

How plaintiffs go about enforcement

Faced with difficulties in collecting the money from the defendant after the court hearing, many plaintiffs simply give up the struggle without taking any further action to enforce the judgment. In this study, over a third of those who had not received payment conceded that they had made no significant effort after the court hearing to recover it. Several of these plaintiffs said that they felt such an acute sense of disappointment after their initial success in the court had come to nothing that they could not summon up the energy to pursue a troublesome defendant further. Others said they had come to realize that it would be a pointless exercise to do so. They saw further action against the defendant as likely not only to prove ineffective but also to exacerbate the anxiety and frustration they had already experienced. 'You can't get blood out of a stone' was a commonly expressed sentiment. The golden rule, before initiating civil proceedings, is that it is imperative to ascertain that the person being sued has the resources to pay. It often seems to be only at the enforcement stage that the meaning and wisdom of this rule strike home to plaintiffs.

Where plaintiffs decided that they would not let matters rest, the commonest course they pursued was to seek a 'warrant of execution' from the court. A warrant of execution is a form of enforcement against a debtor's goods. The creditor pays an initial court fee (at the time of writing set at £40 where the sum to be recovered is more than £125) and completes an application form requesting a warrant of execution, giving the address at which it is to be enforced. A county court bailiff then executes the warrant by visiting the defendant's property and identifies any property which may be sufficient, if it were sold, to cover the debt. Bailiffs are not empowered to enter premises by force, and, since great difficulties would be involved in selling goods which might be seized, the success of the whole system depends to a very large extent upon the threat that goods will be seized and sold. In reality, it seems that few goods are ever seized and sold.[20]

All the available evidence, whether it be from the official statistics or from empirical research, indicates that the use of court bailiffs dom-

[20] See Phipps (1990), at 234.

inates county court enforcement.[21] In 1995, warrants of execution were used in England and Wales four times as often as all other methods of enforcement combined.[22] The *Judicial Statistics* showed that no fewer than 895,301 warrants of execution were issued in 1995. Despite the frequency with which warrants of execution are used, this action may not always be the most appropriate or the most effective step to take in the event of non-payment. But as the interviews conducted in this study suggested, the image of bailiffs visiting a debtor's premises to extract payment—some litigants even picture them arriving with pick-axe handles to force their way into the defendant's house or business premises to seize goods—is deeply ingrained in the public imagination. However arcane and unfamiliar the term 'warrant of execution' may sound, it is nevertheless the only enforcement measure that is readily understood (or, more accurately, misunderstood) by members of the general public. Given the practical difficulties faced by bailiffs and their limited powers, it is not surprising that many plaintiffs are very critical when they appear to have achieved nothing. As Phipps (1990: 235) has noted, 'the warrant of execution procedure is criticised by all parties involved in county court debt enforcement', and she continues:

> Creditors . . . say it is not effective enough, since bailiffs do not have the necessary powers or incentives to make the procedure effective. Courts' administration bemoan the manpower expended on warrants as they are the most labour intensive procedure in enforcement. Debtors' representatives see the warrant as a cruel deception which uses the (empty) threat of seisure and sale to force payment'.

There are three main legal alternatives to warrants of execution available to plaintiffs wishing to enforce a court judgment. These mechanisms were hardly used at all by plaintiffs within the present sample—a picture that is confirmed both by the annual figures given

[21] Phipps (1990: 255) summarizes the reasons for the dominance of warrants of execution in enforcement as follows:

> 'Warrants of execution . . . require minimal information, no application and no hearing and, therefore, they are easy to accommodate within a highly automated and speedy debt collection process. Creditors do not select enforcement procedures logically according to the theoretical objectives of the procedures, but logically according to the practical objectives of their own organization. Within this logic, warrants dominate by default'.

[22] Table 4.16 in the *Judicial Statistics Annual Report 1995* (Cm 3290, 1996).

in the *Judicial Statistics* and by the analysis of enforcement methods conducted by the National Audit Office (1996). These alternative measures include attachment of earnings orders (a court order to the defendant's employers compelling them to make regular deductions from earnings); garnishee orders (an application that money be taken out of a defendant's bank or building society account); or charging orders (an order against the defendant's house or other property, even requiring in extreme circumstances that the defendant sell it to pay the debt so that the plaintiff can be paid out of the proceeds of the sale).

Another possibility that exists is for an aggrieved plaintiff to seek an oral examination of the defendant's resources.[23] This takes the form of an interview conducted in chambers by a court officer, and plaintiffs can attend if they wish and put questions to the defendant. This procedure can be used to assist plaintiffs in determining whether the defendant's financial circumstances are sufficient to justify initiating enforcement proceedings and in deciding on the most appropriate method to be used.[24] Although this is not a method of enforcement as such, the fact that defendants are ordered to attend court to provide details of their means often results (or so it is claimed in the *Judicial Statistics*[25]) in defendants paying up. While the procedure is potentially useful, it was used by only one plaintiff in the present sample.

Major practical difficulties attach to all methods of enforcement, and their application may well be inappropriate in many, perhaps most, situations. For this and other reasons, the plaintiffs interviewed in this sample resorted to legal methods of enforcement to only a limited extent, and, when they did, it seemed to be with no more than moderate levels of success. Table 2 summarizes the principal enforcement action, if there was any, taken by these plaintiffs, and it shows that resort to non-court-based methods of enforcement (even

[23] This is again a procedure for which the county court levies a fee—£30 at the time of writing.

[24] On the basis of interviews with creditors involved in county court judgments, Phipps (1990: 248) notes that they had 'a generally negative attitude' towards the oral examination procedure. She writes:

> 'They prefer to use their own methods of information collection, and even to risk enforcement on very flimsy information. The oral examination procedure is perceived as slow, expensive, unreliable and ineffective'.

[25] See the *Judicial Statistics Annual Report 1995* (Cm 3290, 1996), at 44, where it is also noted that over 90,000 applications for an oral hearing were filed in 1995.

Table 5.2 *Principal enforcement action taken by plaintiffs*

		%
Payment received without need for enforcement action by plaintiff	49	52.1
Payment not received, but little if any effort made by plaintiff to recover it	16	17.0
A warrant of execution used	13	13.8
Plaintiff used other court-based method of enforcement	3	3.2
Plaintiff used a private firm or a solicitor to enforce the judgment	7	7.5
Plaintiff took law into own hands to secure payment	4	4.3
Plaintiff took some other action	2	2.1
No interview conducted	17	—
	111	100.0

plaintiffs taking the law into their own hands) was almost as common as use of legal methods.

Table 2 presents a somewhat over-simplified picture of the enforcement action taken by plaintiffs, since it lists only the principal step they took to enforce the court's judgment. Five plaintiffs in the sample pursued more than one course of action, and, in four of these cases, the action was a combination of legal and private remedies. It is interesting to note that only twenty plaintiffs who had not received payment bothered to pursue the defendant by means of legal remedies.[26] In seventeen of these cases, this was through a warrant of execution. There was also one garnishee order, one charging order, and one other plaintiff who required the defendant to undergo a preliminary oral examination at the court. On less than half of the occasions on which formal legal methods of enforcement were employed did the plaintiffs succeed in recovering the money that was due to them. Table 2 also shows that as many as sixteen plaintiffs made no real effort to enforce the court's judgment, even though some of them had received nothing at all from the defendant. Several simply decided that it was better to cut their losses and forget the matter, particularly if some part of the money had been paid.

Pursuing remedies outside the courts, particularly through a private

[26] In Table 2, the principal enforcement action in four of these cases was classified as a private remedy, however.

debt-collection firm, was viewed by some plaintiffs as likely to be more efficacious than seeking payment through legal channels, and the rates of success were in practice slightly higher than those found in relation to legal remedies.[27] Private remedies of various kinds were adopted by eleven of the plaintiffs who were interviewed. There were four other cases in which plaintiffs decided to take matters into their own hands, although in three of these cases it was only after legal methods of enforcement had failed. Two of these plaintiffs said that they had been forced to resort to strong-arm tactics to get the money that was due to them. They said that they had turned up at the defendants' premises with 'heavies' and issued threats of violence if the money was not paid. Both of these plaintiffs claimed that their methods had succeeded where the courts had failed. Three other plaintiffs said that they had turned the matter over to firms of debt collectors who operated on the basis of 'no questions asked' methods.[28] Some indication of the lengths to which some plaintiffs are prepared to go is given in the following extracts from the interviews that were conducted. These quotations also give some impression of the exasperation felt by respondents in seeking to secure payment from reluctant defendants:

I instructed the bailiffs to go in. The bailiffs knew him reasonably well. They said they would do their best. So I left it in the bailiffs' hands for a number of months but they were getting no joy. The bailiffs tried to gain access to retrieve the money for me but had no success, so I rang him [the defendant] and eventually I caught up with him. I said, 'Look, I've done it all fair and square, I've been to court and won and all I'm asking for now is my money. All I want is my money and then I'll leave you alone.' He said a few impolite words and put the phone down on me . . . . Then I went down to the pub where I'd done the work and spoke to the manager of the place. I told him I wanted the money and he said, 'Get out!' When I refused to go, he got the bouncers to throw me out. I then went to my local pub, I got a couple of my 'debt collecting' friends and we went back and I got my money . . . . I wasn't surprised they paid up in the end. I knew they would pay when I walked in with two guys. The two guys walked in with lump hammers and they basically said to the guy at the bar,

[27] Since numbers were small, these differences between the groups do not reach a level of statistical significance.

[28] Doubts have been expressed about the intimidatory tactics adopted by certain debt collection firms: see, for instance, Rock (1973). The Office of Fair Trading has warned that consumer credit licences will be revoked or refused where such methods are employed: see the 1995 summer issue of *Fair Trading*, at 2. The *New Law Journal* (1996), at 1015 gives details of the steps also being taken by the Lord Chancellor's Department to regulate the activities of private bailiffs.

'You've got money in the till and, in the time that it takes us to walk from here to the room that I tiled, you'd better put the money on the bar or we'll start smashing them up. And after we've smashed them up, you will still have to pay.' He opened the till and gave me the cash. It had been going on for two years which is way too long, so I decided to sort it out myself. I felt obliged to take the law into my own hands . . . . They were helpful at the court, but there was absolutely nothing that they could do. I felt like my hands were tied and the girl at the court was basically asking me write the money off [Northern Circuit, plaintiff an individual trader, Case 33].

We eventually got the money but we had to employ a private investigator (who is an ex-bailiff) to recover the debt. We've had to pay him £250 and we can't recover that. He belongs to one of those firms offering—reading between the lines—someone to go round and break people's legs and things. I don't know if you've come across it; they're employing gangsters to do the job . . . . This outfit specialises in the one o'clock knock on the door [Northern Circuit, Small business plaintiff, Case 35].

Even when I had the judgment in my favour, I was told that, if I wanted to enforce the judgment, I would have to pay for bailiffs to go into the property in question to seize property because the defendants had no intention of paying up. Apparently this was habitual. It was just a game to them. It was clear that the defendants had no intention of paying up. I considered the option of sending bailiffs in, but I was aware that the defendants used this ploy of saying that none of the property on their premises belonged to them, that it was all leased. So I would simply have been out of pocket having sent the bailiffs in. There would have been nothing that they could have seized, or at least the onus would have been on me to prove that the property in fact belonged to them. This would have introduced further legal proceedings and further expenses to me. I was told by one of the bailiffs of the existence of garnishee orders—of which I was totally unaware, not being versed in the law myself. . . . So I slapped a garnishee order on them. Even then they didn't pay up until the very last minute. They tried to get another hearing in court. They introduced all sorts of nonsensical delaying tactics and, as I say, somebody who was less persistent would have simply given up [Northern Circuit, Individual plaintiff, Case 45].

We keep trying and the bailiffs have been round and round and round until they've finally said, 'He's never in'. He does leave one with having to look at the possibility of other alternatives—a couple of big lads to go round and lean on his knee caps. I don't like to get involved in this sort of thing. It's no way to do business. But supplying goods and then not getting paid is no way to do business either. I have still got to pay the supplier, and if you decide that discretion is the better part of valour very often, you find you have to either make one hell of a mark-up on the goods that you supply or you get a shortfall and end up out of business. It's not as though I'm an employee of a multi-national company and can simply say that I've done my best. It's actually cash out of my pocket. It's food off my table [North Eastern Circuit, Small business plaintiffs, Case 69].

To be honest, I have had a bellyful of it in this case. I have just put the whole matter in the hands of a firm of debt collectors. I am not bothering going through the courts again. I could kick myself for putting it in as a small claim in the first place. It has all been a hassle and an aggravation. It has just not been worth it. I am now so exasperated that I have assigned the whole matter to the debt collectors rather than going back to court. They will go and collect the money on my behalf, and whatever means they want to choose to recover the debt is up to them. Whether they put him up in a corner and give him a good smacking, I don't know and I'm not particularly interested. That's a matter for them. They do offer a very good recovery rate . . . . My solicitor has been involved in this case. His fees just about wiped out all the money I got [from the defendant]. It wasn't worth it . . . . It's a waste of time. The debt collectors take 25 per cent of what they collect and that is better than the solicitor taking 100 per cent. It's payment by results. If they don't get any results, they don't get paid . . . . Contact me in another six months and I'll tell you how they got on. Hopefully I shall be able to give you some good news then and perhaps be in a better frame of mind! [Western Circuit, Small business plaintiff, Case 88].

The plaintiffs in the above quotations were exceptional in the sense that they persisted, often for months, in their efforts to obtain the money that was owed to them. When contacted by the writer six months after the court hearing, a few were still actively pursuing matters. But most of those who had not received payment were less determined and had given up at a much earlier stage. In these circumstances, it was surprising to note how infrequently advice was sought about enforcement. Only a third of those who had received no payment sought advice about how they might proceed. There were a few 'repeat players' who knew the ropes from previous experience, but many individuals seemed to run out of steam at an early stage in proceedings and, having taken the matter to the court, did little further to secure payment.

As a result of the difficulties they encountered in enforcing the judgment and the lack of effectiveness, as they saw it, of formal enforcement procedures, some plaintiffs said that they had lost confidence in the small claims procedure itself. The positive views they had expressed when first interviewed at the county court had changed as frustration and disillusionment had set in. An indication of this shift is given by comparing the numbers of litigants who at each stage said that they had been so put off as a result of their experiences that they would not use the procedure again in the future. Whereas only four successful plaintiffs expressed this view immediately following the court hearing, six months later the number had risen to fifteen. Even so, it perhaps says much for the indomitability of the human spirit that, despite the many frustrations they had endured in seeking to secure payment, 70 per cent of the plaintiffs in the sample (compared to almost 90 per cent earlier) said that they would use the small claims procedure again in similar circumstances in the future.

Conclusion

This examination of enforcement procedures supports the observation that, in seeking to provide a forum in which the everyday disputes of ordinary people can be cheaply and expeditiously resolved, it is not enough for courts to provide appropriately informal procedures: enforcement is as important a part of the legal process as any other. It is vital that courts' judgments be binding and authoritative and that they be seen as such by those who are subject to them. Where this is not the case and enforcement proves ineffective, it undermines the value of all that has gone before.[29] The sensitive playing of the judicial role counts for little if it does not produce the final result that the parties seek. If courts are to take seriously the needs and wishes of litigants, as they increasingly claim to do, then they have an obligation, in this writer's view, to assume a much more prominent role in the enforcement of judgments. As Maher (1983: 244) argues in the following powerful passage:

> An important measure of the true worth of any system of civil justice is the mode of enforcing the judgments obtained after recourse to it. No matter how fair the substantive rights conferred by a legal system and no matter how easy is access to its courts or clear its procedures, a system of civil justice stands condemned if its mode of enforcing judgments does not secure effectively the rights of those in whose favour judgments are given or is harsh in operation against those obligated to pay.

[29] As Sir Jack Jacob (1987: 187) puts it:

'The judgment of the order of the court must, so far as possible, be obeyed or complied with, for otherwise the authority of the court would be diminished and the legal order would suffer a breakdown'.

In a study conducted over a decade ago, Steven Weller and his associates (1984: 75) observed that 'nearly all small claims courts [in the United States] could be doing more to help winning parties collect their judgments'. The same point might be made with equal force in relation to county courts in England and Wales, where plaintiffs are commonly disappointed and bemused to find that the court appears to lose interest in their case after the hearing. Although officials at many county courts are ready to offer plaintiffs information about the enforcement options available to them, this falls short of the active involvement in enforcement that plaintiffs seek, and indeed expect, from the courts. When interviewed, few district judges expressed much concern about enforcement procedures, and, in observing hearings, the author came across only one judge who made more than an occasional reference to enforcement at the close of hearings. The more typical judicial response is the one that the author observed at a hearing where a defendant had told the judge, firmly but politely, as he announced his decision that he had no intention of paying the plaintiff the £700 sum that the judge had directed. The district judge's response was revealing: 'That's somebody else's problem, not mine.'

This negative view of enforcement, commonly encountered among district judges and court staff in England and Wales, is of course found in other jurisdictions too. But there is nothing universal or inevitable about it. When one examines what has happened in England and Wales in the past,[30] or what happens in other courts or in other countries, it is apparent that a much more active stance is often adopted (both by judges and by court administrations) as far as enforcement is concerned. One need only consider the procedures that exist to collect the fines imposed by the criminal courts, particularly the use of imprisonment as the ultimate sanction for non-payment,[31] to realize that a passive view towards enforcement by the courts is by no means inevitable. Similarly robust approaches are found in some countries, even in the enforcement of small claims judgments. Some small claims courts, for instance, insist that both parties appear in court within a few weeks of the original hearing for an examination

[30] As every reader of Dickens knows, debtors' prisons were used in the past on a wide scale in this country: see Jacob (1987), at 198–202.

[31] Over 20,000 people are sent to prison annually in England and Wales for non-payment of fines: on this, see Barclay (1995), at 27 and Cavadino and Dignan (1997), at 214–15. Hundreds of people are also sent to prison each year by magistrates for non-payment of the council tax, rates, and the like.

of the defendant's assets if he or she has not paid the judgment by the required date. Others hold an examination of the defendant's assets at the conclusion of the first hearing. The imposition of special sanctions, including the suspension of the defendant's driving licence, in the event of non-payment of the judgment within a certain period, has also been adopted in some jurisdictions.[32] Nor is it by any means universal practice for plaintiffs to be charged a fee if they wish to activate formal enforcement procedures.

In some countries, there are special enforcement agencies or specific court officials, forming part of the court administration, charged with spearheading enforcement strategies. Other countries have sheriffs, Clerks of the Court, or court officials to whom litigants can turn when difficulties arise at the enforcement stage.[33] In yet others, a special office has been set up to offer advice in these circumstances. An Enforcement of Judgments Office exists in Northern Ireland, introduced in 1971, to centralize the enforcement of orders and judgments of all civil courts in the province,[34] and similar agencies exist elsewhere. While there are limitations in the way this Office functions in Northern Ireland (caused particularly by the expense, complexity, and delay in using the procedure), the existence of an office to handle enforcement difficulties ensures that the court itself assumes the primary responsibility for ascertaining debtors' means and for selecting the most appropriate enforcement procedure. Although the idea of introducing an enforcement office has from time to time been mooted in England and Wales, it has never met with the approval of the Lord Chancellor's Department.[35]

The results presented in this chapter point to a short and sombre conclusion. This is that there is a danger that, where (as in England

[32] The latter procedure is used in the New York State Small Claims Court where a claim is based on the defendant's ownership of a motor vehicle, and it is used in disputes about motor vehicle accidents elsewhere: see the discussion in Weller and Ruhnka (1979), at 35–8 on enforcement measures that have been actively considered (and in some cases adopted) in relation to small claims courts in the United States.

[33] Such officials have been appointed, for instance, in certain parts of the United States and Canada.

[34] See Phipps (1990) and the General Consumer Council for Northern Ireland (1992), at 38–44, for some details of how this Office works.

[35] The Payne Committee (1969) on the enforcement of judgment debts recommended the introduction of an enforcement office to co-ordinate and supervise enforcement, but this recommendation was never implemented. The idea was re-examined by the Review Body on Civil Justice (1988) but firmly rejected. For some criticisms of the 'negative approach' adopted by the Review Body on this issue, see Phipps (1990), at 256–61.

and Wales) the processes of small claims adjudication and enforcement are separated so that the courts in effect wash their hands of enforcement, the judicial process takes on the qualities of an empty charade, often producing symbolic, not substantive, justice. Worse, the civil courts come to be seen as impotent bodies, dishing out empty threats to defendants who come to realize that they are able to disregard them at will. This is emphatically not what plaintiffs themselves want when they turn to the courts to resolve their claims. Pyrrhic victories offer no consolation either to individuals or to hard-pressed businesses.

6 Conclusion

During the four years in which the research reported in this book was being conducted, the role of the small claims regime has been transformed in England and Wales, and it has become much more prominent in the debate about the future shape of civil justice. Over that period, this debate has been conducted more vigorously than at any time in the previous twenty years, and, as the unprecedented rise in the small claims limit to £3,000 has demonstrated, the outcome of this debate has proved decisive. From a position of substantial agnosticism, the writer has himself become increasingly convinced, as this study has proceeded, of the merits of the small claims procedure. This does not indicate any particular enthusiasm for the adoption of informal legal procedures in themselves, still less any political commitment to the direct participation of citizens in the resolution of their own disputes. Rather, it reflects the simple, practical consideration that, in the absence of massive increases in government funding of the courts or of legal aid, there is no real alternative to the adoption of certain forms of Do-It-Yourself justice if ordinary people are to use the civil courts to gain redress for their grievances.

It is well recognized that the costs of pursuing many kinds of civil action in the courts are wholly disproportionate to the amounts of money at stake, and it is now widely accepted that it is intolerable for the costs of civil litigation to exceed the sums of money that are in dispute.[1] As was noted at the start of this book, the advent of special small claims procedures represents a major part of a more general movement, now assuming international dimensions, to find simpler and less expensive ways of dealing with civil cases than formal legal procedures have in the past been able to provide. Having observed small claims proceedings in other parts of the world, the author has come to regard the way that hearings are conducted in county courts in England and Wales as falling somewhere between the extremes of formality and informality. The approach adopted by district judges in England is very different from that of their counterparts in many parts of the United States, for example, where a predominantly male

[1] See the discussion in Lord Woolf's reports (1995, 1996) on this question and the research conducted for his Inquiry by Genn (1996) on the costs of litigation.

judiciary can often be seen in shirt-sleeves and braces, seeking to 'knock heads' together, and even addressing litigants as 'you guys'. At the other extreme, most district judges deal with small claims in England and Wales in ways that are quite unlike the formal (and, to be frank, stuffy) approach adopted in certain courts in Scotland, in some provinces in Canada, or other parts of North America. Small claims hearings in some countries are still held in ordinary courtrooms, with judges dressed in gowns, occasionally even in wigs, and legal representation is more common than not. The hearings observed by the author in England and Wales, on the other hand, were held in the judges' own chambers, with the parties ranged around the table, contributing for the most part in an uninhibited way to proceedings.

This said, the district judges in England and Wales are conformists, and there are few, if any, mavericks in the ranks. Hearings are conducted with decorum, and respect for 'the court' is paramount. And while litigants frequently appear at hearings in jeans, sweaters, anoraks, or T-shirts—and one of the small claims leaflets shows a litigant sitting in front of the judge in a boiler suit—the district judges themselves dress smartly for court. For the male judges, this means regulation grey or blue suits and subdued ties. They would, almost without exception, regard it as inappropriate to remove their jackets and unthinkable to have their shirts open at the collar. Female judges invariably assume a similarly dignified stance in such matters.[2] For district judges sitting in county courts in England and Wales (unlike the civil courts in certain other countries that the author has visited), demure solemnity in dress is all but universal.

But appearance often belies practice. In approach and manner, district judges are decidedly down-to earth. When dealing with litigants in person, there is no place for standing on ceremony, for airs and graces, or for pomposity. As was seen in Chapter 3, small claims hearings are in the main characterized by good humour and robust common sense, seasoned with large doses of legal and judicial pragmatism. Notwithstanding the great variations in the methods adopted by district judges in England and Wales, the politeness, courtesy, even gentility, of judges, court staff, ushers, and of most litigants are striking. In all his visits to county courts in England and Wales, the writer never once saw a district judge or a court official barking at litigants in the way that he has seen elsewhere.

[2] Only 4 of the 33 district judges who participated in this study were female.

The methods adopted in determining small claims often prompt the use of metaphor, usually of a pejorative character. District judges often told the writer, for example, that the hearings could not offer Rolls Royce justice. (In discussing judicial procedures, motoring analogies are very common.[3]) They also said that their decisions often took the form of 'rough' justice or 'palm tree' justice, and a few described the proceedings as offering litigants nothing better than 'bargain basement' or 'supermarket' justice. Descriptions of this kind imply that the small claims arena provides only a second-class standard alongside the full-dress, open court trial with which it is unfavourably compared.[4] But the use of pejorative analogy betrays a defensiveness that may be misplaced. Encouraging the development of the interventionist judge in dealing with small claims has not simply been done *faute de mieux*, because it is a cheap alternative to traditional legal procedures and because it saves the costs of employing lawyers: it also provides a means of encouraging ordinary people to bring legal conflicts and grievances to the courts and allows them to participate directly in their resolution. This is after all, what ordinary people seem to prefer to the Rolls Royce end of the market.[5]

As often happens with empirical studies of the courts, events have to a degree overtaken this project. In June 1995, when the fieldwork on this research was nearing completion, Lord Woolf published his interim report on the reform of the civil justice system which contained very important recommendations about the future of small claims in England and Wales.[6] The author had submitted some preliminary

[3] One of the district judges interviewed, stretching this analogy to its limits, made the following point, for example:

> 'People ought not to expect a Rolls Royce decision. But I wonder if we are giving them a Lada or a Skoda. They ought to be entitled to Ford Escort type treatment.'

[4] The heavy reliance in some county courts upon deputy district judges (almost all of whom are solicitors in private practice) to deal with small claims perhaps fosters the idea that small claims are less important than those cases heard by judges in open court. In some jurisdictions, however, private lawyers are much more involved in handling small claims: see Baar (1995) and Lightstone (1995), for instance, on the widespread use of part-time judges to hear small claims in Canada.

[5] See on this National Consumer Council (1995). At the time of writing, the author is conducting a study of the experiences of litigants whose claims of £1,000 to £3,000 were dealt with by formal 'open court' procedures. Preliminary analysis of the results in that study has not revealed any fondness amongst litigants for formal court procedures.

[6] Lord Woolf produced his second, and final, report on *Access to Justice* in July 1996. Although this contains occasional references to small claims, Lord Woolf's main proposals relating to small claims are contained in his interim report produced in June 1995.

findings from his own study of district judges to Lord Woolf, and was pleased to read in both the interim and the final report that they had been taken into account in the recommendations for change that were proposed. Lord Woolf recommended an increase in the small claims limit from £1,000 to £3,000 as 'the primary way of increasing access to justice for ordinary people' (1995: 100). The swiftness with which the Lord Chancellor accepted Lord Woolf's recommended increase—he announced it on the very day of publication of the report—gives some indication of his enthusiasm for the move.[7] In this writer's judgment, it is likely that the small claims limit will rise further to £5,000 in England and Wales within the foreseeable future.[8]

Beyond proposing a substantial rise in the small claims limit, however, Lord Woolf recommended only minor changes to the present arrangements for dealing with small claims in England and Wales.[9] This single step is, however, of the greatest significance, and it will have a fundamental bearing upon the administration of civil justice in the future. The arguments in favour of the extension are the ones marshalled by Lord Woolf himself, in particular the saving of cost and the possibilities of extending citizens' access to justice, especially for those for whom legal aid is not available. With eligibility for legal aid increasingly restricted, access to the courts for such individuals has become more difficult to secure.

While the writer broadly welcomes the expansion of the small claims jurisdiction, he nonetheless entertains certain doubts about how far it will genuinely enhance access to justice in the way that Lord Woolf sought. The author's caution on this key question reflects more than just a customary academic equivocation: rather it illustrates the point that, in considering almost any aspect of small claims proceedings, the arguments that surround the appropriate direction for change seem always to be finely poised. There are many variables that need to be

[7] On the detailed implementation of Lord Woolf's proposals relating to small claims, see Greenslade (1996).

[8] Lord Woolf (1995: 118) proposed that the effects of the increase in the small claims to £3,000 be monitored with a view to a possible further rise to £5,000. Such a move is apparently favoured by the Consumers' Association and the National Consumer Council: see Woolf (1995), at 103.

[9] These modifications included a widening of the discretion exercised by district judges to transfer cases into (and out of) the small claims procedure; somewhat greater use of a paper arbitration option so as to improve access for businesses and the self-employed, and the provision of early evening and Saturday hearings. He also floated some imaginative ideas about the use of mobile courts in smaller country towns.

balanced in the equation, and there is a good deal of research that demonstrates that simple policy prescriptions rarely have the desired effect in solving the problems that dog the courts.

In seeking to expand citizens' access to justice—an objective which, it must be said, has proved largely elusive throughout this century[10]—Lord Woolf assumed a remarkably sanguine view of the small claims procedure. He asserted, rather than demonstrated, that the small claims arena provides 'a forum which is fair and appropriate for litigants in person' (1995: 104). The main weakness that Lord Woolf identified with the procedure is the one noted in the present study—the wide diversity in the approaches adopted at hearings by district judges. Lord Woolf (1995: 109) argued powerfully in favour of greater judicial consistency 'both as a safeguard for the individuals using the system and to increase the esteem in which the jurisdiction is held'. Criticisms were made in Chapter 3 of this book of the limited training in handling small claims available to district judges, and Lord Woolf made out a compelling case for the provision of training in the interventionist role in order to achieve greater consistency in procedure and in applying the substantive law.[11]

It is significant that Lord Woolf envisaged that judges at all levels would in the future play a more interventionist role at hearings, 'to hold the ring', as he put it, 'and ensure the adequate presentation of the litigant's case' (1995: 23). This has important implications for the kind of training that judges will require, and a good deal of thought will have to be given to the kinds of expertise that judges will need in order to play an interventionist role at hearings. It is vital that Lord Woolf's recommendation that there be better training for district judges and a more consistent judicial approach be urgently tackled. It is also imperative that the other main problem on which this study has focused be addressed. This concerns the ways that unrepresented litigants, both in small claims and in hearings of other kinds, are to overcome the disadvantaged position in which they are inevitably

[10] As Lord Woolf (1995: 4) himself acknowledged, the prospects of effecting any radical re-thinking of current practices in civil justice are distinctly unpropitious. Indeed, more than 60 reports on aspects of civil procedure and the organization of the courts in England had preceded Lord Woolf's, yet none could be said to have succeeded in producing fundamental change.

[11] Lord Woolf (1996: 97–100) reports that some progress is being made in achieving these goals.

placed as a consequence of their ignorance of the law in determining whether they have a legal case.[12]

Though exacerbating this latter problem, the raising of the small claims limit to £3,000 in January 1996 was well received by almost all commentators.[13] Little more than murmurs of dissent were heard from legal practitioners about it. There is of course much to be said in favour of the rise. Indeed, the results of the present research show that, in terms of most of the criteria which Lord Woolf argues are needed to ensure adequate access to civil justice—equality of access regardless of resources to assert or defend legal rights; just delivery of results; a system seen to be fair; costs proportionate to the nature of issues; speed; procedures that are understandable, responsive, certain, and effective—the small claims procedure in England and Wales can be said to perform quite well.

Yet it is important to be alive to the dangers. By no stretch of the imagination can small claims hearings be said to provide a refined brand of justice. Instead, such claims are as a rule resolved by means of quick decisions, based upon the assembling and presentation of inadequate evidence by lay people. This approach can be defended in relation to claims which involve small sums of money, and it emerges clearly from talking to litigants that most are well satisfied with the results that these methods achieve. But questions must be raised about whether this rough-and-ready judicial approach, the resort to inspired guesswork to reach decisions, and the occasional cavalier disregard of the law will be appropriate or acceptable where much larger sums are at stake. 'How far can we go in relying on common sense to get us through?' is how one district judge put it in an interview with the author.

The expansion of the small claims regime inevitably means that unrefined legal procedures, based as they are upon simple and crude forms of Do-It-Yourself case preparation and presentation, will need to be stretched to encompass an ever-growing range of civil disputes. The

[12] See also Lord Woolf (1995), at 118. Lord Woolf put forward many interesting, if somewhat vague, ideas about how the difficulties that confront lay litigants might be tackled. For instance, he foresaw the possibility that, as court staff are liberated by new technology from time-consuming and repetitive work, they will be able to 'undertake the higher quality and more demanding work of assisting litigants and providing support to judges on cases management' (*ibid.*: 122). He also raised the possibility that information might be conveyed to litigants by means of self-service legal 'kiosks', interactive videos, and legal information systems.

[13] See Baldwin (1995), at 187. Grosskurth (1995: 935) referred to the 'unrestrained enthusiasm' amongst solicitors for Lord Woolf's package of proposals.

insistence that the costs incurred in resolving civil disputes be proportionate to the sums at issue has rightly become a prominent theme in current debates about the reform of civil justice, and one of the guiding principles of the Woolf Inquiry was that procedures and cost should be proportionate to the nature of the issues involved. 'Cadillac-style procedures are not needed to process bicycle-size lawsuits' is how an American commentator has more colourfully, if less elegantly, made the same point.[14] There has been a good deal of debate of late, in part stimulated by the Woolf Inquiry itself, about whether the resolution of civil disputes might be made less 'adversarial'. Indeed, the unbridled 'adversarialism' of lawyers is regarded by some commentators (Lord Woolf included) as a main factor in producing the delays which result in the high costs of litigation.[15]

Much of this discussion overlooks, however, the plainer truth that civil justice in England and Wales is becoming to an extraordinary extent lawyer-free. Expanding the scope of small claims means expanding the scope of the 'no costs' rule which inevitably diminishes the role for lawyers. It is no exaggeration to say that, in the determination of a majority of civil actions dealt with by the county courts in England and Wales, we shall soon witness the virtual disappearance of professional legal representation.[16] If one includes, under the broad heading of 'civil actions', the hundreds of thousands of cases determined annually by the range of administrative tribunals—something that most commentators, including Lord Woolf, omit to do—the point is even more dramatically made.[17] It is true that, since personal injury claims over £1,000 are specifically excluded from the expanded small claims regime,[18] much lucrative bread-and-butter litigation for lawyers will

[14] Maurice Rozenberg, cited by Armstrong (1995).

[15] On this point, see the discussions in Zuckerman (1995, 1996); Armstrong (1995); and Jolowicz (1996). Andrews (1995: 172) sees Lord Woolf as a negative critic of the adversarial system, and he argues:

> 'Lord Woolf does pay some scant respect to the traditional adversarial model of English civil justice, but his compliment (in the context of a 270 page report) is so fleeting that it is unclear what he thinks is admirable and worthy of preservation'.

[16] With the advent of the 'procedural' judge, following Lord Woolf's recommendations, the role of lawyers will be further reduced, even in complex civil actions: see Andrews (1995), at 179–80.

[17] On the neglect of the role of tribunals in contemporary debate about access to civil justice, see Sainsbury and Genn (1995).

[18] The extent to which personal injury claims might be dealt with as small claims had been the subject of considerable controversy before Lord Woolf's Inquiry. In 1993,

remain. But in the post-Woolf era, with much greater emphasis placed on judicial rather than on party control, the diminishing role of lawyers is becoming increasingly evident. Andrews (1995: 179) asks, 'What will be the fate of litigators engaged in ordinary or even medium-sized actions?', and it is surely only a matter of time before the legal profession asks itself the same question.

The sensible answer to this question is that solicitors should continue to play a significant part in the preparatory stages of civil actions. They might, indeed, even expand this role, perhaps by offering advice to litigants on a fixed fee basis.[19] But with legal aid unavailable for the court representation of small claims litigants,[20] it will be left more and more to litigants to go it alone at hearings. It is an unfortunate truth that lawyers are now simply too expensive to play much of a role in the determination of civil claims that involve even substantial sums of money. If the quality of justice that is dispensed by the county courts in such cases suffers as a result, then we must face up to the fact—sad but inevitable—that the chill winds of market forces affect the admin-

the Lord Chancellor issued a consultation paper on proposals to deal with many personal injury claims under modified small claims procedures, and in 1994 he announced, in the light of the important Court of Appeal judgment in *Afzal and others* v. *Ford Motor Co. Ltd* [1994] 4 All ER 720 (which was one of 21 similar appeals on the suitability of dealing with small personal injury claims under the small claims regime), that he did not intend to take further action on that question (see (1994) 144 *New Law Journal*, 935 and 1122.) The place of personal injury cases in the new order was examined by Lord Woolf (1995), at 114–17, and he reported that the Association of Personal Injury Lawyers was 'particularly emphatic as to the inappropriateness of the small claims procedure for personal injury cases' (*ibid.*: 46). He acceded to the line taken by this powerful pressure group, which had for years vociferously argued that personal injury claims are qualitatively different from other claims, and for that reason unsuitable for a procedure operating largely without legal representation. Instead of personal injury cases being dealt with under the small claims procedure, they are to be placed on the 'fast track', unless one of the parties wishes to invoke the small claims jurisdiction and the court agrees: see further Allen (1994, 1996); Saggerson (1996); and Hemsworth (1996).

[19] A Law Society official has been quoted by Smerin (1996: 14) as saying:

> 'Solicitors must think about how they will give potential clients the quickest possible advice when they first come through the door. They will have to do a rapid benefit analysis of the cost to the client of employing a solicitor on the assumption that the client is not going to get any of that back'.

[20] The Legal Aid Board issued a notice in January 1996, at the time the small claims limit was raised, stating that it would be unreasonable for legal aid to be granted for small claims cases 'unless there are exceptional circumstances and there will be a tangible benefit to the assisted person': see the *Law Society's Gazette*, 10 January 1996, at 19.

istration of justice as they affect other areas of public finance. As Zuckerman (1995: 74) has observed:

> A country can no more maintain an absolute commitment to reaching the truth in civil litigation than it can maintain an unlimited commitment to the best possible health system, regardless of cost, or to the most efficient transport system. The provision of adjudication, like the provision of any other amenity, must be subject to what the country can afford and necessitates compromises.

Virtually all commentators are agreed that the raising of the small claims limit from £1,000 to £3,000 will produce a substantial increase in the number of cases handled as small claims with a consequent reduction in formal 'open court' hearings.[21] Raising the limit is likely to reinforce the trend for small claims hearings increasingly to dominate the determination of defended actions in the county courts, a phenomenon that was discussed in Chapter 1 of this book. The precise effects of a change of this magnitude are, however, extremely difficult to predict, since, in the history of small claims in this country, there has never been an increase on anything like this scale before. Despite the popular appeal that the small claims procedure undoubtedly enjoys, the limit has been raised only five times since the procedure was introduced in England and Wales in 1973. The periodic raising of the small claims limit in the past (with consequent automatic referral of claims within that limit to the small claims procedure) has strengthened the trend for more claims to be dealt with under the procedure, and, in the process, to reduce the number of full trials in the county courts. It is curious, however, that, at the very time that a massive increase in the small claims limit is implemented, a substantial (and disquieting) reduction in numbers of small claims hearings has occurred. The figures published in the official *Judicial Statistics* show that the increases in the numbers of small claims that have been recorded in every year since the procedure was introduced over twenty years ago did not arise in 1994 or in 1995.[22] Although the reason for this change is not at all clear, it may well have something to do with a reluctance on the part of district judges to conduct ever-greater numbers of small claims hearings. It is a mistake to assume that, simply because most district judges have come to play the interventionist role at small claims hearings with

[21] See, for example, the (1995) 145 *New Law Journal.*

[22] The figures given in the *Judicial Statistics* for 1994 reveal a 17 per cent reduction on the 1993 figure, and the 1995 figure is only marginally higher than that for 1994: see further Baldwin (1995), at 191–2.

some enthusiasm, they will want to do much more of it. On the contrary: dealing with small claims was regarded by most of the judges who were interviewed in this study as difficult and demanding work, tolerable only in relatively small doses and when balanced by other more intellectually satisfying judicial work.

The popular appeal of small claims can scarcely be said, therefore, to extend to the district judges themselves. 'Arbitration day is not the most popular day in the judge's calendar' is how one judge on the Northern Circuit put it when discussing with the author whether the small claims limit should be increased. Few of his colleagues in courts in other parts of the country expressed a markedly different view. Almost a half of the district judges interviewed said that they would be opposed to any increase from the existing limit (which at that time was set at £1,000), and a further fifth wanted no more than expansion in line with rates of inflation. Only just over a quarter of the judges could be described as sympathetic to an increase in the small claims limit on the present scale. Although the Association of District Judges has broadly welcomed the recommendations of Lord Woolf—and the author has not subsequently detected any silent opposition within the rank-and-file to the increase in the small claims limit—it might be that district judges nonetheless have reached saturation point in the number of small claims hearings that they are prepared, or indeed are able, to conduct. One consequence of this lack of judicial enthusiasm might be that delays, already experienced at some county courts in dealing with small claims,[23] might be reproduced in many other courts in the longer term. If this happens, it will of course defeat one of the main objectives of dealing with more cases under the simplified small claims procedure.

The problem of delays will also be exacerbated if there are demands for greater refinement in the procedures adopted by district judges. It is hazardous to assume that the judges will be able to perform just as competently and efficiently when obliged to take on growing numbers of small claims, especially where higher sums of money are at stake. Their response, when confronted with the inadequate evidence that most parties now produce at hearings, may be to order more adjournments or to resurrect the idea of pre-trial reviews, both of which are heartily disliked by most litigants and are at present officially discouraged. Although district judges are the work-horses of the civil justice

[23] See the discussion at 41–2.

system, there are limits to what they can do, particularly since they are to assume under the new order much greater responsibility than hitherto for case management.[24] Without large numbers of judicial appointments—something that is not apparently seen as necessary[25]—concern must be expressed about the capacity of district judges to cope with the additional burdens that are now being placed upon them.

It is interesting to consider what light the academic literature can shed on the consequences of the substantial raising of the small claims limit. It has to be said that the findings of research concerned with the prospects of court reform producing real change are not encouraging. Enough is already known about the ineffectiveness of court reform measures to make one feel uneasy about radical, common sense proposals for change. 'Legal institutions change slowly', writes Richard Marcus (1995: 242), 'getting them to adopt significantly different methods of operation requires persistent effort'. In support of this contention, Marcus cites Arthur Vanderbilt's aphorism that 'judicial reform is no sport for the short-winded'. The available empirical research, most of which has been carried out in the United States, has shown that fundamental court reform is extremely difficult to effect, and reading this material quickly dispels any optimism about 'quick-fix' solutions. One might note, indeed, that the bolder the proposals for court reform, the more likely they are to be ineffective, to backfire, or to have unanticipated consequences.[26] As Dingwall and Durkin (1995: 379–80) put it:

> The history of attempts at court reform in the US is littered with examples of local judges and lawyers colluding to maintain the status quo in the face of outside attempts at change. The courtroom work group of lawyers and judges have long been recognised as the enemy of victims and reformers alike . . . . The list of unexpected results can be multiplied.

[24] For the proposals relating to the need for judicial case management, see Woolf (1995, 1996) and the critique by Scott (1995).

[25] Lord Woolf (1995) was vague about whether new judicial appointments, especially at district judge level, would be needed to give effect to the greater responsibilities of case management they will have to assume. While he conceded that 'there may need to be some increase in the number of judges' (*ibid.*: 70), no indication was given of the numbers of extra judges who might be required. Instead of judicial appointments, Lord Woolf emphasized the importance of providing judges with additional assistance from the court administration, team working, the greater use of technology, and the attachment of law clerks to management teams. In the 2-page chapter on resources in the interim report, he made a few tentative references to compensatory savings that might be achieved by these means.

[26] See in particular Feeley (1983); Feeney (1987); Matthews (1988); Menkel-Meadow (1991); and Dingwall and Durkin (1995).

In Chapter 1 of this book, a number of the theoretical perspectives, particularly those developed by writers concerned with the expansion of 'informal justice', were examined. While one might predict, on the basis of the American research literature, that raising the small claims limit will indeed serve to enhance access to civil justice, an immediate fear, voiced by several academic writers, is that such expansion will primarily serve to promote and reinforce dominance of the procedure by commercial and business interests. One should be alert to the danger that attempts to widen access to the courts may be at the expense of the lay litigant, so much so that the latter may become the victims, not the beneficiaries, of the expansion of cheap and informal court procedures.[27] In other words, the proliferation in simplified legal procedures, such as small claims, may serve more to weaken the lay litigant's position than to strengthen it.

The literature on 'access to justice' also indicates how difficult it is for ordinary people to surmount the formidable barriers that impede access to justice. Plaintiffs who make it as far as a small claims hearing have had to overcome a number of obstacles and inhibitions, the most prominent of which is the fear of the cost that might be incurred in pursuing an action through the courts. Furthermore, going to court is inconvenient, it may well be disagreeable, perhaps acrimonious, and the prospects of a successful outcome are very uncertain. Rather than face a court appearance, the strong temptation is either to forget the whole thing—to 'lump it' in the socio-legal vernacular[28]—or simply to pay up whatever sum is claimed. The temptation exists regardless of the rights and wrongs of litigants' cases.

Plaintiffs who reach the county courts represent, then, the tip of a very large iceberg. There are many other members of the public with serious legal grievances who do not pursue matters at all, let alone to the courts, even though, for many types of action, it is probable that they would be successful if they did so.[29] No one wants to see people

[27] See, in particular, Abel (1982); Trubeck (1984); and Matthews (1988).

[28] As was noted in the Scottish study of small claims procedures, the inclination of litigants is 'to "lump it" rather than face the "hassle" of a court action': see Scottish Office, Central Research Unit (1991), at 28. On the tendency of individuals to 'lump it', see also Felstiner (1974); Nader (1979); Felstiner, Abel, and Sarat (1981); Harrell-Bond and Smith (1983); Cranston (1986); and Merry (1990).

[29] See the discussion in Genn (1995: 401) who shows that:

> 'Of those who do take steps to bring a claim the chances of succeeding in obtaining some sort of settlement are quite high among road, work and other accidents . . . ; however, among those attempting to secure damages for injuries caused by medical negligence cases the majority of cases commenced fail'.

using the county courts as other than a last resort, and, in almost all situations, alternative solutions to legal problems will probably be more appropriate. But it is vital in any democratic society that people who feel that they are the victims of injustice or have a grievance can turn to the courts to seek a remedy when other efforts to resolve matters have failed. Yet all the research evidence demonstrates that there are innumerable potential litigants who are simply unwilling to use the courts for this purpose or do not recognize the courts as offering an avenue that is available to them. The Consumer Complaints Surveys, carried out by the Office of Fair Trading, have consistently demonstrated that a negligible proportion of consumer complaints ever reach the civil courts.[30] Although it was outside the scope of this study to explore the reasons why people do not use the courts, it was nonetheless clear from talking to small claims litigants that many had found it an uphill struggle to pursue the action as far as the county court.[31] Only those sufficiently experienced or determined are likely to overcome the difficulties that such a course inevitably involves. In seeking to facilitate citizens' access to justice, therefore, it is not enough to provide improved facilities or to expand the scope of informal procedures or to encourage judges to become pro-active: the greater problem is to persuade people confronting serious legal difficulties to make use of the courts and other legal processes. Public awareness of small claims procedures and alternative methods of resolving disputes is very low, and public attitudes to the courts in general remain stubbornly resistant.[32]

[30] See Office of Fair Trading (1991), at 123–5 for details of these surveys and a more general discussion of barriers to justice. See also the study conducted in the United States by Best and Andreason (1977), which also showed that people only infrequently took action over complaints about consumer goods and services, and that by Miller and Sarat (1981) which reached a somewhat different conclusion.

[31] The same point was made in the study of small claims procedures conducted in Northern Ireland: see General Consumer Council for Northern Ireland (1992), at 45–6.

[32] Studies measuring the extent of 'unmet legal need' have been out of fashion for many years, and most of the research which sheds light on the scale of the problem in England and Wales was carried out in the 1970s: see, for example, Morris, White, and Lewis (1972); Abel-Smith, Zander, and Brooke (1973); and Byles and Morris (1977). An important study of accident cases, carried out more recently by members of the Oxford Centre for Socio-Legal Studies, examined why so many potential plaintiffs fail to pursue actions: see in particular Genn (1984, 1995). There are, however, signs of a re-awakening of interest in large community surveys of unmet legal need: see National Consumer Council (1995). At the time of writing, Professor Hazel Genn of University College, London, is directing a national study on access to justice, supported by the Nuffield Foundation, and in this survey she is examining use of the courts and other methods of resolving disputes.

It is questionable whether expanding the small claims jurisdiction of the county courts in England and Wales in the past has succeeded to any significant degree in extending citizens' access to justice. It is probably truer to say that such expansion has enhanced access to justice for only a limited segment of the population. Most litigants contacted in this study, especially those who appeared as plaintiffs, were relatively well-heeled and articulate individuals. Over two-thirds of those in paid employment were in professional or managerial occupations, and the same applied to well over half of all defendants. Many litigants were of course businessmen and women. Almost three-quarters were car owners who had driven to the hearing. Very few litigants were from ethnic minority groups.[33] The genuinely 'poor' make few appearances at small claims hearings, and, when they do, it is typically as defendants to face landlords or money-lenders.

This depiction of small claims contradicts another common image of the civil courts: as the arena in which the rich are commonly pitched against the poor or the powerful against the powerless. Given the backgrounds of the litigants who most often appear in the county courts, this characterization is at best a crude over-simplification, at least as far as England and Wales is concerned. It would be an over-statement—but only a slight one—to describe the small claims arena as being a predominantly middle-class preserve, and the county courts as places to which others are as a rule invited to appear only as defendants. For the most part, small claims hearings involve well-to-do people suing other well-to-do people.

It is easy for an academic researcher, who has become familiar with the relaxed regime operated nowadays by most district judges in resolving small claims, to overlook the simple point that the courts remain for large sections of the population uninviting, even forbidding, institutions, to be visited only in extreme circumstances. This applies

[33] An attempt was made in the study to explore the question whether there were discernible trends as far as the gender of court users is concerned. However, it was not considered worth pursuing this in much detail as the interpretation of findings was inevitably blurred and complex not just because a large proportion of plaintiffs and defendants were businesses, but also a sizeable number of plaintiffs and defendants (1.9 per cent and 4.6 per cent respectively) were husband and wife teams. Of the minority of cases involving private individuals, about twice as many featured males both as plaintiffs and defendants. A somewhat different picture was painted by Merry (1990), in the study she conducted in the United States, where it was noted that disproportionate use was made of the courts by women as part of 'the general pattern of relatively vulnerable and powerless people turning to the courts for help in those relationships in which they feel at a disadvantage' (*ibid.*: 178).

no matter how informal judicial procedures may be and regardless of the amount of money that is at stake. Irrespective of any apprehensions about the outcome of the hearing, the court appearance itself represents an ordeal that is frequently dreaded by lay litigants, the more so if they are making their first appearance. The county courts are fixed in the public imagination as places where people are 'taken', not somewhere they go of their own volition.[34] They are seen by large sections of the population as out of bounds, not places where decent people go to resolve their differences. Indeed, going to court is often seen instead by litigants as carrying a social stigma. In the eyes of many defendants, 'being taken to court' is abhorrent, and use of the term 'defendant' reinforces this stigma. 'I've never been in trouble before in my life' is how one middle-aged defendant expressed his thoughts in interview with the author. Furthermore, the fear of 'not being believed' by a judge is sometimes perceived even as carrying quasi-criminal connotations.

Nor are the county courts commonly viewed by members of the general public as the arena in which rights may be asserted or in which wrongs may be remedied. Much earlier research has demonstrated that large sections of the population do not regard the courts as an appropriate arena in which to resolve their disputes, although there is certainly a serious problem to be addressed in what Nader (1979: 1019) has called 'the low-profile, petty exploitation suffered by large segments of the population' where the courts may be expected to play an important role. The civil courts have a serious image problem, and, until this is tackled, citizens' access to the courts (and to a large extent their access to justice as well) is bound to be limited.[35] 'Access to Justice' is a powerful and evocative rallying cry, but to most of the populace it carries little meaning or relevance. Worse, there is a danger that the phrase 'access to justice' may become no more than a mere catch-phrase, devoid of substance. 'In the end', as Genn (1995: 394) writes, 'it means everything and perhaps nothing'.

[34] This point was well made in the report on consumer redress mechanisms by the Office of Fair Trading (1991: 46), where it was noted that:

> 'The courts have to overcome their image as the place where ordinary people are taken, commonly by creditors, rather than as one to which they resort on their own initiative to resolve a dispute'.

[35] The National Consumer Council (1979, 1989, 1995) has complained for years about the poor image of the courts and their unapproachability in the eyes of members of the public. See also National Audit Office (1996), at 13–19.

The main problem with informal court procedures, as it has been identified in this book, is that, while they may be relaxed and easy to follow, they are nonetheless inherently legal. At all stages of the process, litigants who have been encouraged to go it alone at small claims hearings run up against the law. They cannot be expected to have any grasp of the legal complexities raised by their cases or to know what evidence they will need to prove the case to the satisfaction of the judge. Basing their claim or defence on common sense or the moral rectitude of their position provides merely a quicksand foundation. Litigants' difficulties are not by any means confined to the hearing: serious problems can arise well before that stage, and they can surface subsequently at the enforcement stage. Access to justice means nothing if Do-It-Yourself litigants find out only when they reach the court that their case is not well founded in law. And it means no more when they are unable to enforce the court's judgment. Without effective enforcement mechanisms, the court procedure is negated, and, where this happens, successful plaintiffs feel let down, if not cheated. The official literature available to the litigants in small claims plays down the nature of the difficulties that are likely to arise at the enforcement stage. This crucial issue was also overlooked in the reports produced as a result of Lord Woolf's inquiry (1995, 1996). Access to justice implies more than the fair, expeditious, and inexpensive resolution of disputes: for judicial procedures to have meaning, the courts must in addition have regard to the problems that arise for litigants seeking to enforce court judgments.

As the small claims regime in England and Wales enters a new era of expansion, its success will depend to a critical extent upon the attitudes adopted by the judges. This study shows that the district judges who participated in this study were no-nonsense in approach, civilized in manner, and determinedly pragmatic in orientation. Although adopting a pro-active judicial role at hearings may give rise to many dilemmas and difficulties, the advent of the interventionist judge has at least succeeded in providing an informal setting in which lay litigants can put their own cases, without legal representation, and for the most part effectively. It is unrealistic and misleading to regard the alternative to interventionism as being Rolls Royce justice: the alternative may well be no access to justice at all.

Bibliography

ABEL, R. L. (1982), 'The Contradictions of Informal Justice', 267–320 in R. L. Abel (ed.), *The Politics of Informal Justice* (New York: Academic Press).

ABEL-SMITH, B., ZANDER, M., and BROOKE, R. (1973), *Legal Problems and the Citizen* (London: Heinemann).

ALLEN, P. (1994), 'Small Personal Injury Claims', *Journal of Personal Injury Litigation* 57–64.

—— (1996), 'Gambling in the Three Grand Lottery', *Law Society's Gazette*, 10 January, 16.

ANDREWS, N. (1995), 'The Adversarial Principle: Fairness and Efficiency: Reflections on the Recommendations of the Woolf Report', 169–83 in A. A. S. Zuckerman and R. Cranston (eds.), *Reform of Civil Procedure: Essays on 'Access to Justice'* (Oxford: Clarendon Press).

APPLEBEY, G. (1978), *Small Claims in England and Wales* (Birmingham: Institute of Judicial Administration).

—— (1979), 'Small Claims in England and Wales', 683–763 in M. Cappelletti and J. Weisner, *Access to Justice Vol 2: Promising Institutions* (Alphenaandenrijn: Sijthoff and Noordhoof).

—— (1992), 'Lay Representation in Small Claims', 11 *Civil Justice Quarterly* 343–45.

—— (1993), 'New County Court Rules for Small Claims', 12 *Civil Justice Quarterly* 20–3.

—— (1994), *A Practical Guide to the Small Claims Court* (Croydon: Tolley).

ARMSTRONG, N. (1995), 'Making Tracks', 97–118 in A. A. S. Zuckerman and R. Cranston (eds.), *Reform of Civil Procedure: Essays on 'Access to Justice'* (Oxford: Clarendon Press).

ASHWORTH, A., GENDERS, E., MANSFIELG, PEAY, J., and PLAYER, E. (1984), *Sentencing in the Crown Court: Report of an Exploratory Study* (University of Oxford: Centre for Criminological Research).

AUERBACH, J. S. (1976), *Unequal Justice: Lawyers and Social Change in Modern America* (London: Oxford University Press).

BAAR, C. (1995), 'The Problematic Growth of "People's Justice"', 4 *National* 17–22.

BALDWIN, J. (1985), *Pre-Trial Justice: A Study of Case Settlement Procedures in Magistrates' Courts* (Oxford: Blackwell).

—— (1988), 'How Solicitors Use the Green Form—Adapting to Local Policies', 138 *New Law Journal* 928–30.

—— (1995), 'Raising the Small Claims Limit', 185–99 in A. A. S. Zuckerman and R. Cranston (eds.), *Reform of Civil Procedure: Essays on 'Access to Justice'* (Oxford: Clarendon Press).

—— (1996), 'Consumers' Access to Justice: Small Claims Procedures in the County Courts', 8–22 in Office of Fair Trading, *Developments in Consumer Redress* (London: Office of Fair Trading).

—— and McConville, M. (1977), *Negotiated Justice* (London: Martin Robertson).

—— and —— (1979), *Jury Trials* (Oxford: Clarendon Press).

——, Wikeley, N., and Young, R. (1992), *Judging Social Security* (Oxford: Clarendon Press).

Barclay, G. C. (1995), *The Criminal Justice System in England and Wales* (London: Home Office).

Bawdon, F. (1994), 'Dealing with DIY-ers', *Law Society's Gazette*, 26 October, 8.

Bell, K. (1969), *Tribunals in the Social Services* (London: Routledge and Kegan Paul).

—— (1975), *Research Study on Supplementary Benefit Appeal Tribunals* (London: HMSO).

Best, A., and Andreason, A. R. (1977), 'Consumer Response to Unsatisfactory Purchases: A Survey of Perceiving Defects, Voicing Complaints, and Obtaining Redress', 11 *Law and Society Review* 701–42.

Bingham, T. (1994), *The Price of Justice*, Holdsworth Club lecture, University of Birmingham.

Birks, M. (1984), *Small Claims in the County Court: How to Sue and Defend Actions Without a Solicitor* (London: Lord Chancellor's Department).

Bland, R. (1987), 'Progress in the Introduction of a Small Claims Procedure in Scotland', 6 *Civil Justice Quarterly* 199–204.

Browne-Wilkinson, N. (1988), 'The Independence of the Judiciary in the 1980s', *Public Law* 44–57.

Bundy, S. M. (1992), 'The Policy in Favour of Settlement in an Adversary System', 44 *Hastings Law Journal* 1–78.

Byles, A., and Morris, P. (1977), *Unmet Need* (London: Routledge).

Cain, M. (1983), 'Where are the Disputes? A Study of a First Instance Civil Court in the U.K.', 119–33 in M. Cain and K. Kulscar (eds.), *Disputes and the Law* (Budapest: Kaido).

—— (1986), 'Who Loses out on Paradise Island? The Case of Defendant Debtors in County Court', 101–46 in I. Ramsay (ed.), *Debtors and Creditors* (Abingdon: Professional Books).

Camley, M. (1995), 'Judicial Statistics—Past, Present and Future', 146 *New Law Journal* 1123.

Caplovitz, D. (1974), *Consumers in Trouble: A Study of Debtors in Default* (New York: The Free Press).

Cappelletti M., and Garth, B. (1978), *Access to Justice: A World Survey* (Alphenaandenrijn: Sijthoff and Noordhoof).

CAVADINO, M., and DIGNAN, J. (1997), *The Penal System: An Introduction* (London: Sage).

CHRISTIE, N. (1977), 'Conflicts as Property', 17 *British Journal of Criminology* 1–15.

CHURCH, T. W. (1990), *A Consumer's Perspective on the Courts* (Melbourne: Australian Institute of Judicial Administration Incorporated).

——, CARLSON, A., LEE, J., and TAN, T. (1978), *Justice Delayed: The Pace of Litigation in Urban Trial Courts* (Williamsburg, Va: National Center for State Courts).

CIVIL JUSTICE REVIEW (1988), *Report of the Review Body on Civil Justice*, Cm 394 (London: HMSO).

CONSUMER COUNCIL (1970), *Justice Out of Reach: A Case for Small Claims Courts* (London: HMSO).

COTTERRELL, R., DAVIES, R., GOODE, R., GRAVELLE, H., and PHIPPS, J. (1986), 'The Recovery of Judgment Debts in the County Court: Some Preliminary Results', 68–100 in I. Ramsay, *Debtors and Creditors* (Abingdon: Professional Books).

CRANSTON, R. (1986), 'What Do Courts Do?', 5 *Civil Justice Quarterly* 123–43.

—— (1995), '"The Rational Study of Law": Social Research and Access to Justice', 31–59 in A. A. S. Zuckerman and R. Cranston (eds.), *Reform of Civil Procedure: Essays on 'Access to Justice'* (Oxford: Clarendon Press).

DICKENS, L., JONES, M., WEEKES, B., and HART, M. (1985), *Dismissed: A Study of Unfair Dismissal and the Industrial Tribunal System* (Oxford: Basil Blackwell).

DICKINSON, T. (1994), 'Dispute Designs', *Law Society's Gazette*, 9 February, 19–20.

DINGWALL, R., and DURKIN, T. (1995), 'Time Management and Procedural Reform: Some Organizational Questions for Lord Woolf', 371–92 in A. A. S. Zuckerman and R. Cranston (eds.), *Reform of Civil Procedure: Essays on 'Access to Justice'* (Oxford: Clarendon Press).

ECONOMIDES, K. (1980), 'Small Claims and Procedural Justice', 7 *British Journal of Law and Society* 111–21.

EISENBERG, M. E. (1976), 'Private Ordering through Negotiation: Dispute-Settlement and Rulemaking', 89 *Harvard Law Review* 637–81.

ERVINE, W. C. H. (1991), *Small Claims Handbook* (Edinburgh: Sweet and Maxwell).

—— (1993), *Settling Consumer Disputes: A Review of Alternative Dispute Resolution* (London: National Consumer Council).

FEELEY, M. M. (1983), *Court Reform on Trial: Why Simple Solutions Fail* (New York: Basic Books).

FEENEY, F. (1987), 'Evaluating Trial Court Performance', 12 *The Justice System Journal* 148–69.

FELSTINER, W. L. F. (1974), 'Influences of Social Organization on Dispute Processing', 9 *Law and Society Review* 63–94.

——, ABEL, R., and SARAT, A. (1981), 'The Emergence and Transformation of Disputes: Naming, Blaming, Claiming', 15 *Law and Society Review* 631–54.

FISS, O. M. (1984), 'Against Settlement', 93 *Yale Law Journal* 1073–90.

FRAME, A. (1990), 'Fundamental Elements of the Small Claims Tribunal System in New Zealand', 73–98 in C. J. Whelan (ed.), *Small Claims Courts: A Comparative Study* (Oxford: Clarendon Press).

FREEMAN, M. (1995), 'Introduction', pp. xi-xvii in M. Freeman (ed.), *Alternative Dispute Resolution* (Aldershot: Dartmouth).

GALANTER, M. (1974), 'Why the Haves Come Out Ahead: Speculations on the Limits of Legal Change', 9 *Law and Society Review* 95–160.

—— and CAHILL, M. (1994), '"Most Cases Settle": Judicial Promotion and Regulation of Settlements', 46 *Stanford Law Review* 1339–91.

GENERAL CONSUMER COUNCIL FOR NORTHERN IRELAND (1992), *How to Make Small More Beautiful: The Small Claims Procedure in Northern Ireland* (Belfast: General Consumer Council).

GENN, H. (1984), 'Who Claims Compensation: Factors Associated with Claiming and Obtaining Damages', 45–78 in D. Harris, M. Maclean, H. Genn, S. Lloyd-Bostock, P. Fenn, P. Corfield, and Y. Brittan (eds.), *Compensation and Support for Illness and Injury* (Oxford: Clarendon Press).

—— (1987), *Hard Bargaining: Out of Court Settlements in Personal Injury Actions* (Oxford: Clarendon).

—— (1995), 'Access to Just Settlements: The Case of Medical Negligence', 393–412 in A. A. S. Zuckerman and R. Cranston (eds.), *Reform of Civil Procedure: Essays on 'Access to Justice'* (Oxford: Clarendon Press).

—— (1996), *Survey of Litigation Costs* (London: Lord Chancellor's Department).

—— and GENN, Y. (1989), *The Effectiveness of Representation Before Tribunals* (London: Lord Chancellor's Department).

GILVARRY, E. (1995), 'Court Doors Closing', *Law Society's Gazette*, 1 February, 7.

GLASSER, C., and ROBERTS, S. (1993), 'Dispute Resolution: Civil Justice and its Alternatives', 56 *Modern Law Review* 277–81.

GREENSLADE, R. (1996), 'Small Claims Arbitration and the Solicitor', 146 *New Law Journal* 118–20.

GREER, D. (1990), 'Small Claims in Northern Ireland', 133–66 in C. J. Wheelan (ed.), *Small Claims Courts: A Comparative Study* (Oxford: Clarendon Press).

GRIFFITHS, J. (1986), 'What Do Dutch Lawyers Actually Do in Divorce Cases?', 20 *Law and Society Review* 135–75.

GROSSKURTH, A. (1995), 'Plaudits with Provisos', 145 *New Law Journal* 935–6.

HARRELL-BOND, B., and SMITH, A. (1983), 'Dispute Treatment in an English Town', 55–65 in M. Cain and K. Kulscar (eds.), *Disputes and the Law* (Budapest: Kaido).

HARVEY, B. W., and PARRY, D. L. (1996), *The Law of Consumer Protection and Fair Trading* (London: Butterworths).

HEILBRON, H. (1993), *Civil Justice on Trial—The Case for Change* (London: General Council of the Bar and the Law Society).

HEMSWORTH, M. C. (1996), 'Pitfalls for the Small Claims Litigant', 146 *New Law Journal* 1319–20.

HOLLAND, K. M. (1982), 'The Twilight of Adversariness: Trends in Civil Justice', 17–29 in P. L. Dubois (ed.), *The Analysis of Judicial Reform* (Lexington, Mass.: D. C. Heath).

HOOD, R. (1992), *Race and Sentencing* (Oxford: Clarendon Press).

INGLEBY, R. (1993), 'Court Sponsored Mediation: The Case Against Mandatory Participation', 56 *Modern Law Review* 441–51.

ISON, T. G. (1972), 'Small Claims', 35 *Modern Law Review* 18–37.

JACOB, H. (1992), 'The Elusive Shadow of the Law', 26 *Law and Society Review* 565–90.

JACOB, Sir Jack I. H. (1986), 'Active Role of the Parties—Small Claims Procedure', 5 *Civil Justice Quarterly* 182–3.

—— (1987), *The Fabric of English Civil Justice* (London: Stevens).

JETTINGHOFF, A. (1986), 'Debt Enforcement in Dutch Courts', 147–61 in I. Ramsay (ed.), *Debtors and Creditors* (Abingdon: Professional Books).

JOLOWICZ, J. A. (1996), 'The Woolf Report and the Adversary System', 15 *Civil Justice Quarterly* 198–210.

JUSTICE (1971), *Litigants in Person* (London: JUSTICE).

—— (1992), *The Judiciary in England and Wales* (London: JUSTICE).

KEE, H. P. (1988), 'Small Claims Process: The Singapore Experience', 7 *Civil Justice Quarterly* 329–42.

LEGG, T. (1996), 'The Management of the Law', Annual G.K.N. Lecture, Magdalene College, Cambridge.

LIGHTSTONE, S. (1995), 'Staying on Track in the People's Court', 4 *National* 25–8.

LIND, E. A., MACCOUN, R. J., EBENER, P. A., FELSTINER, W. L. F., HENSLER, D. R., RESNICK, J., and TYLER, T. R. (1990), 'In the Eye of the Beholder: Tort Litigants' Evaluations of their Experiences in the Civil Justice System', 24 *Law and Society Review* 953–96.

—— and TYLER, T. R. (1988), *The Social Psychology of Procedural Justice* (New York: Plenum).

LORD CHANCELLOR'S DEPARTMENT (1986), Consultation Paper No 2, 'Civil Justice Review: Small Claims in the County Court' (London: Lord Chancellor's Department).

—— (1986), Consultation Paper No 4, 'Civil Justice Review: Enforcement of Debt' (London: Lord Chancellor's Department).

—— (1993), 'Small Personal Injury Claims: A Consultation Paper on Proposals for Changes to the Treatment of Small Unliquidated Claims in the County Court' (London: Lord Chancellor's Department).

McBarnet, D. J. (1981), *Conviction: Law, the State and the Construction of Conviction* (London: MacMillan).

McConnell, B. (1995), 'Watch these LIPs', 145 *New Law Journal* 1549–52.

McConville, M., Sanders, A., and Leng, R. (1991), *The Case for the Prosecution* (London: Routledge).

——, Hodgson, J., Bridges, L., and Pavlovic, A. (1994), *Standing Accused* (Oxford: Oxford University Press).

McEwan, C. A., and Maiman, R. J. (1982), 'Mediation and Arbitration: Their Promise and Performance as Alternatives to Court', 61–76 in P. L. Dubois (ed.), *The Analysis of Judicial Reform* (Lexington, Mass.: D. C. Heath).

—— and —— (1984), 'Mediation in Small Claims Court: Achieving Compliance through Consent', 18 *Law and Society Review* 11–49.

McGuire, S. C., and Macdonald, R. A. (1994), 'Of Magic Wands, Presto Justice and Other Illusions' (Unpublished manuscript, McGill University).

—— and —— (1995), 'Wizards of Oz' (Unpublished manuscript, McGill University).

Macauley, S. (1979), 'Lawyers and Consumer Protection Laws', 14 *Law and Society Review* 115–71.

Malleson, K. (1996), 'Appeals Against Conviction in the Court of Appeal (Criminal Division)' (unpublished Ph.D thesis, University of London).

Marcus, R. L. (1995), '"Déjà Vu All Over Again"? An American Reaction to the Woolf Report', 218–43 in A. A. S. Zuckerman and R. Cranston (eds.), *Reform of Civil Procedure: Essays on 'Access to Justice'* (Oxford: Clarendon Press).

Mather, L., and Yngvesson, B. (1981), 'Language, Audience, and the Transformation of Disputes', 15 *Law and Society Review* 776–821.

Matthews, R. (1988), 'Reassessing Informal Justice', 3–24 in R. Matthews (ed.), *Informal Justice?* (London: Sage).

Mayer, G. (1983), 'The Enforcement of Judgments in Scots Law', 2 *Civil Justice Quarterly* 244–56.

Menkel-Meadow, C. (1991), 'Pursuing Settlement in an Adversary Culture: A Tale of Innovation Co-opted or "The Law of ADR"', 19 *Florida State University Law Review* 1–46.

—— (1995), 'Dream or Nightmare? Lessons from the American Experience', 220–36 in R. Smith (ed.), *Shaping the Future: New Directions in Legal Services* (London: Legal Action Group).

Merry, S. E. (1990), *Getting Justice and Getting Even: Legal Consciousness among Working-Class Americans* (Chicago, Ill.: University of Chicago Press).

Miller, R. E., and Sarat, A. (1981), 'Grievances, Claims, and Disputes: Assessing the Adversary Culture', 15 *Law and Society Review* 525–65.

Mnookin, R. H., and Kornhauser, L. (1979), 'Bargaining in the Shadow of the Law', 88 *Yale Law Journal* 950–97.

Morgan, P. M. (1996), 'User Satisfaction and Waiting Times in Magistrates' Courts', 38 *Home Office Research Bulletin* 57–63.

MORRIS, P., WHITE, R., and LEWIS, P. (1972), *Social Needs and Legal Action* (London: Martin Robertson).

MULVANEY, A., and GREER, D. S. (1987), 'Small Claims: The Northern Ireland Experience', 6 *Civil Justice Quarterly* 56–67.

NADER, L. (1979), 'Disputing Without the Force of Law', 88 *Yale Law Journal* 998–1021.

NATIONAL AUDIT OFFICE (1996), *Handling Small Claims in the County Courts* (London: HMSO)

NATIONAL CONSUMER COUNCIL (1989), *Ordinary Justice: Legal Services and the Courts in England and Wales* (London: HMSO).

—— (1995), *Seeking Civil Justice: A Survey of People's Needs and Experiences* (London: National Consumer Council).

——/WELSH CONSUMER COUNCIL (1979), *Simple Justice: A Consumer View of Small Claims Procedures in England and Wales* (London: National Consumer Council).

O'BARR, W. M., and CONLEY, J. M. (1985), 'Litigant Satisfaction versus Legal Adequacy in Small Claims Narratives', 19 *Law and Society Review* 661–701.

OFFICE OF FAIR TRADING (1991), *Consumer Redress Mechanisms* (London: Office of Fair Trading).

—— (1986), *Consumer Dissatisfaction: A Report on Surveys Undertaken for the Office of Fair Trading* (London: Office of Fair Trading).

OTTON, LORD JUSTICE (1995), *Litigants in Person in the Royal Courts of Justice, London* (London: Judges' Council's Working Party).

PANNICK, D. (1988), *The Judges* (Oxford: Oxford University Press).

PATERSON, A. (1982), *The Law Lords* (London: Macmillan).

—— and STEDWARD, G. (1989), 'Monitoring of the New Small Claims Procedure in Scotland', 8 *Civil Justice Quarterly* 301–2.

PAYNE COMMITTEE (1969), *Report of the Committee on the Enforcement of Judgment Debts*, Cmnd. 3909 (London. HMSO) .

PEDLEY, F. H. (1994), 'The Small Claims Process', 144 *New Law Journal* 1217–18.

PHIPPS, J. (1990), 'Warrants of Execution in the Recovery of Consumer Debts in the County Court. A Lost Opportunity for Change?', 9 *Civil Justice Quarterly* 234–61.

PLOTNIKOFF, J., and WOOLFSON, R. (1993), *From Committal to Trial: Delay at the Crown Court* (London: Law Society).

PRICE, J. (1993), 'Small Claims—Major Challenge', *Legal Action*, September, 8.

PURCHAS, F. (1993), 'The Constitution and the Market Place', 143 *New Law Journal* 1604–9.

RAMSAY, I. (1990), 'Small Claims Courts in Canada: A Socio-Legal Appraisal', 25–48 in C. J. Whelan (ed.), *Small Claims Courts: A Comparative Study* (Oxford: Clarendon Press).

RICKMAN, N., and GRAY, A. (1995), 'The Role of Legal Expenses Insurance in Securing Access to the Market for Legal Services', 305–25 in A. A. S.

Zuckerman and R. Cranston (eds.), *Reform of Civil Procedure: Essays on 'Access to Justice'* (Oxford: Clarendon Press).

ROBERTS, S. (1995), 'Litigation and Settlement', 447–57 in A. A. S. Zuckerman and R. Cranston (eds.), *Reform of Civil Procedure: Essays on 'Access to Justice'* (Oxford: Clarendon Press).

ROCK, P. (1973), *Making People Pay* (London: Routledge and Kegan Paul).

—— (1993), *The Social World of an English Crown Court* (Oxford: Clarendon Press).

ROHL, K. F. (1990), 'Small Claims in Civil Court Proceedings in the Federal Republic of Germany', 167–81 in C. J. Whelan (ed.), *Small Claims Courts: A Comparative Study* (Oxford: Clarendon Press).

ROSS, H. L. (1970), *Settled Out of Court: The Social Process of Insurance Claims Adjustment* (Chicago, Ill.: Aldine).

ROYAL COMMISSION ON CRIMINAL JUSTICE (1993), *Report*, Cm 2263 (London: HMSO).

ROZENBERG, J. (1994), *The Search for Justice: An Anatomy of the Law* (London: Hodder and Stoughton).

SAGGERSON, A. (1996), 'Automatic Arbitration and Holiday Claims', 146 *New Law Journal* 1016–18.

SAINSBURY, R. and GENN, H. (1995), 'Access to Justice: Lessons from Tribunals', 413–29 in A. A. S. Zuckerman and R. Cranston (eds.), *Reform of Civil Procedure: Essays on 'Access to Justice'* (Oxford: Clarendon Press).

SANDER, F. E. A. (1985), 'Alternative Methods of Dispute Resolution: An Overview', 37 *University of Florida Law Review* 1–18.

SARAT, A. (1976), 'Alternatives in Dispute Processing: Litigation in a Small Claims Court', 10 *Law and Society Review* 339–75.

—— and FELSTINER, W. L. F. (1986), 'Law and Strategy in the Divorce Lawyer's Office', 20 *Law and Society Review* 93–134.

—— and —— (1988), 'Law and Social Relations: Vocabularies of Motive in Lawyer/Client Interaction', 22 *Law and Society Review* 739–69.

—— and —— (1989), 'Lawyers and Legal Consciousness: Law Talk in the Divorce Lawyer's Office', 98 *Yale Law Journal* 1663–88.

—— and —— (1995), *Divorce Lawyers and Their Clients: Power and Meaning in the Legal Process* (Oxford: Oxford University Press).

SCOTT, I. R. (1995), 'Caseflow Management in the Trial Court', 1–30 in A. A. S. Zuckerman and R. Cranston (eds.), *Reform of Civil Procedure: Essays on 'Access to Justice'* (Oxford: Clarendon Press).

SCOTTISH OFFICE, CENTRAL RESEARCH UNIT (1991), *Small Claims in the Sheriff Court in Scotland: An Assessment of the Use and Operation of the Procedure* (Edinburgh: Scottish Office).

SHERR, A. (1986), 'Lawyers and Clients: The First Meeting', 49 *Modern Law Review* 323–57.

SILBEY, S. (1989), 'Dispute Processing in Law and Legal Scholarship: From

Institutional Critique to the Reconstruction of the Juridical Subject', 66 *Denver Law Review* 499–543.

SMERIN, J. (1996), 'Small Claims', *Law Society's Gazette*, 10 January, 14.

SMITH, P. (1986), 'Small Claims: Back to an Adversarial Approach?', 5 *Civil Justice Quarterly* 292–7.

THIBAUT, J., and WALKER, L. (1975), *Procedural Justice: A Psychological Analysis* (Hillsdale, NJ: Erlbaum).

THOMAS, R. (1982), 'A Code of Procedure for Small Claims: A Response to the Demand for Do-It-Yourself Litigation', 1 *Civil Justice Quarterly* 52–63.

TOUCHE ROSS (1986a), *Civil Justice Review: Study of the Small Claims Procedure* (London: Touche Ross).

—— (1986b), *Study of Debt Enforcement Procedures* (London: Lord Chancellor's Department).

TRUBECK, D. (1984), 'Turning Away from Law?', 82 *Michegan Law Review* 824–35.

TWINING, W. (1993), 'Alternative to What? Theories of Litigation, Procedure and Dispute Settlement in Anglo-American Jurisprudence: Some Neglected Classics', 56 *Modern Law Review* 380–92.

TYLER, T. R. (1988), 'What is Procedural Justice?: Criteria Used by Citizens to Assess the Fairness of Legal Procedures', 22 *Law and Society Review* 103–35.

VIDMAR, N. (1984), 'The Small Claims Court: A Reconceptualization of Disputes and an Empirical Investigation', 18 *Law and Society Review* 515–50.

—— (1987), 'Assessing the Effects of Case Characteristics and Settlement Forum on Dispute Outcomes and Compliance', 21 *Law and Society Review* 155–64.

WELLER, S., and RUHNKA, J. C. (1979), *Practical Observations on the Small Claims Court* (Williamsburg: National Center for State Courts).

——, ——, and MARTIN, J. A. (1984), 'In-Court Assistance to Small Claims Litigants', 3 *Civil Justice Quarterly* 62–76.

——, —— and —— (1990), 'American Small Claims Courts', 5–23 in C. J. Whelan (ed.), *Small Claims Courts: A Comparative Study* (Oxford: Clarendon Press).

WHELAN, C. J. (1987), 'The Role of Research in Civil Justice Reform: Small Claims in the County Court', 6 *Civil Justice Quarterly* 237–47.

—— (1990a), 'Small Claims in England and Wales: Redefining Justice', 99–132 in C. J. Whelan (ed.), *Small Claims Courts: A Comparative Study* (Oxford: Clarendon Press).

—— (1990b), 'Small Claims Courts: Heritage and Adjustment', 207–34 in C. J. Whelan (ed.), *Small Claims Courts: A Comparative Study* (Oxford: Clarendon Press).

WHITE, R. C. A. (1985), *The Administration of Justice* (Oxford: Blackwells).

WILLIAMS, G. (1973), *The Proof of Guilt: A Study of the English Trial* (London: Stevens).

WOOLF, LORD (1995), *Access to Justice: Interim Report to the Lord Chancellor on the Civil Justice System in England and Wales* (London: HMSO).

—— (1996), *Access to Justice: Final Report to the Lord Chancellor on the Civil Justice System in England and Wales* (London: HMSO).

YALE LAW JOURNAL (1974), 'Note: Toward Principles of Jury Equity', 83 *Yale Law Journal* 1023–54.

YIN, C. N., and CRANSTON, R. (1990), 'Small Claims Tribunals in Australia', 49–71 in C. J. Whelan (ed.), *Small Claims Courts: A Comparative Study* (Oxford: Clarendon Press).

YNGVESSON, B., and HENNESSEY, P. H. (1975), 'Small Claims, Complex Disputes: A Review of the Small Claims Literature', 9 *Law and Society Review* 219–74.

—— and MATHER, L. (1983), 'Courts, Moots, and the Disputing Process', 51–83 in K. O. Boyum and L. Mather (eds.), *Empirical Theories about Courts* (New York: Longman).

ZANDER, M. (1989), *A Matter of Justice* (Oxford: Oxford University Press).

ZUCKERMAN A. A. S. (1995), 'Reform in the Shadow of Lawyers' Interests', 61–77 in A. A. S. Zuckerman and R. Cranston (eds.), *Reform of Civil Procedure: Essays on 'Access to Justice'* (Oxford: Oxford University Press).

—— (1996), 'Lord Woolf's Access to Justice: Plus ça Change . . .', 59 *Modern Law Review* 773–96.

Index